Nevermore

Nevermore: The Hymen and the Loss of Virginity

DEANNA HOLTZMAN, PH.D.

AND

NANCY KULISH, PH.D.

JASON ARONSON INC.
Northvale, New Jersey
London

The authors gratefully acknowledge permission to reprint the following:

"The Wedding Night," in *Live Or Die* by Anne Sexton. Copyright © 1966 by Anne Sexton. Reprinted by permission of Houghton Mifflin Co. and Sterling Lord Literistic, Inc. All rights reserved.

Fragments from the poetry of Sappho from *Sappho: A New Translation*, trans. Mary Barnard. Copyright © 1958 The Regents of the University of California; © renewed 1984 Mary Barnard.

This book was set in 11 pt. Fairfield Light by Alpha Graphics of Pittsfield, New Hampshire.

Library of Congress Cataloging-in-Publication Data

Holtzman, Deanna.
    Nevermore : the hymen and the loss of virginity / by Deanna
Holtzman and Nancy Kulish.
       p. cm.
    Includes bibliographical references and index.
    ISBN 0-7657-0037-9 (sc : alk. paper)
    1. Defloration   2. Hymen (Gynecology)   3. Virginity—Mythology.
I. Kulish, Nancy. II. Title.
HQ23.H726 1997
306.7—dc20   96-30401

Printed in the United States of America. Jason Aronson Inc. offers books and cassettes. For information and catalog write to Jason Aronson Inc., 230 Livingston Street, Northvale, New Jersey 07647. Or visit our website: http://www.aronson.com

For David and Harold,
David, Susan, Karen, Daniel, and Arlene
Alexander and Emma
Melinda and Jonathan

Contents

viii

Contents

Foreword

Considering the importance of virginity in different eras, cross-culturally, and in markedly different civilizations, there has been a striking scarcity of psychoanalytic literature on the subject. If there has been changing concern about virginity as well as about the loss of virginity, it may be said that despite changes in customs, mores, ideals, education about sex and birth control, and the availability of contraception, concerns about virginity have hardly disappeared. The maintenance of virginity has powerful social and psychological determinants, and its loss is always meaningful, with powerful psychological and social reverberations. Admired and feared, protective and destructive, virginity has been regarded as a gift and a prize as well as a barrier and a taboo. Clearly related to rites of passage and initiation from adolescence to adult sexual experience, the veil of virginity is only now being lifted in continuing psychoanalytic investigation.

Here, in a multidimensional and fascinating set of studies, Deanna Holtzman and Nancy Kulish provide a very scholarly, systematic exposition of this relatively neglected aspect of psychosocial development. Of primary significance in feminine development, virginity has been noted to have greater psychosocial importance in patriarchal societies. The authors present evidence from analysis as well as etymology and folklore, anthropology and sociology, biography and literature, metaphor and symbolism. The symbolism of flowers and fruit, veils and membranes, the breaking of glass and enmeshment in spider webs, and crossing irreversible thresholds converge with data from psychoanalysis. They demonstrate that the psychoanalytic process may be represented as penetrating the dark and forbidden "virgin" territory of the unconscious.

The initiated patient is an analytic virgin, first immersed in a psychoanalytic primal scene. Beginning analysis may be representative of defloration and initiation into the mysteries of adult sexuality. Adam and Eve were expelled from Paradise by first experiencing sex and initiating original sin. Virgin goddesses were worshipped and Christianity has virtually deified the Virgin Mary and held premarital virginity as a religious idea. Virginity was associated with personal and familial pride, demonstrating purity and unblemished sexual innocence. It was a badge of honor and an emblem of virtue, proof of a girl's readiness for devoted monogamous marriage. The avoidance of premarital sex was to be followed by the avoidance of extramarital sex. Virginity also protected the girl from the dangers of unwanted pregnancy and venereal disease. The anatomical representative of virginity, the hymen, was "a girl's best friend," since loss of virginity was associated with internally generated anxiety and guilt and grave external dangers. In many cultures the bride is required to be a virgin, and a nonvirgin is "damaged goods" who could be returned to her family. The premarital loss of virginity is then associated with shame and disgrace, narcissistic mortification, and social devaluation. A girl could be beaten by her husband or relatives, and in some societies, even killed with impunity. Akin to chastity belts of medieval times, virginity could be enforced by anatomical as well as social strictures. A girl may be violated in some cultures through genital mutilation and sewing together of the labia, inflicting injury while ensuring virginity.

Virginity has represented a moral, legal, and religious barrier and boundary. The boundary is also psychological, social, and political. The bride has often been bartered for political and socioeconomic advantage. Insistence on the virginity of the bride has its own powerful, unconscious determinants. Reviewing the analytic literature, the authors begin with Freud's own self-analysis. Indeed, Freud indicated his own fantasies concerning virginity and defloration in the analysis of his dreams and screen memories. He thought of himself as a "conquistador," a pioneer who opened the first pathways into the hitherto unknown virgin territory. He unconsciously linked the unconscious mind to the maternal body. Defloration was associated not only with anticipatory excitement and gratification, but also with inevitable anxiety and guilt. Our authors infer the importance of oedipal conflict behind conflicts about virginity. Virginity had to be exalted and extolled, protected and safeguarded, to protect the child from sexual abuse and incest. Virginity was a barrier that unconsciously represented the incest barrier. The anatomical membrane, the hymen, was a boundary that was not to be violated without such violation threatening the core of familial regulation and morality. The idealization of virginity had the function of upholding the family honor and saving parent and child from the stain, that is, the shame and guilt of incest. Throughout the ages, families lived in one room or the closest quarters with sexual exposure, seduction, and all manner of overstimulation. All too frequently there was actual experience of sexual molestation and outright rape. A hymen was a bodyguard, symbolic of safe avoidance of sexual abuse and incest. In this connection, the commandment against adultery is derivative of the prohibition of incest. The danger of damaging the hymen fortified the inhibition of unconscious incestuous masturbation. The commandment prohibiting adultery is necessary because of the temptation toward intrafamilial adultery. Sexual relations were to be confined to the boundaries of the marriage, and only between the parents and no other members of the family.

Expanding their fertile investigation, Holtzman and Kulish consider their theme in relation to overall female development and feminine psychology. Although defloration is often accompanied by discomfort and variable pain and bleeding, the combination of pleasure and pain does not confirm for them feminine masochism. Painful experiences are inevitably associated with the reactivation of sadomasochistic fantasy, but this does not mean that defloration is primarily feared and sought in terms of masochism. The willingness to accept and to endure pain may be the price of love, respect, and adult sexual pleasure. The consummation of marriage also means a changed identity and status as well as separation from the original objects. Defloration may be concurrent with major change in social role and life situation. Further, virginity may be unconsciously preserved as in the unconscious fantasy of the virgin mother, concurrent with its irreversible conscious loss and change in self and body image. Reactions to such transformation are hardly determined by a primary feminine masochism. Similarly, childbirth is hardly the masochistic orgy implied in some of the pioneer analytic literature. Rather, childbirth is ambivalently endured for the reward of having a baby and becoming a mother.

The authors infer that the bleeding associated with defloration is unconsciously linked to menstruation and fertility, birth and death. Although bleeding and pain of defloration may be culturally representative of an idealized "purity," they may also unconsciously represent punishment for forbidden sexual fantasy and activity. Childhood conflicts concerning masturbation are reawakened. Display of bloody bedclothes is simultaneously a display of the woman's virginity, and of the male's virility and conquest. The "macho" male who particularly seeks to deflower virgins also seeks to reverse oedipal defeat with oedipal victory and to prove that it is the woman and not himself who has been castrated. The linkage between fantasies of castration, bisexuality, and gender reversal can be inferred in the rites of defloration and circumcision. The hymen and foreskin are biologically insignificant tissues that represent momentous psychological issues. Highlighting new perspectives without overgeneralization or oversimplification, these issues are analytically elaborated and elucidated in this original and scholarly survey.

—Harold P. Blum, M.D.
May 1997

Preface and Acknowledgments

$\mathcal{F}$reud asserted, "Anatomy is destiny," a statement for which he has been denounced by feminists and scholars from all disciplines. We would add our dissent to these voices, but our objection is not with the concept of "anatomy" but with that of "destiny." We do not think that anatomy alone, any more than physiology, individual narratives, family dynamics, sociological influences, religion, culture, or history determines a person's destiny. One's life course is a matter of many forces, including individual choice and the operation of chance. All of these are significant influences and legitimate sources of investigation in understanding human behavior and feelings.

We believe that the body and its psychological meanings to the individual are important aspects of the personality. We find that bodily events and processes constantly entwine with and impinge upon women's psyches. As psychoanalysts we are interested in understanding both the conscious and especially the unconscious meanings of such phenomena. We focus on mental phenomena and the psychological meanings of the body because these are our areas of expertise and interest. We do not wish to imply by this focus that other ways of understanding the data are not equally important.

We have chosen what to us is an interesting and important subject pertaining to the body, a subject which we also feel has been greatly neglected by psychoanalysts. Defloration, sometimes marked by the breaking of the hymen, is a significant milestone in the psychology of women. It has important meanings for both men and women across cultures and throughout history.

Many people have contributed to our thinking and to the writing of this book. Dale Boesky, M.D., Jean Flood, Ph.D., Linda Goettina, D.M.H., Alexander Grinstein, M.D., Daniela Roher, Ph.D., Rhonda Shaw, M.D., and Barrie Ruth Strauss, Ph.D. read early drafts of chapters and provided helpful and careful criticism about the content and presentation.

We would like to thank Sylvia Iwrey, M.S.W., for her careful editing of the manuscript. Karen Holtzman provided particularly appreciated help in searching the literature and obtaining references. David's Holtzman's technical expertise on the computer made the project possible.

Invaluable comments and insights about conceptual content were made by Barnaby Barratt, Ph.D., Marianne Goldberger, M.D., Jack Miller, M.D., and Phoebe Mainster, Ph.D.

Our husbands, David and Harold, provided us with a steady supply of carry-out food and cheerfully put up with it themselves. They and our children gave us support, encouragement, and humor throughout this project.

1

Introduction

*I*n the fourth century A.D. St. Jerome (Jeffrey 1992) described the loss of virginity as an irreparable fall from perfection. He asserted that even an all-powerful God cannot restore virginity. Perhaps nowhere else is there such a definite and dramatic statement of the idea that the loss of virginity is irreversible. Once lost it can *never* be restored. Even God who performs all sorts of miracles, parts the seas, raises the dead, indeed, creates the world, cannot, in this credo, reverse its finality. We have discovered that the loss of virginity across time and across cultures inevitably evokes words like *never*, or *nevermore*. The loss of virginity is an important developmental milestone that marks the passage to adult sexuality. Thus, on one side of the threshold lies Peter Pan's Never-Neverland, a world of perpetual childhood. On the other side lie adult sexuality, procreation and parenthood, and ultimately death. *Never* is the language of death and loss, as in the refrain of Edgar Allan Poe's famous poem "The Raven" (1849), a lament for a lost love:

For the rare and radiant maiden whom the angels name Lenore—
Nameless *here* for evermore. . . .
Tell this soul with sorrow laden if, within the distant Aidenn,
It shall clasp a sainted maiden whom the angels name Lenore—
Clasp a rare and radiant maiden whom the angels name Lenore.
Quoth the Raven "Nevermore."

In our clinical work in psychotherapy and psychoanalysis we have been struck and puzzled by the fact that whenever the subject of defloration or the hymen was approached by our patients, which in fact was quite frequently, it was inevitably introduced by or couched in language of negation: "I never experienced that," or "I never heard of the hymen," and so on. It was this clinical phenomenon that first drew our interest to the subject. When we turned to the psychoanalytic literature to see what had been written about the loss of virginity, we found very little. There was almost nothing written by psychoanalysts about the hymen. Since the loss of virginity is a major developmental milestone in people's lives, and virtually all female human beings have as a part of their anatomy the hymen, this absence, this "never" is particularly intriguing.

It was only afterwards that we discovered a consistent occurrence of negations and nevers in psychoanalytic writings, cross-cultural material, classical mythology, fairy tales, and many literary works. We were not disappointed in the wealth of material we found. But what was especially interesting was that in all of these areas, the negations and "nevers," the theme of "nevermore," repeatedly appeared in conjunction with defloration and the hymen. The psychoanalyst Yates spoke of defloration leaving the woman with a wound, "*never* the same again." Literature is replete with references to the loss of virginity as a stain that will *never* go away.

The striking occurrence of the word "never" in connection with material about the hymen and defloration calls for investigation. One explanation for the theme of "never" is that the loss of virginity represents a passage or a transformation in life that is irrevocable. Such a passage implies a step toward inevitable death, as in the refrain from Poe's "The Raven." In Peter Pan's Never-Neverland children escape the step from childhood to adulthood. They *never* grow up to be adults. In the biblical story of Adam and Eve, transgression from innocence into sexual knowledge leads to being cast out of Eden forever. Breaking of the hymen is associated in many cultures with an irreversible crossing from closed to open, from clean to unclean, from treasured to devalued, as illustrated in marriage rituals in primitive cultures. Defloration, like birth and death, is a one-time occurrence that cannot be repeated.

While classical myths abound with stories about virgins and defloration, classical scholars argue about whether ancient Greeks knew of the existence of the hymen. Similarly, anthropologists argue about whether a given culture had knowledge of the hymen, even as they describe rituals around defloration which mark a threshold that can *never* be reversed. Stories like *Peter Pan*, "Sleeping Beauty," and "Blue Beard" graphically link the themes of sexual awakening and *nevermore.* They create worlds from which children do not grow up, in which princes awaken enchanted princesses to the world of adult romance by a kiss, or young damsels cross over forbidden thresholds to witness bloody scenes.

The experience of the loss of virginity is one that the great writers in world literature from Shakespeare to James Joyce have described in poetry, drama, and fiction. They give voice to the themes of negation through their characters' lament for steps *never* to be retraced or for experiences negated and undone. The image of the threshold particularly conveys the idea of "never." We were particularly interested in the work of the great American writer Edith Wharton. In her novels and short stories, irreversible thresholds, lost innocence, and sexual awakenings are particularly salient and are beautifully depicted. What's more, we found in Wharton's life a clear conflict about virginity and its loss that we feel made its way into her writings and produced a fascinating set of symptoms, including a phobia about thresholds. We will devote some time to examining her life and work.

When we turned to our medical colleagues for information, we were astounded to find the "nevers" again. We pursued the question of the anatomical and physiological functions of the hymen. "*Never* heard of its function" or "*Never* thought of it" was their reply. A thorough search of the gynecological literature by the librarian at a local hospital turned up nothing.[1] The conclusion was that there is no known anatomical or physiological function for the hymen. Perhaps something could be learned from the study of other mammals. Did apes or monkeys have hymens, we asked, and if so what was their function? Again, we were astounded by the answer—another "never." A biologist whose specialty is mammals (J. Mitani, personal communication, November 1995) reported that as far as he knew the female mammals closest to Homo sapiens did not have hymens. The well-known evolutionary biologist Margie Profet, who has speculated about the possible evolutionary adaptive functions of menstruation, also had a "never" for us (personal communication, spring 1995). When asked if she knew of an evolutionary function for the hymen, she was intrigued but confessed that she had never thought of it herself nor had she heard of anyone who had. We are left with the somewhat dissatisfying conclusion that the hymen is some kind of vestigial organ with no actual anatomical function. Gilbert Tordjman (1981), in a treatise on the loss of virginity, called the hymen an embryologic relic without physiological function. A sexologist (Bouris 1993) commented that she found nothing about loss of virginity when looking through shelves of women's books in bookstores.

This absence of a known function for the hymen, of course, leaves room for idle speculation that it was placed in female human beings just to make trouble for them. Dattner (cited in Federn and Nunberg 1912), in a meeting of the Vienna Psychoanalytic Society on November 6, 1912, objected to an opin-

---

1. We are indebted to Alan Berlin, M.D., and the librarians at Sinai Hospital in Detroit for this information.

ion about the formation of the hymen. A footnote in the recordings of the minutes explains: "The objection refers to Sadger's thesis that the hymen came into being because the anthropoid monkey female wanted to force the male to inflict pain upon her, thus increasing sexual pleasure. Sadger then presents a number of examples in order to show that in the human sex is linked with pain" (p. 116).

This is not to say that nothing has been written about the hymen in the medical area. A book on *Ideal Marriage* written for the general public in the 1920s by Theodoor Van de Velde (1930) tried to dispel misinformation about the hymen. Van de Velde wrote that the hymen is the membrane that partly closes the vagina in the normal unmarried woman. (This was an era when women were expected to remain virgins until marriage.) Though the hymen usually disappears in married life (i.e., in sexual life), it plays an important part in the first act of intercourse that may have a lasting effect. The hymen, he tells his audience, varies enormously in different individuals, both in size and shape. It is usually crescent-shaped and very thin. There are, however, other not infrequent variations of form, for example, ring-shaped hymens or hymens with two or even more congenital perforations. During the first act of sexual intercourse, under normal circumstances, the hymen is torn or at least perforated, generally in two places. This penetration is usually, but not always, accompanied by a slight loss of blood. The bleeding may also be quite considerable. The pain that accompanies this penetration depends on the size, thickness and tension of the membrane itself, quite apart from, the good doctor tells us, "such preventable mistakes as nervous terror on the woman's part and roughness on the man's" (p. 59).

As for errors of popular belief or superstition about the hymen, Van de Velde was emphatic: "The nonsense talked and credited here, not only by primitive savages, but among modern educated people, is beyond belief. And not only absurd, but often dangerous. For these erroneous ideas can lead to quite false and unjust conclusions as to the chastity of women or the reverse"

(p. 59). He continued to describe variations of form in the membrane, such as deep scallops on the inner edge that cannot be distinguished from perforations caused by intercourse. On the other hand, the hymen may be so dilatable that it may not be perforated during intercourse and, in exceptional cases, can even survive the passage of a child at birth.

In spite of the fact that virginity cannot always definitely be determined by examination of the hymen, it remains charged with considerable psychological, social, and cultural significance. The following news item appeared in the *Detroit Free Press* of March 6, 1996:

> Virginity has been declared compulsory for female cadets entering the Indonesian police and military forces, the Pos Kota newspaper said on Wednesday. Indonesian police chief General Banurusman Astroemitro was quoted as telling a parliamentary commission on Tuesday that a woman's virginity would have to be verified before she could enter academies for the military, which includes the police. "If needed, the examination can be done by a woman doctor." [p. 4A]

Of course, such verifications and tests for virginity are still widespread throughout much of the world today. We will describe some of these in Chapter 4, which focuses on cross-cultural studies.

A physically intact hymen is not synonymous with virginity, nor does a perforated one necessarily mean loss of virginity. Certainly in the psychological and philosophical realms, just as in the physical, the meanings of *hymen* and *virgin*, although integrally linked, are not equivalent. In ancient Greece, for example, there was a strong concept of virginity, which was understood as something spiritual to be treasured, but at the same time it is not certain whether the Greeks had a clear idea of the anatomical existence of the hymen. Psychologically, a woman whose hymen has been broken can still feel herself to be a virgin, consciously and/or unconsciously. We will see this in our clinical material as well as in our study of Edith Wharton, who had a sexual awakening in her mid-forties, twenty years after her marriage was probably consummated.

While the word *virgin* also refers to men, its historical and most consistent reference is to women. Virgin, from the Latin, originally referred to an unmarried woman. In the *Old Testament*, two words are translated as virgin. The word commonly used for a woman who has never had sexual intercourse is *betulah*; the word is also sometimes used metaphorically to refer to a vulnerable city or country seen as too weak and defenseless to avert the lust and destruction of a conquering army. In the Jewish culture of the *Old Testament*, a permanent state of virginity for the woman was not considered desirable. To deny marriage was thought to deny the image of God, who created the marriage of male and female. In the first centuries of the Catholic Church, however, virginity became a Christian ideal for both men and women. The early fathers of the Church speculated that originally humanity was created virginal and asexual (Jeffrey 1992).

It is a matter of definition and some controversy, therefore, whether loss of virginity must be accompanied by the break of the hymen and only accomplished through heterosexual intercourse. Of course, the rupture of the hymen, through sexual intercourse with a man, has been heralded and used as the absolute marker and proof of a girl's previous virginity and chastity. What about lesbian sexuality? Can a lesbian "lose her virginity" in her relations with other women? In this case, the breaking of the hymen through heterosexual intercourse cannot be the marker of a sexual initiation. Many contemporary women object to the entire concept of virginity as a state that can be lost: "Losing your virginity no longer has any reality. . . . The inception of sexual relations is the beginning of new experience gained, our sensuality now shared" (Bouris 1993, p. 189). Other women resent the emphasis on penile-vaginal intercourse in the definition of loss of virginity. "If the idea is that a woman's a virgin until she has penile-vaginal intercourse, there is also an idea that the only sex that counts is intercourse. I beg to differ"

(Bouris 1993, p. 12). We see these questions as ones of arbitrary and cultural definition. In fact, what we are interested in studying are the variety of meanings, in addition to shared cultural ones, that individuals attach to defloration and the hymen. Our focus in this book will be the attitudes of men and women to defloration and the hymen in primarily heterosexual women.

The idea of loss of virginity is riddled with ambiguity and fantasy. In *La Première Fois* (Tordjman 1981), a treatise by a group of scholars on defloration that has not been translated from the French, these ambiguities are discussed. A virgin is perceived as in a "zone of undecided," that is, being neither mother nor whore but potentially both at the same time. The key concept that characterizes virginity is that of transparency, a notion of Kierkegaard. In this sense, a man is fascinated less by what he sees in a virgin than what he projects onto her. She can be characterized, thus, as a mirror that reflects his desire. For example, Vladimir Nabokov's (1955) character, Humbert Humbert, says of his obsessive love, Lolita, that she has no other reality than that of a man's desire. The authors of this study stress that virginity is an invention of men. Like Narcissus, they see themselves in the virgin and cannot cease this looking. According to the myth, Narcissus sees his image in the water, falls in love with this reflection of himself, and wants to possess it. Thus he falls in and drowns. In his place is a flower. We have found that *mirror, flower,* and *death* are words associated with loss of virginity. "To have a virgin" carries with it the connotations of being the first, educating, exerting control, and possessing.

In *The Second Sex*, Simone de Beauvoir (1974) explored the nature of men's desire to possess women by deflowering them. If men see women as their personal property, as has been the case historically, then some means must be established to assert this possession. Since today it is not rationally possible to realize the possession of another human being, ownership is established in a negative fashion. No one else can use the object. Nothing seems more desirable to a man than what has never belonged to any other human being. The conquest of virgin land

or an untouched peak seems absolute and unparalleled. As de
Beauvoir so beautifully puts it:

> A virgin body has the freshness of secret springs, the morning
> sheen of an unopened flower, the orient luster of a pearl on which
> the sun has never shone. Grotto, temple, sanctuary, secret gar-
> den—man, like the child, is fascinated by enclosed and shad-
> owy places not yet animated by any consciousness, which wait
> to be given a soul: what he alone is to take and to penetrate seems
> to be in truth created by him. And more, one of the ends sought
> by all desire is the using up of the desired object, which implies
> its destruction. In breaking the hymen man takes possession of
> the feminine body more intimately than by a penetration that
> leaves it intact; in the irreversible act of defloration he makes of
> that body unequivocally a passive object, he affirms his capture
> of it. This idea is expressed precisely in the legend of the knight
> who pushed his way with difficulty through thorny bushes to pick
> a rose of hitherto unbreathed fragrance; he not only found it, but
> broke the stem, and it was then that he made it his own. The
> image is so clear that in popular language to "take her flower"
> from a woman means to destroy her virginity; and this expres-
> sion, of course, has given origin to the word "defloration."
> [pp. 174–175]

Through the clinical material that arises during psychoanalysis,
we will examine the unconsciously defensive and dynamic meanings of these concepts that de Beauvoir expresses so poetically.

The sexual revolution has not seemed to relegate to obscu-
rity old phallocentricities, anguished questions and confusions,
or distorted fantasies and myths. Contrary to the popular notion that girls are eager to give up their virginity because it is of
little importance to them, we see that young girls ply advice
columnists with their questions about virginity. Here are some
questions sent to *Seventeen Magazine* recently: "I had sex when
I was sixteen. I recently met another guy, and I told him that I
was a virgin, because I'm ashamed of having sex and I don't want
anyone to know. Could he tell if I'm a virgin or not by having
sex with me?" Another girl asks, "Are you still a virgin if you use

tampons? I'm somewhat confused by tampon commercials that claim you can use them without losing your virginity." Or, "My boyfriend and I were starting to have sex when we decided not to. He already put it in and tore the hymen. I was a virgin before this. Am I still? I feel different physically. Is there a reason? I am emotionally and mentally confused about this." (Kent 1993, p. 66). Note this question to a columnist in the *Detroit Free Press* (Hacker 1994): "I think I'm a virgin, but I have to ask you something. Do you lose your virginity if you do anal sex? What is virginity, really?"

In addition, the confusion expressed by these adolescent girls over how one loses virginity and what virginity is reveals anxieties about the moral and personal values they and society attach to virginity. Alleen Nilsen (1990), in an article discussing the attitudes about virginity that appear in jokes about defloration, notes that the concept of virginity is an important cultural metaphor, a metaphor that contributes to its own reality. She sees references to virginity in current jokes about it as having three semantic features. The first is the value of virginity as something rare and ephemeral. An example of this value is contained in the joke about the man who called his girlfriend "Virge for short, but not for long." Second, there are positive connotations associated with virginity as a state of innocence in contrast to negative connotations associated with virginity as a permanent condition, as in an "old maid" or spinster. Nilsen tells the story of an unmarried woman who did not want "Miss" written on her tombstone because she had not missed as much as people thought she had. Third, virginity is used as a medium of exchange and symbol of control. In a humorous vein, Nilsen says that paradoxically, the most active thing a woman can do with her virginity is to keep it. It is commonly said that a man "deflowers" a woman but not that she offers him her flower or that she forces her virginity upon him. We would argue with this latter idea of a woman's necessary passivity around defloration, which is a defensive distortion based on more fearful fantasies about her aggressiveness.

Several research studies and surveys in the United States have focused on women's first sexual experience. David Weis (1985) explored the notion that the loss of virginity commonly involves the experience of pain. He gave an anonymous questionnaire to 200 college women that asked them to rate the degree to which they experienced a set of twelve possible feeling states (pleasure, tension, pain, sadness, etc.) during the first intercourse. The results indicated that 33 percent of the sample experienced severe pain, 25 percent no pain. Other subjective reactions were experienced at least as commonly as pain. As would be expected, Weis reported that women who described their first coital partner as loving, tender, and considerate experienced more positive affects during their first intercourse. A recent sociological research study (Honnet 1990) had similar findings. Men reported more positive and fewer negative first sexual experiences. For women, the proportions shifted toward more negative first experiences. The rite of passage for both men and women, but especially for women, was experienced as more positive in the context of a loving relationship. However, these conscious reactions are only part of the picture. As psychoanalysts, we look at other meanings and layers as well.

Sharon Thompson (1990) conducted 400 in-depth interviews with teenage girls to study the quality of their sexual initiation. Family and sexual histories of girls who described sexual initiations as painful, boring, or disappointing were compared with those of girls who emphasized curiosity, desire, and pleasure. The researcher concluded that the more negatively tinged stories were dominant. We were particularly interested in the manner and details of how the stories were told. Many girls froze and shifted into the passive voice: "I don't know what came over me that night. I really don't. I mean, I can't really answer it. But it happened" (p. 343). That is to say, they denied sexual volition. "I didn't really know what I was doing. I knew what I was doing but I didn't actually *know* what I was doing" (p. 344). What is also interesting to us is the repeated use of negatives in these accounts—didn't, don't, and so on. Many reported pain: "It felt

like there was a knife going through me" (p. 345), or disappointment: "It wasn't really that good. There was nothing I really liked
about it." Often even the pleasure was muted or negated: "It
was all right. It wasn't nothing to brag to my mother about, but
it was nice" (p. 346). Negations abound: "I almost was 15 and
that was, that was at a party and, uhm, it wasn't—I didn't even
really sleep with him. I really didn't. It was just like for two sec-
onds. And it was just really strange, you know. And I was like
Nope" (p. 348). Again: "I had never thought about it like that.
At all" (p. 349).

Among the girls who told pleasurable narratives, negation still
appears, although perhaps less frequently: "And I did want to. I
was glad I wanted to, and you know, the moment was right . . .
It wasn't very different from what I thought but . . . I hadn't
thought of it really that far. . . . So it was kind of no surprise,
but, you know, something new. I wasn't thinking of it. But—I
liked it" (p. 355).

As these research surveys show, more and more adolescents
are engaging in sexual experiences at a younger age. Yet we
believe that the valence attached to loss of virginity is strong,
and that the experience remains an important one. Young people
seem to speak among themselves more freely about the loss of
virginity, but in spite of their denials, its value is highly charged
and carries with it traces of older notions. As Tordjman put it,

> the loosening of morals, the liberalization of mores, the profu-
> sion of means of contraception, the end of the "dirty little se-
> cret," the widening of sexual education are not the same as epi-
> sodes in a novel, which tell of a casual sexuality, a first time like
> a banal hygienic procedure, not more important than the loss of
> a first tooth. No, today like yesterday, the first coming together
> of bodies is not nothing. Neither for the boy nor for the young
> girl. It raises the stakes, it evokes hopes and dreams, it awakens
> fears, apprehension, doubts, and it represents a conspicuous and
> prominent event, an indelible date which will be inscribed in the
> memory of a life. . . . [p. 21]

A strong negation—"no"—organizes the idea expressed in this commentary on the importance of defloration in contemporary life. Individuals' experience of defloration and the loss of virginity may reverberate throughout their lives, even when conscious denials and disavowals of their importance are the manifest expression. In the 1995 movie *French Kiss*, the character played by Kevin Kline opens a conversation with Meg Ryan by asking: "You were how old when you lost it—the flower?" The movie *Kids* has as a main theme the notion of how a young teenage boy makes it his sport to deflower young virgins. In the film *Clueless* one sexually experienced girl comments in disbelief to two inexperienced ones about their still being virgins. One replies that the politically correct term for virgin is "the hymeneally challenged." She goes on to explain that she is not interested in "doing it" until she finds the right person and adds, "You see how picky I am about my shoes and they go on my feet!" In the Tony award-winning play *Three Tall Women* (Albee 1995) there is a lengthy rumination by an older character on her loss of virginity. She reexamines the impact of the experience from the vantage point of three stages of her life, youth, middle-age, and old age. We, too, find that all ages of women and men in psychoanalytic treatment inevitably raise the issue of their initiation into active sexual life.

Men's and women's experiences of this initiation, although sharing certain similarities, do differ in ways upon which we will elaborate in future chapters. These differences are evident both in the ways men and women write about defloration and in the ways they talk about it in psychoanalysis. We have found that the topic appears with regularity in our patients, both in the content of their thoughts and in metaphors about the therapeutic process and interaction. These important clinical phenomena, however, are often missed. Not taking the subject up means the therapist loses an important opportunity for empathy and full understanding of the patient and the therapeutic relationship.

The meaning of the loss of virginity is important in understanding the relationship between the sexes and how each feels about the other. For women loss of virginity and the hymen constitute significant bodily experiences and mental representations. Thus, our findings about defloration have important implications for theories of female sexuality. They challenge the older psychoanalytic notions of masochism as an integral part of female sexuality and try to amend phallocentric biases and misinterpretations.

Throughout this book we will trace the idea of "never" and its connection with defloration and the hymen. We will begin with a discussion of classical myth and literature, and some of the origins of the concept of virginity and defloration. We will follow with a brief summary of the psychoanalytic literature on the subject, which is very sparse. Explorations of anthropological writings about the experience of defloration and the meaning of the hymen in different cultures will follow. We will turn to fairy tales as a rich source of common fantasies about human experience to look for symbolic representations of defloration and the hymen. We will then examine the life and work of two famous women writers, Edith Wharton and Beatrix Potter, for whom loss of virginity was especially significant. Next, we will illustrate from a wide literary sample the ubiquity and concurrence of certain themes and images of defloration. We will then present clinical data that demonstrates the meanings of defloration in the clinical process for male and female patients. Finally, we will conclude with the implications of our findings for clinical practice, for education, and for theories of female sexuality. We hope in these ways to throw light on the meaning of *nevermore*.

CHAPTER

2

؎

The Origins of the Concept of Defloration in Classical Mythology

We will start our exploration of the subject from the beginning by tracing the origins of words. This search provides some interesting clues to the psychological and historical meanings of virginity and its loss. The word *hymen* is derived from the Greek word for membrane, akin to the Sanskrit word for a band (Partridge 1958). The Greek word for bridal song, from which the word *hymn* is derived, is identical, although ethnolinguists are cautious about making inferences about a link between the two words. The second meaning of the word comes from ancient marriage customs. The bride was accompanied to her new husband's home by well-wishers, who sang and cried, "O hymen hymenaii," words whose original meaning has been lost (Rose 1959). Sissa, a classicist, concludes that, "In spite of such an obvious and unavoidable vocalic similarity, the relationship between the wedding song 'Hymenaie' and the hymen of histol-

ogy remains obscure" (p. 352).* Partridge speculates that the
bridal song might have originated as the cry greeting the an-
nouncement of the loss of virginity. Another, more accepted,
explanation suggests it is an exclamation that wishes the couple
a happy and inseparable life (Sissa 1990).

Marriage is personified by Hymen, the god of marriage, typically represented as a male youth carrying a torch and veil
(Bulfinch 1979). Sissa (1990) tells us that Hymen died on his
wedding night, as did Hymenaios, a mythical figure whose suggestive name inevitably turned him into an allegory for the dangers of nuptial deflowering. In one account he was crushed under
the walls of his house on his wedding day. Hence, his name may
have been offered at weddings by way of expiation to the gods.
In another tale, Hymenaios of Athens, a handsome youth of such
beauty that he could be mistaken for a girl, hid himself among
a group of young virgins to be close to the girl he loved. When
pirates carried off the virgins, Hymenaios was also abducted.
He was able to slay the thieves and return the girls to their
homes. His deeds won him the hero's prize—the virgin he de-

---

*In a feminist encyclopedia of mythology (Walker 1983), the hymen
is likened to the veil of the temple of the virgin goddess Aphrodite.
The author clams that the vagina was conceptualized as a sanctuary
of Aphrodite. The veil of her temple was "rent in the midst" by the
passion of her doomed bridegroom at the moment he entered her
chthonian womb, and the sun, the male principle, was darkened. All
these elements appear in the account of Christ's crucifixion. Another
link is to bees and honey. Bees are called *hymenopteria* (veil-winged)
after the hymen or veil that covered the inner sanctum of the fertility
goddess's temples. Honeymoon evokes these images. The honeymoon
spanned a lunar month, usually May, the month of pairings. The honeymoon of a lunar month also spans a menstrual period. Both honey and
menstrual blood were once considered magical and life-giving. This
suggestive chain of associations and interpretation, however, is not to
be found or corroborated in other etymological sources, and therefore
should be considered cautiously.

sired for his wife. Because this marriage was a blessed one, it is speculated that the name of Hymenaios was used at weddings as a form of blessing. We note here that Hymenaios, a beautiful youth who passes himself off as a girl, exemplifies the bisexuality that we found repeatedly in clinical, literary, and anthropological material about defloration. Bisexuality will be explored further in subsequent chapters.

The veil carried by the god of marriage, Hymen, figures prominently in the ancient Greek wedding ceremony, as it does today in many modern societies. The Greek bride remained very strictly veiled throughout the ceremonies until a crucial moment when she rose and faced her bridegroom and the men of his household and took off her veil. This action signified the official consecration of the marriage. Anne Carson (1990) states that the moment of unveiling meant that the intact boundary of the bride's person was violated by contact of man's vision. She was no longer *parthenos*, a maiden. That is to say, she was symbolically deflowered. We find further collaboration for the unconscious meaning of such customs in the fact that frequently in our clinical material the hymen is unconsciously equated or represented by a veil or gauzelike material.

There is disagreement among classical scholars about whether or not ancient Greek and Roman scientists knew of the existence of the hymen, anatomically. Sissa (1990), for example, argues that tests for virginity were not made anatomically, but rested on beliefs that others had in the girl's spiritual integrity. According to Sissa, the early Greeks viewed defloration as the opening of a preexisting wound, rather than the breaking of a closed barrier. She describes a common metaphoric view of the female genitals as closed by lips pressed together. She cites Galen (second century A.D.) who wrote that the womb was shielded from harm by the labia or lips and the clitoris or *nymphe*, as it was called, which owes its name to being veiled like a bride. The metaphor of closed lips is illustrated by the story of the oracle of Apollo at Delphi who was obliged to preserve her virginity in order to maintain the secrecy of the oracles she delivered, that is, to keep her lips sealed. Hanson (1990), in contrast, points to the Roman medical writer of the second century A.D., Soranos, who criticized popular anatomy's picture of the uterus as sealed off by a membrane. He attributed the bleeding and pain suffered by the girl in first coitus to stretching of vaginal folds and attacked an older belief that the hymen was a thin membrane that grew across the vagina. This more primitive view of the hymen as an impervious membrane fostered analogies between defloration and the break of the city walls by an invading army, as in Aeschylus' play *Agamemnon*. Hanson gives evidence of a popular and long-standing conception in ancient Greece of the uterus as an upside-down jug closed by a stopper. It was believed that for women's good health, excess fluids needed to drain out of their bodies as in the flow of blood during menstruation. (As we will see, views about the hymen are often mixed with ideas about menstruation.) Thus, the knowledge of a hymeneal membrane was clearly established only with later and more sophisticated anatomy and dissection. We note with interest this scholarly debate among classicists about the ancient Greek and Roman knowledge of the existence of the hymen. This debate echoes a theme of obsessive doubting and negation that we will see repeatedly whenever the subject of the hymen comes up, be it in the clinical situation or among academicians in various disciplines.

The word *virgin* in antiquity meant a woman who was not married, one unattached, and referred to social role rather than a physical fact. Since girls in ancient Greece and Rome married very young, being unmarried and inexperienced sexually were one and the same. The Latin root of the word *virgin* carried the meaning of strength and skill as in *virile* and did not necessarily refer to sexual chastity. These connotations came with later Christian translations (Sjoo and Mor 1987). The heroine of Sophocles' drama *Antigone* epitomizes this concept of a girl "unto herself," that is, unbridled, in defying the ruler of the land to give her brother an honorable burial. As she is led away to be buried alive for her treason, she cries that she will die,

"Unwept, unfriended, without marriage-song" (Sophocles 1988, p. 137). In ancient Sumerian, *virgin* was also synonymous with a young unmarried girl. Sumerian words for virgin are translated literally as "does not know the penis," "who is not penetrated," or "unopened" (Leick 1994, n.p. 47).

Greek thinking about virginity also included the idea that a woman's life had no prime, but rather consisted of a season of unripe virginity followed by a season of overripe maturity, with the "single occasion of defloration and marriage as the dividing line" (Carson 1990, p. 144). The presexual or asexual female was thought part of the wilderness, like an untamed animal or a swelling bean or a ripening apple. After sexual initiation, the woman is pictured as an overripe or spoiled fruit.

Readings of classical literature and mythology yield a concept of *parthenia*, an abstract concept, translated as virginity, which is treasured and can be lost or taken. The paradox of the coexistence in Greek writings of the concept of parthenia, virginity, and the word *parthenos*, a virgin, which could be used to refer to a girl who had been raped or who had given birth to a child out of wedlock, has fed scholarly speculations about the lack of knowledge among the Greeks of the hymen. The Christian belief in the virgin birth has been linked to these earlier pagan concepts. Sissa (1990) in her essay, "Maidenhood without Maidenhead," argues rather convincingly that the Greeks did not know explicitly, that is, anatomically, of the hymen. Rather, they conceived of virginity as a state of mind and being, an innocence of sexual knowledge and experience, of not being opened, which harmonized with what she says was their idea of the female genitals as sealed or closed like lips. Virginity was something that had to be divined and was not easily or manifestly apparent. "Parthenia is the object of a seizure; it is a treasure to be guarded and a value that must be respected" (p. 342). Virginity, whatever it was, was highly valued and was to be safeguarded by a girl's father; its loss could be discovered by pregnancy, by being caught in the act, or in magical ritual. That is, any sexual activity of the girl had to remain outside the sphere of consciousness for her virginity to remain unchallenged. Yet the classical myths and literature that writers such as Sissa use to bolster their arguments that there was no sense of a physical membrane or closure also convey a sense of a barrier that is breached in the "deflowering" of the virgin.

The origin of the word *defloration* is Latin, probably colloquial. Why loss of virginity or the physical breaking of the hymen should be associated with a deflowering is an interesting question, which we shall try to address in later chapters. Images of flowers are frequently associated with the loss of virginity in ancient myths and literature. In the well-known myth of Demeter and Persephone, for example, flower imagery is woven into a tale of loss of virginity by rape. Persephone, the daughter of Demeter, is a young girl on the verge of womanhood. The other name by which she is known, Kore, is virtually synonymous with the Greek for "maiden" or "virgin." Persephone is playing near a spring and gathering baskets of flowers. *The Homeric Hymn to Demeter* (Foley 1994) sets the scene with the words, ". . . as she [Kore] played with the deep-breasted daughters of Ocean, plucking flowers in the lush meadow —roses, crocuses, and lovely violets, irises and hyacinth and the narcissus, which Earth grew as a snare for the flower-faced maiden in order to gratify by Zeus's design the Host-to-Many [Hades], a flower wondrous and bright. . . . The girl marveled and stretched out both hands at once to take the lovely toy" (5–16). Then Pluto, stung by Cupid's arrow, tears off her garments and ravages her. According to Ovid's "Metamorphoses" (Ovid 1955), "the loosened flowers fell and she in simple innocence, grieved as much for them as for her other loss" (5, 399–400). In vain, the girl calls for her mother's help. Cyane, a water nymph, tries to save her and to stop Pluto. The story, resonant with sexual metaphor, continues: In anger Pluto smites the pool of the nymph open with his scepter, and his chariot plunges down to Hades. Grieving for the violation of the girl and for her fountain, Cyane dissolves into tears, "And in her silent spirit kept the wound incurable" (5, 427–428).

The classical romance, *Daphnis and Chloe* (Longus 1977), composed in the second century A.D., draws a graphic and sensual picture of defloration. Daphnis asks Lycoenium, an experienced woman, to teach him "the sweet craft of love." After the lesson, Lycoenium says,

> thou must know, Daphnis, that [I] being a grown woman thou hast not hurt me; for another man a long while back taught me what I have taught thee, and for his pains he had my maidenhead. But Chloe, when she will struggle with thee, will cry out and will weep, and will bleed as if she had been killed. But do not be afraid. And when she would give herself to thee bring her hither so that if she cries out nobody will hear and if she weeps nobody will see, and if she bleeds she can wash herself at the spring. But never forget that it was I, and not Chloe, that made thee a man. [p. 13]

Later, Daphnis and Chloe "lay under the same goatskin, flesh to flesh. Then Chloe might easily have been made a woman if Daphnis had not been frightened at the thought of blood. He had such great fear of it, and was in such doubt that he might not always be master of himself, that he did not suffer Chloe to be naked often" (p. 150). Here, defloration is depicted as painful to the girl and frightening to the boy. There is no clear indication of the actual anatomical source of the bleeding, but the blood itself creates anxiety. Sexuality between men and women involves violence and pain in this work.

Later a disappointed rustic suitor for Chloe's hand, Lampis, vandalizes Daphnis's gardens. The deed is done out of spite and in an attempt to spoil his rival's impending marriage to Chloe. The flowers are smashed and broken, irrecoverably lost, "never to bloom again in spring, grow tall in summer, or garland a brow in autumn" (4.8.3–4). Froma Zeitlin (1990), a classicist, interprets this violence against the flowers as a suggestion of the impending loss of Chloe's virginity and a displacement onto the unworthy Lampis of the destructive potential of erotic desire. Zeitlin also argues that the structure of the plot can be taken as a parallel to early childhood psychosexual experiences that are laid down unconsciously. She reads the whole work as depicting "an eros, inaugurated, deferred and finally attained, a direct result of an innate maturational process that is required in the psychological and social domains" (p. 423). As psychoanalysts we share similar ground with Zeitlin in our assumption of a

libidinal development that goes through stages, including a necessary postponement and working through of infantile desires
from childhood until adulthood.

When at last the lovers are married, they "lay naked in bed,
where they exchanged kisses and embraces without closing an
eye all the night, . . . Daphnis practicing with Chloe all that
Lycoenium had taught him, and Chloe coming to understand
that all they had done hitherto in the woods was but the play of
children" (p. 222). With the acceptable status of marriage, un-
abashed sexual pleasure is allowed and the attainment of adult
sexuality is achieved.

As we will see, these tales contain common themes—defloration as an irrevocable loss or incurable wound, the loss of virginity associated with rape and violence, and the daughter turning to the mother for help.

A similar set of images occurs in a lesser known work, the
drama *Ion,* by Euripides. In it, Ion's mother, Creusa, tells poignantly how her long-lost son was conceived in a rape by Apollo.
She laments:

> Yet how unveil that dark amour and lose the name of honor? . . .
> You came to me with the sunlight in your golden hair when I
> was gathering the yellow flowers in the folds of my robe, the flow-
> ers that shone like golden sun. You caught the white wrists of
> my hands and drew me, screaming "Mother, mother," to the bed
> in that cave. Divine seducer, you drew me there, and shamelessly
> you worked the pleasure of Cypris. And I bore you a son—O
> Misery!—and in fear of my mother I cast him . . . upon the cruel
> couch where cruelly you ravished me, the hapless girl. . . .
> [ll. 892–901]

Note that the girl calls for her mother to prevent the rape, yet
later fears her mother's punishment for her becoming pregnant.
We feel the latent oedipal implications are thinly disguised: this
feared punishment would result from the discovery of a shameful, oedipal crime of having a baby by Apollo, a god who represents the father. Even if a victim of rape, the girl often feels guilt

over oedipal fantasies and expects punishment from her mother. In addition, it should not be forgotten that in ancient Greece disgrace and actual punishment did come to unmarried girls who became pregnant, no matter what the circumstances.

A forcible conquest—a rape or an attack—frequently is the means by which virginity is lost in ancient literature. In her argument that the ancient Greek anatomy pictured the uterus as a sealed vessel, Hanson (1990) cites frequent themes of the breaching or breaking of a virgin. For example, in fifth-century tragedy the violation of virginal figures such as Priam's daughters is repeatedly juxtaposed with the breaching of the walls at Troy. In her death scene the empress Agrippina Minor, in a vulgar manner, parodies the words and gestures of an attacked virgin raped in the sack of a city. Hanson interprets the more subtle scene from the Odyssey—Nestor's serving vintage wine from a sealed jug, whose seal is broken and the cover removed— as another image of the loss of virginity. Thus, we would conclude from our outsiders' view of such classical debates that, while the ancient Greeks may not have had actual detailed knowledge of a hymen, in their notions of the loss of virginity by deflowering there was an unconscious sense of an anatomical as well as an abstract spiritual breach.

Loss of virginity meant another important loss in ancient Greece. Childhood was the happiest time for the Greek female, who lived in a secure nest with her mother, siblings, and playmates. Upon her early marriage she was wrenched away from this unity into a new family and role, where she had very little status, and her husband was distant from family life. Thus the loss of virginity alluded to in the early Greek poetry and drama signified a loss of the earliest ties to loved ones, especially to the mother. According to Philip Slater (1968), the mother– daughter bond seems to have been the "closest, most affectionate, and least conflicted of all familial dyadic relationships, as is true in most sex-segregated societies" (p. 29).

The Greek poet, Sappho, from the sixth century B.C., puts these themes of defloration and loss into her verse:

"Lament for a Maidenhead"

Like a quince-apple
ripening on a top
branch in a tree top

not once noticed by
harvesters or if
not unnoticed, not reached

Like a hyacinth in
the mountains, trampled
by shepherds until
only a purple stain
remains on the ground
You wear her livery

Shining with gold
you, too, Hecate,
Queen of Night, hand-
maid to Aphrodite

Why am I crying?

Am I still sad
because of my
lost maidenhead?

In this beautiful verse the purple stain is an allusion to the blood which can mark the loss of virginity. In this translation (Sappho 1958) the word *maidenhead* is used, which evokes the image of the bleeding at the rupture of the hymen. Another writer (Balmer 1993) translates the end of the fragment as "Am I still longing for my lost virginity?" Balmer writes that Sappho's poems reflect the idea that chastity was a symbol of female honor in Greek culture. She also stresses the difficult social condition

of married women in Greek society: "Sappho stresses the physical trauma of loss of virginity but more importantly her poems
symbolize the emotional trauma of marriage and its effect on
women's lives—the separation from family" (p. 22). Since
Sappho's poetry survives only in fragments, however, its translation and interpretation are treacherous and variable. It is saf-
est to say that the poetry of Sappho blends spirituality, emotion,
and physicality, as well as the cultural values of the time.

Orestes in *The Choephoroe*, by Aeschylus, also voices the prohibition against violating a virgin and the stain of blood. As he
is about to step over the threshold into the palace to avenge the
killing of his father by his mother, he says:

> As he who treads the virgin bower can find
> No cure, so too, though stream on stream should pour
> Their swift-cleansing waters on the hand of blood, the old
> Stain shall not be wiped away. [69–74]

In mythology the blood of defloration is frequently linked with
menstrual blood, parturition, or castration. An example of this
linkage can be found in the tale of Persephone. Demeter grieves
ferociously for her abducted daughter. The agreement between
Zeus and Demeter is that Persephone will be released if she eats
nothing, but she eats a pomegranate seed. As in the biblical story
of Adam and Eve, the girl brings on her downfall by eating the
forbidden fruit, traditionally depicted as a red apple. Bruce Lincoln (1991) suggests that in Greek mythology the bright red of
the pomegranate is associated with blood—the blood of mortal
wounds, of menstrual blood, of the blood of defloration, and the
blood of parturition—and its prodigious number of seeds with
female and male fertility, life, and rebirth. Lincoln points out
that the heroine's name, Kore, becomes inappropriate when her
virginity is lost and only then does she take on the new name,
Persephone.

The themes of trouble caused by woman's disobedience and
of a fatal, irreversible step are illustrated by another well-known
Greek myth, that of Pandora (Bulfinch 1979). Pandora, which

means "all gifted," was the first woman. She becomes the instrument of revenge on man for having accepted the fire which Prometheus stole from heaven. The gods all give her gifts that will make her attractive and hence dangerous to man. Zeus entrusts her with a jar or box, which he tells her not to open. Curious, she opens it and out fly all the ills of humanity, leaving behind only hope. The story of Pandora's box is commonly read, like the story of Adam and Eve, as a cautionary tale in which woman is the source of all evil. We see in the tale a sexual metaphor for loss of virginity: once the seal of the jar or box is opened, it can never be closed again. Only hope—perhaps for a baby—remains. The feared sexuality is released in the evils of the world.

While we are on the subject of words and their origins, we think it might be interesting to take a look at the current English slang for *hymen* and *deflower*. For a synonym for hymen, dictionaries on slang (Lewin and Lewin 1994, Spears 1991) direct us to *bean*. Is this bean as in hit or as in "a seed"? In ancient Greece the unwed, presexual female was described as "a swelling bean" by Aristophanes (Carson n.p. 144). Under *bean* and *hymen*, we find *cherry, bug, claustrum virginale, flower, maiden gear, maidenhead, maid's ring, rose, tail feathers, that, toy, virginal membrane*, and *virginal knot*. (*Cherry* also is slang for the nipple.) "Cherry picker" can mean both a man who pursues virgins and a penis. It is interesting that according to this dictionary *bean* also can refer to the penis, just as is the case with many slang terms that can signify either male or female genitals. Again *hymen* seems paradoxically to have bisexual connotations. Also, we find the ancient link to flowers in this modern slang. Under *virgin* we find cherry again, and cherry tree, bug, canned goods, roni. In a history of "dirty" words (Hugh 1989) the reasons the cherry has so long been associated with virginity are delineated. The cherry is an old symbol of the shortness of life and the fleeting nature of its pleasures. From medieval times, moreover, the cherry tree is associated with the Virgin Mary. In the ballad "The Cherry Tree Carol" from the fifteenth century, Mary asks Joseph to pick a cherry for her. He refuses and the unborn child causes the tree to bend down to bear the Virgin its fruit. This story seems to be yet another disguised tale of immaculate conception, but the sequence is reversed. The child causes the birth, that is, gives the Virgin the fruit from the tree. It is also a disguised oedipal wish in which the child, not the father, impregnates the mother.

The synonyms for *deflower* in a dictionary of slang (Spears 1991) are interesting. The dictionary traces the word to the thirteenth century, although, as we have seen, the association to flowers and flowers being plucked can be found much earlier, in Greek myth. It then lists the following: *break, cop a bean, crack a cherry, crack a Judy's teacup, crack a pitcher, dock, double event, pick her cherry, ease, get through, pluck, punch, ransack, ruin, scuttle, trim, trim the buff*, and *violate*. Here, again, as in the classical references are many allusions to a violent attack or breach. While unfortunately many countless millions of young girls have lost their virginity through rape and violence, the linguistic equation of loss of virginity with violence is striking and not necessarily self evident.

3

Defloration and the Hymen in the Psychoanalytic Literature

The loss of virginity and the breaking of the hymen have received very little attention in psychoanalytic literature. This paucity is interesting and may reflect some of the anxieties and conflicts about defloration that we will elaborate upon in our clinical discussions in later chapters. Not only is there little written about the loss of virginity, but it is in the context of these early writings about female sexuality by both men and women that we find several ideas that are erroneous and outdated. Throughout most of the psychoanalytic literature on female sexuality there is a phallocentric bias. This bias has unfortunately been infused with residues of childhood conflicts and fantasies about sex, which are then expressed as scientific fact. Possession of, or lack of, the penis are defining aspects of development in these theories, which ignore the reality of the female genitals: the hymen, the clitoris, and so on. This theoretical perspective has thus been uneven and incomplete. We feel, for example, that the idea that women are innately masochistic is based on a phallocentric confusion or distortion. That is, the phallocentric or infantile notion that penetration necessarily means inflicting pain or discomfort produces a corresponding view that being penetrated means being hurt. In this view a feminine desire to be entered or penetrated is viewed as masochistic. To be interested in receiving or in being penetrated in an assertive manner, however, should not be equated with a desire for subjugation or submission or a wish to be hurt. We will return to these clinical questions in later chapters.

The following is a review of the psychoanalytic literature on defloration. Sigmund Freud examines the topic of defloration in "The Taboo of Virginity" (1918a), the last of three contributions to his study of the psychology of love. In the third essay, he introduces the subject of virginity with the statement: "Few details of the sexual life of primitive peoples are so alien to our own feelings as their estimate of virginity, the state in a woman of being untouched" (p. 193). The defloration (rupturing of the hymen) of girls in these "primitive" cultures occurs outside the marriage and before the first act of marital intercourse. The performance of the ritual is handed over to a surrogate (an elder, priest, or holy man). This designated surrogate, not the bridegroom, initiates or deflowers the virgin bride. Freud likens this important act to a type of religious prohibition. He attributes the avoidance of virginity to the horror of blood, its link to menstruation, and ideas of sadism. Additionally, he says, there is the neurotic anxiety surrounding every new undertaking—"on the threshold of a dangerous situation."

In this work Freud goes on to attempt to explain frigidity and its possible links to defloration. He states that frigidity may, first, be due to the narcissistic injury from the "destruction of an organ" (the hymen) (p. 202) but not to the pain of defloration itself; secondly, to the infantile sexual wishes fixed on the father or brother, which make the husband "only a substitute, never the right man" (p. 203) ("primitive" people are seen as taking account of this and utilizing a substitute for the father);

and thirdly, to envy of men, which originates in childhood and which can produce uncontrolled aggression toward the husband after intercourse. We do not agree with this idea that after mutually-agreed-upon defloration, women frequently have hostile and aggressive feelings toward men. We feel this idea is another example of a fantasy projected onto the female by the male. We do find this scenario in literature written by men about defloration. We did not, however, find this attitude generally in our women patients. When women do express anger, it is at emotional or physical abandonment by men after the sexual act, particularly after the first time.

Freud provides a literary example demonstrating these dynamics, citing Friedrich Hebbel's tragedy *Judith* (1840). In this story, Judith's first husband is unable to consummate the marriage due to a paralysis in reaction to the appearance of an apparition on their wedding night. As a result of this paralysis/impotence, Judith says "My beauty is like belladonna, Enjoyment of it brings madness and death" (Freud 1918a, p. 207). Thus it is as a virgin/widow that Judith plans and carries out the seduction of the Assyrian general, Holofernes, who threatens her city. After she has been deflowered by him, she cuts off his head and becomes a heroine to her people. Freud reads the ancient motive, the taboo of virginity, beneath the story line of a girl's saving her people. According to Freud's interpretation, deflowering leads to the general's castration due to Judith's anger. Freud notes that in the unconscious, beheading is a well-known substitute for castration.

Freud thinks women frequently have a paradoxical reaction to defloration that may bind them lastingly to the man and that may at the same time provoke an intense reaction of hostility toward him. This may cause women to cling to their first husbands (assumed to be their first lovers) not in affection but in a state of bondage and desire for revenge via castration. Thus, in his view, second marriages may fare better after the frigidity and unhappiness of the first troubled marriage has been dissipated.

In his discussion of virginity Freud also describes the ubiquitous and defensive fantasy of the child who denies the sexuality of parents and turns the mother into an "untouched virgin" or a perpetual virgin. We will not take up the extensive topic of the Madonna/whore paradigm here. This dynamic has been explored by Estela Welldon (1988), Marina Warner (1983), and others. Freud (1912) says about this phenomenon: "The whole sphere of love . . . remains divided in the two directions personified in art as sacred and profane (or animal) love. Where they love they do not desire and where they desire they cannot love" (p. 183).

Throughout Freud's writings (1893, 1900, 1901, 1905, 1913, 1914, 1916a,b, 1917, 1922) virginity, defloration, and their symbols are delineated. In dreams, red and white flowers represent purity and innocence as well as their opposite. Flower pots and vases represent the female genitals, and, of course the word *defloration* itself employs flower symbolism. The dream element "violet" is connected to "violate" and "violence." Flowers thus represent virginal femininity, defloration by violence, and the sexual organs themselves (both male and female) just as blossoms are the sexual organs of plants. The gift of flowers between lovers may have these meanings. Other examples of defloration are described, such as the ceremonial breaking of crockery at weddings and/or betrothals. We see these symbols reflected in myths and fairy tales as well.

In "A Fragment of an Analysis of a Case of Hysteria" (1905), Ida Bauer (given the pseudonym Dora by Freud) is the 18-year-old young woman who was virtually forced by her father to see Freud for treatment. She had hysterical symptoms of migraine, dyspnea, coughing attacks, a limp, and vaginal discharge. Freud reports two famous dreams that in the main constituted his understanding of this case. He interprets these dreams as reflecting wishes and fears about defloration. In regard to the first recurrent dream, Freud's language itself reflects these underlying themes: "we are here concerned with unconscious processes of thought which are twined . . . much as festoons of flow-

ers are twined around a wire" (pp. 84–85).* In the first dream
Dora flees a burning house. Her mother argues with her father
over saving her jewel case. Freud felt that Dora's unconscious
intention stated in the dream could be phrased as, "I must fly
from this house, for I see that my virginity is threatened here"
(p. 85). In regard to Dora's associations to this dream of "locking or not locking a room," Freud expresses his suspicion that
the symbolic meaning of the word *Zimmer* (room) often stands
for a derogatory word for woman. Therefore he concludes, "The
question whether a woman is 'open' or 'shut' can naturally not
be a matter of indifference." He goes on to imply that "key" referred to the male genital which "effects the opening in such a
case" (p. 67).

About the second dream, which occurred a few weeks later,
Freud says, "Here was a symbolic geography of sex!" (p. 99). This
was an anxiety dream in which Dora wanders about a strange
town. She ends up in a cemetery, her father dead. Freud refers
to the dream elements, such as "railroad station" and "cemetery,"
and Dora's associations to pictures of "thick woods" and "nymphs,"
as representations of the female genitals. He deduces that,
"there lay concealed . . . in the dream a phantasy of defloration,
the phantasy of a man seeking to force an entrance into the
female genitals" (p. 100). He adds an important additional
understanding in a footnote: that in the dream the phantasy of
defloration is represented from the masculine point of view
(p. 111). That is, Dora was also unconsciously identified with
the man or the man's role in the act of defloration.

Additional associations to the dream centered around a picture gallery in Dresden where Dora had stared at the picture of
the Sistine Madonna for two hours. This, Freud says, reflects
her concern about her own virginity as well as her attraction to
the virgin mother. In a footnote (p. 104) Freud adds another

---

*Some of our clinical material specifically links the image of wire
with the hymen.

interpretation to those in the text. He says that the Madonna was Dora herself.

Freud attributes to the phrase "he is dead" in the manifest content of the dream the meaning of a "craving for revenge" upon her father and other men (p. 98). Thus he links the woman's desire for revenge to defloration as in his later writing on virginity, although he does not describe it in the same terms. Dora's quitting treatment was seen by Freud as partially motivated by a desire for revenge upon all men, including Freud himself.

We would note that in this second dream there are several negations in the manifest content, as for example, "I know nothing about that" (p. 94). Certainly anatomical and sexual knowledge are apparent in this material. It would be plausible for Dora to have had specific knowledge of the hymen and defloration. She was also well aware of the dangers of venereal disease, which raged epidemically in the era and from which her father suffered. These realities lend greater urgency to Dora's fears of heterosexual intercourse, fears that came out in the dream. Dora's fear of childbirth was also noted by Freud (p. 110).

Feminist writers have commented on Freud's insistence on a male-dominated discourse and mastery over the material in the case of Dora. They point to his stated desire for complete knowledge and his confession in his prefatory remarks that where gaps in the material existed, he restores what is missing or fills them in (p. 12). They argue that his insistence on an intelligible, consistent, and unbroken case history, which he contrasts to Dora's hysterically disjunctive narrative, is related to his repudiation of femininity (Bernheimer and Kahane 1985). From this perspective, Freud's approach to the case can be seen as a masculine penetration and dominance of its feminine object, a kind of defloration of the text and the case. In October 1900, Freud wrote to his friend Fliess about his new patient (Dora), "a case that has smoothly opened to the existing collection of picklocks" (Masson 1985, p. 427).

Other writers (Decker 1982, Malcolm 1981, Sprengnether 1985), give additional evidence for Freud's manner of approaching the case as a penetrating male. These writers have traced the origins of the pseudonym "Dora." The name Dora referred to a girl who was employed in Freud's home who was not allowed to keep her own name because it was the same as that of a member of the family (Freud 1901, p. 241). Dora may refer also to the Greek root of her name meaning gift, *Theodora*, which also means a gift from the gods, or the mythological Pandora who loosened the evils on the world when she opened her gift from Zeus. The name given the case, therefore, has references to the theme of defloration as a gift.

An additional reference to the hymen occurs in Freud's "From the History of an Infantile Neurosis" (1918b). Here the patient's fantasy of a torn veil is interpreted by Freud as a birth veil and in terms of a wish for rebirth. In a footnote Freud adds: "A possible subsidiary explanation, namely that the veil represented the hymen which is torn at the moment of intercourse with a man, does not harmonize completely with the necessary condition for his recovery. Moreover, it has *no* bearing on the life of the patient, for whom virginity carries *no* significance" (p. 101, italics added). It strikes us that this interpretation, which Freud considers and rejects, is indeed plausible, given the patient's strong feminine identifications. Striking, also, is the appearance of negations. It is puzzling to us that in his paper on "The Taboo of Virginity," Freud (1918a) stresses the importance placed on virginity, yet here clinically he disavows it.

We turn now to other early psychoanalytic writers. Karl Abraham (1922), in his clinically rich essay on the female castration complex, states that girls frequently perceive their genital as a wound, which represents the effect of castration. Menstruation and defloration, which are connected with the loss of blood, "reanimate" this idea of a wound and reinforce the sense of castration. Abraham stresses that the continuation of such attitudes and the accompanying vengeful castrating feelings are found in neurotic women. He agrees with Freud that defloration reinforces the sense of castration, which promotes accompanying vengeful feelings toward the man who deflowers her.

As we have said, in our own clinical material, we have not found vengefulness toward men by women in this situation. In our view, the fantasy that women are vengeful at being penetrated may be another example of phallocentric bias. Vengefulness will not be found when there is no tendency to attribute or project such anger onto women.

The most extensive psychoanalytic study on the subject was done by an early English analyst, Sybille Yates (1930). She notes that the historical emphasis on virginity swings between two polar opposites, that of a high positive value or a negative value. Typically, virginity is prized because women are regarded as property and must enter marriage undamaged. Yates agrees with Freud's explanations of ritual defloration but feels that they are not sufficient. She also concurs with Freud that an avoidance of the woman's revenge may be a factor, but she feels it is not the most significant factor in virginity taboos and rituals.

Gathering material from psychoanalyses and primitive cultures, Yates examines the dynamics of the underlying attitudes toward virginity, which differ between women and men. She suggests that for females, the desire to preserve virginity for the "ideal man," God, the Father (the infantile incestuous wish), is accompanied by the idea that they would lose something precious. Defloration leaves a wound and they are "never the same again" (p. 168). Note the occurrence of the word *never* and the idea of irrevocable change.

Yates explains that for males there is a double taboo—defloration and the first intercourse. After ritual defloration, the husband does not shed the woman's blood and thus avoids the necessity of having intercourse with a virgin, which is considered dangerous. This perception of danger is due to the fact that in women there is almost always an actual injury that causes in some men a fear of the perpetration of a sadistic injury to a woman, equivalent to castration. In this case guilt feelings and therefore fear of retribution via castration are aroused. In addition, the view that intercourse with a virgin may be seen as intercourse "with a woman who belongs to a god or spirit or other father substitute" revives the fear of father's revenge for the wish to take the mother away from the father—the infantile oedipal fantasy. The initiation rite allows the man to escape these guilt feelings and fears of castration, sadism, and death.

As another reason that defloration outside of marriage becomes the custom, Yates cites one of the many versions of stories, artistic images, and so on, that warn of the mortal danger for a man in defloration. In one such story, a maiden has one or more serpents in or on her body that will sting the man on his penis so that death is the result of deflowering. In this story, we believe the familiar phallic symbol in dreams and myths of the snake to be representative of the paternal phallus.

Karen Horney (1933), an early female psychoanalytic pioneer, attributes one form of feminine genital anxiety to early attempts at vaginal masturbation, when the little girl will "incur pain or little injuries obviously caused by infinitesimal ruptures of the hymen" (p. 68). Such experiences are revealed in memories of injuries to the genital region. We wonder if such memories are more usefully understood as reflecting fantasies of genital harm rather than actual physical ruptures of the hymen, as our own data does not concur with her hypothesis. That is, these "obvious but infinitesimal ruptures" can never be verified nor have we found reports of these phenomena clinically. It is true, however, that an environment that is sexually overstimulating frequently produces excessive masturbatory behavior on the part of little girls, which can and does produce vulvar and vaginal tissue discomfort, redness, and soreness. In unusual instances, the introduction of large items into the girl's vagina can cause hymeneal as well as tissue damage.

Helene Deutsch (1945), one of the early followers of Freud, describes in her study of female psychology what she believes are three basic traits of femininity: narcissism, passivity, and masochism. She states, "A painful bodily injury—the breaking of the hymen and the forcible stretching and enlargement of the vagina by the penis—are the prelude to woman's first complete sexual enjoyment." Thus pain, which is secondarily linked with pleasure, "endows the sexual experience with a masochistic character" (p. 81). The masochistic trend in females seen by Deutsch as an essential of femininity is organized around the breaking of the hymen. This juncture between pain and pleasure produces what she called a "masochistic reflex mechanism." We believe that the assumption that a once-felt pain, that is, the breaking of the hymen, must lead forever to a commingling of pain and pleasure is an erroneous and unsubstantiated one. Once the way is opened to enable pleasure, it does not necessarily carry with it the connotation of pain.

Deutsch finds that even more damaging to marital relations than reactions of anger and revenge by deflowered women are those of contempt for men who failed to gratify women's deeply felt need to be overpowered. This failure would occur because of some men's fears of the act of defloration. According to Deutsch, these fears are motivated by inhibitions related to men's own aggression or of the anticipated hatred by their brides.

Freud, Abraham, Horney, and Yates reassert the connection between the first menstruation and defloration, blood and injury (or wound), castration and death.

In *Female Sexuality* (1953), Marie Bonaparte, another early follower of Freud, describes the "perforation complex," the fear of penetration, which she believes is a common cause of frigidity. "We may not be surprised then, when we turn to the human race, if we find that women react with anxiety and terror to their sexuality far more often than do men" (p.186). She attributes this to the real dangers of female sexuality—by pregnancy and childbirth, and the pain that is a part of menstruation, defloration, and childbirth.

We disagree with the notion that women's sexual anxieties and terrors are more frequent than men's conflicts over their sexuality. The frequency of perverse phenomena in males is clear reflection of such terrors. Bonaparte also states, "Pain cannot always be spared the woman and, if not too intense may, in any case, favour that erotogenic masochistic attitude which should be that of the woman in the sex act" (p. 137). But elsewhere she says, "actually, normal vaginal coitus does not hurt a woman: quite the contrary" (p. 175) and "[she] must dissociate passive coitus from other feminine reproductive function (menstruation, pregnancy, parturition)" (p. 174). Also, "It is true that in woman's acceptance of her role there may be a slight tincture—a homeopathic dose, so to speak—of masochism, and this, combining with her passivity in coitus, impels her to welcome and to value some measure of brutality on the man's part" (p.174). Fortunately, contemporary psychoanalytic views of female sexuality have abandoned these early ideas. We differentiate between assertive, potent behavior, and brutality. But, *De gustibus non disputandum est!*

Muriel Gardiner (1955), another female analyst, argues that except for defloration, intercourse should be a pleasurable experience for the woman and that pain is an indication of conflict. Like us, she does not support the notion that women are innately masochistic.

Among more contemporary analysts, Philip Weissman (1964) presents clinical material regarding neurotic virginity and "old maidenhood." In the case he presents, the unconscious fear of intercourse and penetration is based on the woman's early and excessive preoedipal attachment to her mother. What seems to be her heterosexual object choice is seen by Weissman as expressing a concealed and unconscious tie to the mother. He contrasts this interpretation to what he feels is a more familiar explanation of the virginity of "the old maid," which is based on a fixed erotic (positive oedipal) tie to the father.

Harriet Lerner (1977), a contemporary female analyst, points to incomplete and poorly differentiated knowledge of the female genitalia as having serious psychological consequences for women, such as penis envy and learning inhibitions. She notes that denial of the external female genitals occurs in its most extreme form as clitoridectomy and the ablation of the labia. As we will describe in Chapter 4, millions of women have been and still are subjected to these mutilations. Yet it is interesting that in this important and insightful article Lerner makes no men-tion of the hymen in a list of the denied, unnamed, and unmentioned parts of the female anatomy, such as the clitoris, vulva, and so on. It is striking to us that the hymen is omitted as a recognized and named part of the female anatomy in a psychoanalytic paper devoted to the psychological importance of the mislabeling of the female genitals. This omission is prevalent in psychoanalytic and clinical material as well as educational efforts. Toni Morrison, the contemporary American author, pointed out in her 1993 acceptance of the Nobel Prize in Literature that words empower and fend off "the scariness of things with no names" (Darnton 1993, p. 17c).

Didier Anzieu (1986), a French psychoanalyst, asserts that a defloration which is "phantasied" as destructive and sadistic is the core of the screen memory that was interpreted by Freud in 1899 (pp. 303–322). In this memory (which has later been attributed to Freud himself), Freud and his nephew John "snatch a bunch of flowers from Pauline." Anzieu deciphers this as "they 'deflower' her" (p. 304). Anzieu also points out that Freud's new discoveries of psychoanalysis carry a metaphoric meaning of defloration: "being the first to examine a subject."

We turn now to contributions by those who emphasize the textual characteristics of the unconscious. One such prominent writer uses the hymen as a central metaphor in his arguments. Jacques Derrida (1981), French philosopher, founder of deconstructionism, displaces Hegelian dialectics with what he calls a "logic of the hymen." He challenges the notion of polarities such as inside/outside, masculine/feminine, identity/"differance." Dialectics cannot account for the graphics of the hymen:

> The hymen, consummation of differends, the continuity and confusion of the coitus, merges with what it seems to be derived from: the hymen as protective screen, the jewel box of virginity, the vaginal partition, the fine, invisible veil which, in front of the hystera, stands *between* the inside and the outside of a woman, and consequently between desire and fulfillment. It is neither desire nor pleasure but in between the two. Neither future nor present, but between the two. It is the hymen that desires dreams

of piercing, of bursting, in an act of violence that is (at the same time or somewhere between) love and murder. If either one *did* take place, there would be no hymen. But neither would there simply be a hymen in case events go *no* place. With all the undecidability of its meaning, the hymen only takes place when it doesn't take place, when nothing *really* happens, when there is an all-consuming consummation without violence, or a violence without blows, or a blow without marks, a mark without a mark (a margin), etc., when the veil is, *without being*, torn, for example when one is made to die or come laughing. [Derrida, 1981, pp. 212–213]

Thus, phallocentrism is restructured through a feminine logic. In "The Unhappy Hymen" (1990), the French feminist critic Leslie Rabine argues that Derrida does not succeed in overcoming phallocentrism. For Rabine the "tearing of the hymen is the institutionalization of men's violently taking ownership of women" (p. 36).

In "The Double Session" (1981), Derrida explores the questions of representation in Western literature and philosophy by utilizing the juxtaposition of a passage from the short text "Mimique" by Mallarmé with a segment from Plato's "Philebus." He attempts to demonstrate that any text functions against its own assertions and that what is said is necessarily related to what is not said. Derrida analyzes Mallarmé's texts of Mimique and other works with their hymeneal images that utilize the hymen as a referent. Derrida describes many of his own associations to Mallarmé's images of the hymen, "the white as yet unwritten page . . . tainted with vice yet sacred, between desire and fulfillment, perpetration and remembrance . . ." (p. 175). For example, Derrida demonstrates a play on the French words (pronounced identically) of the *entre* as the between and the *antre* as the deep dark cavern. He contributes many important images of the hymen: spider web and a masked gap, windowpane or glass that does not simply conceal or reveal, and membranes or wings of certain insects called hymenoptera. Leaving aside philosophical questions, what is striking to us is that this text captures the rich and numerous images seen throughout fairy tales, literature, myths, and our own clinical material.

Sarah Kofman (1991), a contemporary French literary critic who works in the areas of feminism and psychoanalysis, is critical of "the disorder of the Freudian discourse" in her essay on Freud's literary interpretation of Hebbel's *Judith*. She claims that Freud arrives at his analysis by dismemberments and dissections, and finally by discovering "a hidden truth, concealed beneath the veil of a seductive beauty whose charms must be stripped away" (p. 5). She does not comment on the metaphor of defloration she uses to describe Freud's analysis. She goes on to argue that explanations of defloration that emphasize loss of blood and thus the taboos of blood and menstruation repress the specifically sexual aspect of the taboo. She argues that "Freud's conceptions about women coincide with those of the literature that he exploits" (p. 82). That is, the relationship between analytic theory and literature is an indication that they are both under the influence of the same phallocentric ideological and cultural prejudices, and that literature, therefore, does not prove the truth of Freud's ideas.

Thus, as this brief review of the psychoanalytic literature about defloration and the hymen demonstrates, very little attention has been paid to the subject. Early insights of Freud have focused primarily on understanding defloration rituals and on decoding of symbols for virginity in dreams. Most of the psychoanalytic literature has emphasized the masochistic meanings of defloration for women and the castration anxieties for men.

CHAPTER

4

ৎৎ

Cross-Cultural Studies of Defloration and the Hymen

$\mathcal{B}$eginning with Freud, psychoanalysts have turned to anthropological data for confirmation or inspiration for their hypotheses about the nature of the mind. We think cross-cultural data can indeed be suggestive and illuminating. On the one hand, awareness of the tremendous variety of behaviors and customs across cultures keeps us mindful of general claims about the biological, "essential," or universal nature of man or woman. On the other hand, finding common themes, fantasies, and symbols across cultures lends support for our ideas, which are usually drawn from a relatively small number of cases in certain narrow contexts.

THE VALUE PLACED ON VIRGINITY

In most societies, past and present, virginity is a highly prized commodity, to be guarded until marriage. Research studies published in the 1960s through the 1980s (Ames 1953, Burgos and Diaz-Perez 1986, Christensen 1952, Erlich 1966, Halpern 1958, Hutchinson 1957, Lambek 1983, Levine 1965, Mernissi 1982, Obermeyer 1969, Shapurian and Hojat 1985, Somchintana 1979, Yap 1986) demonstrate that virginity was very much valued in Brazil, the Philippines, Puerto Rico, Serbia, Iran, Morocco, Egypt, Fiji, Nigeria, Thailand, and Africa. For those of us in Western societies, for whom virginity is a private and individual matter, it may be hard to grasp that in many other parts of the world, it is a matter of concern for the family or the larger group. In many societies, especially in the Middle East, a family's honor rests on the virginal integrity of its daughters (Masters 1953). Anthropologists believe that some non-Western peoples do not place high values on virginity, but these cultures are in the minority. Examples of these societies include the Garo in Asia (Burling 1963), the Hopi Indians in the United States (Titiev 1971), the Yakuts in Asia (Kharuzin 1898), the Aymara in South America (Bouroncle-Carreon 1964, Tschopik 1946), the Tarahumara in Mexico (Bennett and Zingg 1935) and the Truk in Oceana (Goodenough 1949). In such societies, there seem to be no major strictures against premarital sex or no special importance placed on a girl being a virgin when she marries.

In modern industrialized societies, attitudes about the importance of virginity are changing. For example, Mereille Bonierbale-Branchereau (1985) concluded that in France the value placed on virginity for females is decreasing. Another researcher (Ramsey 1982) wrote that loss of virginity is a contemporary initiation rite for American boys and girls devised by adolescents themselves. One large survey found that a white female virgin in the United States whose best friends of both sexes were sexually experienced was almost certain to have sexual intercourse within two years (Billy and Udry 1985). That is to say, pressure from peers pushes a young girl toward loss of her virginity. Nevertheless, a double standard still applies. A 1992 study of first intercourse by Darling and colleagues showed that young American males feel less guilty than females after their first intercourse.

Changes in behavior, which are documented by these surveys, undoubtedly reflect changes in attitudes, but as psychoanalysts we are skeptical that such surveys can always tap into unconsciously held deeper feelings. We have clinical experience and anecdotal evidence of adolescent girls who make up their minds to rid themselves of their virginity. On the surface they seem unconflicted about their spur-of-the-moment decision. This decision might appear to agree with the statistics showing that contemporary adolescent girls do not value virginity any longer. Yet, in some instances the decision to give up being a virgin is carried out in a counterphobic manner in order to conquer a fear, to prove one is liberated, or to be "like the guys." The adolescents long to put an anticipated frightening experience behind them. As one of our patients put it, "I just wanted to get it over with."

Even in traditional cultures in Africa the older attitudes toward virginity are crumbling. Fifty years ago, in the Hausa society, for example, a respondent lamented that few girls came to marriage as virgins. The old word for a virgin had come to mean only an unmarried girl (Hassan and Shuaiba-Na'ibi 1952). A contemporary study of regional differences in sexual behavior across sub-Saharan Africa found a trend toward greater similarity in sexual practices and toward greater sexual freedom in general (Caldwell and Caldwell 1992).

The value of a virgin can be concretely assessed crossculturally in the price paid for a bride, the dowry, or in wedding gifts. Formerly in the Twi society of Africa, gifts were sent to the bride's family after the test for virginity was made. Gifts were a bottle of drink, or more recently a bottle and a white cloth (Christensen 1952). In the Lozi society of Africa the law until the 1900s decreed that two beasts should be given as the marriage price for a virgin and one for a girl who is not (Gluckman 1950). In the Kurdish traditions, an expensive gift accompanied the white handkerchief stained with the hymeneal blood sent to the mother of the newly deflowered bride (Masters 1953). In French Guiana (Hurault 1961) the price of virginity paid to

the mother of the girl after consummation of the marriage included seven pieces of cloth, rum, and various other objects.
While all these tangible gifts or prices paid for a virgin indicate
virginity is a valued attribute of a woman and a badge of a family's
honor, the meaning is paradoxical. The girl as virgin is valued,
but as object, a commodity. The placing of a high material value
on virginity reflects a demeaning and dehumanizing attitude
toward women.

In studies of the judicial process in both industrialized na-
tions and in underdeveloped countries, it has been shown that
penalties are higher for sexual crimes against virgins than against
other women (Fulero and Delara 1976, Gluckman 1950, Kanekar and Kolsawalla 1977, Kanekar and Vaz 1988). Among the
Bedouins, fines assessed for rape were higher when the victim was a virgin (Obermeyer 1969). From an old volume on
sex offenses and crimes among the Indians of Bogota (Wafer
1934) comes this rather lurid description: "If a man debauches
a virgin they thrust a sort of Bryer [sic] up the passage of his
penis and turns it round [sic] which is not only a great torment,
but commonly mortifies the part, and the Person dies of it"
(p. 96).

Studies of attitudes toward rape victims show a similar atti-
tudinal bias. Moral and social fault is more likely to be attributed to non-virginal rape victims than to virginal rape victims.
In fact, in a study in the United Kingdom of appeal cases, the
court all but held the daughter responsible in father–daughter
incest unless she was a virgin (Mitra 1987). These differences
have been empirically sustained in experimental studies in which
subjects are asked to comment on, and make judgments about,
fictional vignettes with different types of victims. Non-virgins
are judged more harshly and held to be more responsible for
crimes inflicted upon them than are virgins (Kanekar and Vaz
1988). These findings in experimental studies are not consistently replicated, however.

Anthropologists tell us that the value placed on the virginity
of the bride reflects societal attitudes about the roles of women

and men. Ronald Cohen (1967), for example, suggests that the value placed on virginity in the Kanuri demonstrates the status of women there as inferior and subordinate. Kanuri men want complete obedience from docile subordinates. A family's honor is measured in many societies by the integrity of its women, as it is among the Kurds (Masters 1953). Indeed, it is the male-dominated, patrilineal societies that tend to place the highest values on virginity. Female genital mutilations, virginity tests, and female initiation rites are more commonly found in societies with strong fraternal interest groups (Ericksen 1989). In societies in which patrilineal descent was the norm, it was crucial that the virginity of the bride be established so that the legitimacy of the first-born son and heir could be verified (Michalowski, personal communication, 1995).

The anthropologist Otto Nemecek (1958) believes that the concern over virginity is peculiar to patriarchal societies. (A patriarchal society is one in which men are accorded economic and social preeminence.) There may be a further differentiation in that foraging societies tend to be more sexually permissive, whereas horticultural societies give rise to tension and hostility between the sexes, thus creating rules about sexual segregation and rituals governing the relationships between the sexes. Nemecek states that for a society of food-gatherers all value attaching to virginity is an alien concept and even the word for "virginity" is lacking (p. 51). According to Nemecek, there is only one example of a matriarchal family organization in existence, a tribe inhabiting the central highlands of Sumatra; however, there are many matrilineal groups, that is, ones in which the position of the individual is determined by descent through the maternal side. In such societies the value placed on virginity may not be as strong as in patrilineal and patriarchal societies.

In many societies in Africa, a young girl's virginity is safeguarded by extreme measures. Ritual circumcisions and clitoridectomies, in which the clitoris and the labia are removed, are performed to inhibit the girls' sexual desires. Often, in addition, the labia are sewn together to further safeguard the girl against sexual intercourse until marriage (Lewis 1962). These practices are still very common, especially in Muslim Africa, and affect 20 to 70 million women (Shaw 1985). Hanny Lightfoot-Klein's (1989) study of female genital circumcision provides compelling evidence that such operations are practiced because they are believed to attenuate or to abolish sexual desire in women. In a six-year journey through the Sudan, Kenya, and Egypt, she interviewed large numbers of women and men concerning their personal experiences and feelings about genital mutilations. Marie Assaad (1980), in her careful study of such practices in Egypt, comes to similar conclusions. She quotes religious leaders in Egypt who sanction circumcisions "in view of its effect of attenuating the sexual desire in women and directing it to the desirable moderation" (p. 5).

The idealization of virginity reaches its pinnacle in the worship of the Virgin Mary. In her comprehensive and excellent book, Warner (1983) explores the role of the Virgin Mary in history, theology, culture, and myth. She asserts that the Christian religion used the idea of virgin birth, which was a common belief in the ancient world, to bolster its argument that Jesus was divine. Moreover, in theological arguments of the fourth century, the dogma of the Immaculate Conception spared Mary of the stain of original sin. Eve's sin of disobedience and the resultant evils of sexual passion were attributed to woman. The son of God thus could enter the world without sin. Warner shows the depth of the belief among early Catholic theologians in the lowliness and evil of women:

> In the faeces and urine—Augustine's phrase—of childbirth, the closeness of woman to all that is vile, lowly, corruptible, and material was epitomized; in the "curse" of menstruation, she lay closest to the beasts, the lure of her beauty was nothing but an aspect of the death brought about by her seduction of Adam in the garden. St. John Chrysostom warned that the whole of her bodily beauty is nothing less than phlegm, blood, bile, rheum, and the fluid of digested food. [p. 58]

Thus, the image of the Virgin is a paradoxical one, she argues. It extols the virtue of the mother even while it rests on the belief in the depravity of women, sex, and childbirth. Warner believes that psychoanalytic explanations for the belief in the virgin mother, such as the oedipal need to keep the mother pure and untouched, are not adequate. Instead, she sees the more powerful influences in the social and historical circumstances in which these beliefs emerged. Like Warner, Nancy Breuner (1992) refutes the assertion that the Virgin Mary cult is understandable simply as an expression of the oedipal conflict. She states that the virgin provides women with a culturally sanctioned means of achieving power through self-abnegation and denial of sexuality. We would agree that no one interpretation is satisfactory in the study of these complex phenomena.

One of the most popular subjects of European art in the late Middle Ages and Renaissance was the legend of the unicorn, whereby the mythical beast, otherwise not able to be captured, was lured into the lap of a beautiful virgin and then killed by hunters, an allegory of Christ's incarnation. Ildiko Mohacsy (1988) relates the curiously double nature of the virgin in this tale, her purity versus her duplicity, to the infantile image of the all-bad versus the all-good mother. Again, the image of the virgin here reveals a deeply ambivalent feeling toward woman.

The modern martyr Saint Maria Goretti, canonized in 1950, epitomizes the idealized honor attributed to virginity. She was a 12-year-old virgin who was stabbed to death when she refused to submit to having sex with a young man (Young 1989). The idea that death is preferable to dishonorable sex is held up as a saintly ideal.

RITUAL TESTS

In many societies across the world, both in the past and the present, customs dictate there be proof of virginity on the wedding night as part of the wedding ritual. A passage in Deuter-

onomy (22:14–20) decrees that the garments of a Jewish bride
are to be spread before the elders as "tokens of virginity." If she
does not pass the test, she is to be stoned to death. In modern
times among more Orthodox Jews, a white cloth called the *edes*,
translated as *witness*, is substituted. As recently as the early
1950s the Kurdish bride had to demonstrate her virginity or be
sent back to the family, who would slay her (Masters 1953). The
evidence was obtained from the white bedclothes. The groom
sometimes would smear a handkerchief with the blood from the
hymen and present this to his mother. Henny Hansen (1961)
reports that the white cotton material that comprised the actual detachable bridal sheet would be kept by the bride's family
for a year as proof for the bride's in-laws in case any doubt should
be raised about the bride's honor. The test of virginity among
Bedouins (Peters 1965), was done manually with the toga of the
husband wrapped around his fingers. Then the toga was dis-
played. The men, waiting outside the tent during this time, cele-
brated wildly and loudly. The bride was said to cry out for her
mother, reminiscent of the story of Persephone. Showing a bloodstained sheet was also customary among the Wolos in Africa
(Ames 1953).

Proof of virginity was demanded of young brides among Gyp-
sies in Bulgaria. Blood on the bridal sheet, however, was not
enough to prove the bride's virtue. The bloodstained sheet was
laid out and sprinkled with rakia or plum brandy. The women
of the bridegroom's family then watched to see if the rakia moved
the blood into the shape of a flower. A desperate couple might
try to use animal blood to fool the experts, but as one Gypsy
woman put it, "Pig's blood doesn't bloom right" (Fonseca, 1995,
p. 130). These practices were still prevalent in 1978.

A white cloth was spread on the bridal mat in the Twi society in Africa (Rattray 1927). If there were doubts about the wife's
virginity the husband would accuse the wife with the words, "Has
anyone eaten you?" If she maintained her innocence or refused
to name her lover or seducer, another ritual was performed. She
and her husband and parents would go to a crossroads. Here

the girl would cast an egg onto the ground and utter an oath, "If anyone has eaten me may my god kill me!" (p. 86).

In the Amhara society in Africa, girls found not to be virgins were sent back to their families and beaten. The Amhara male cherished the sense of conquering his women. A girl was taught to resist her husband's advances as fiercely as possible. The groom also was socialized to regard the nuptial night as a battle in which the bride must be forcibly overcome. If he was unable to accomplish the defloration, he called in a *mize*—a male helper, usually a married relative or friend—who performed the task. The mize took a bloodstained cloth to show the wedding guests and chanted triumphantly: "He has broken the silver bracelet for you!" (The "you" referred to the bride's parents.) The girl, who would respect neither herself nor her husband without a good fight, had now become a woman. Researchers note that this dramatized ritual did not mean that both the Amhara women and men did not enjoy sex in their subsequent married lives (Levine 1965). These particular rituals put into rather dramatic terms the fantasy of defloration as a battle between man and woman, a fantasy we find throughout various literary and historical sources as well as in our clinical material.

Versions of this type of ritual were also found in the Kanuri society in Africa (Cohen 1967). There the consummation was a semi-public affair in which relatives of the husband whispered to the young bride that she must resist the advances of her husband until very late at night and until the proof of her virginity was forthcoming. Then a clatter and cry were set up. In the Kanuri society there are two types of marriages, primary marriages with virginal girls at puberty and secondary marriages with divorcees. Cohen discusses the ambivalence toward women in the Kanuri society that was evidenced in these customs. Mature women were more sexually attractive to the Kanuri men than the young girls with whom the first marriages were made; first marriages also cost more and put the man into great debt. Yet men felt that marriage to a virgin represented the attainment of unblemished and complete obedience from docile subordinates. Virgins were valued because they were "not used." As one respondent put it, he was the "first": no man had touched the girl; he could train her as he wished.

The color white is often used as a symbol or test of virginity, but not necessarily in the form of bed linens. In Tipopia, in Polynesia, virginal girls wore a white shell in the septum of the nose but the researcher reported that he was not sure exactly what this meant (Firth 1936). If after intercourse with a virgin, a man saw the blood flow, he referred to her as "my *surusuru*." This term referred to a dancing ornament of leaves splayed out at the back. If he found his mate untouched by other men, then the next morning he appeared in public with a back ornament or a white frangipani bud in his hair over his forehead. The baby frangipani bud was said to be "not opened," like the woman. The man's attitude was one of great pride that he was the *first* one. In former times the man would dip his finger in the hymeneal blood and smear it on his forehead, whether the couple was married or not. On seeing the mark the people would say that the man had broken his *surusuru*. A man's reputation spread with each broken *surusuru* about whom he could brag. Typical songs might have satirized or taunted a girl as "a pierced vessel." A woman being deflowered was described as being "broken in her genitals" and she shrieked until, according to Raymond Firth, the hymen was perforated. Songs spoke of the loss of virginity or reputation, "cast aside and trodden by the young men," or, like food, consumed or destroyed. We note that here again is the idea of virginity as something that once gone is lost forever, as in Greek and Roman mythology.

While there is in many societies this sense of pride and triumph over being the "first," in others there is a more obvious sense of fear. Nemecek (1958) states that in some cultures everything done for the first time is closely bound up with danger from magic. Thus, defloration in many societies was done ritually by another man rather than the husband. The unconscious meaning of such ritual deflorations has been a subject of speculation for Freud and other psychoanalysts, as discussed in Chapter 3. In an Indian tribe in Bogota, for example, a man was hired by the girl's family to break the hymen gradually over a period of days. If the procedure was not gradual, it was feared that the girl would be sterile (Reichel-Dolmatoff 1951). Among the Ijca of South America the first coitus was viewed as dangerous, and so it was performed by a surrogate, the *mama* (Bolinder 1925). In some tribes the hymen was ruptured ritually at puberty; in one tribe in Mexico priests deflowered babies with their fingers within the first month after birth, a procedure repeated by mothers six years later (Becher 1960).

For the Ojibwa Indians of North America (Landes 1938), the proof of virginity was not an intact hymen, but the inability of any man to "talk about" a girl, that is, to talk about sexual experience with her. Among other North American Indians the test for virginity was a verbal vow given ritually. At the insistence of their husbands, wives had to "vow the tongues" (Wissler 1918). We will see how commonly this notion of speaking or "knowing" is equated in the mind with a concrete sexual "knowing."

We think that this common need to be first and dominant over women may allow men to hide from competitive, oedipal fears toward the father. It also soothes narcissistic vulnerabilities that would be aroused by an older, experienced, and perhaps more dominating and threatening mother figure.

Anthropologists have offered different sorts of explanations for this need to subjugate women. Mary Douglas (1966), for example, suggests that ideas about separating women and men and exaggerating their differences is one way a given people tries to impose order on its experience of the world. The female body becomes the symbol of the dangers the society faces. Dangers attributed to the woman, by this reasoning, mirror real dangers, such as warfare, famine, and so on. Also, men's need to be dominant over women may reflect the fact that often many women were originally taken from enemy groups that were considered hostile. As a result, the women, posing an internal danger, had to be kept subjugated.

Social biologist-anthropologists offer another more convincing and interesting explanation for the high value placed on virginity and the need for ritual tests of chastity. Like other mammals, humans need to control the access of others to potential
mates. This control can be direct, as in the physical herding of
potential mates and the physical exclusion of other members of
the same sex from these mates seen in certain animal species.
Human beings often engage in more indirect and elaborate
mechanisms of mate control, bolstered by cultural practices. In
many societies high status grooms with economic wealth attract
brides, whose families compete for these mates with dowries.
Guarantees that the paternal investment of wealth will not be
wasted on the offspring of others are established. Mildred
Dickemann (1979) suggests that the practices of veiling, nuptial virginity tests, or even wedding rings are all "probability of
paternity mechanisms," a biological term. The higher the family's
status the earlier, more intense, and longer these practices of
"claustration" are imposed on its females. She feels that this
covert aspect of dowry competition gives rise to all the ideological
obsessions with masculine honor and feminine purity.

All of these defloration rituals that we have discussed, however, are changing, although the wedding night tests for virginity are still present in many Arab countries. Western writers may
falsely assume a particular society's knowledge of a hymen because there are ceremonies around the wedding night blood,
although ceremonies around blood do not indicate in themselves
any particular anatomical or accurate knowledge.

BLOOD

We have found that the fears and fantasies about menstrual
blood are consistently mixed up with those about hymeneal
blood. Janice Delaney and colleagues (1988), in their comprehensive review of cross-cultural attitudes and practices regard-

ing menstruation, point to the widespread taboos about contact with menstruating women, including prohibitions against sexual intercourse or even eye contact. For example, orthodox Jews consider menstruating women as "unclean." Delaney and colleagues cite psychoanalytic theories about the fear of blood that must underlie these taboos, including Freud's concepts about fears of castration, Reik's ideas about unconscious, ambivalent attitudes toward women and the "animal" attraction they exert on men, or Bruno Bettelheim's ideas about men's envy of women's capacities for childbearing. Bettelheim (1954) believes that menstrual taboos will arise wherever there is a fear of the mature, sexual woman. Thus in some tribes it is believed that the glance of a menstruating woman will, like the glance of the Medusa, turn a man to stone or otherwise render him immobile or impotent (Briffault 1927). Menstrual blood is universally seen as very dangerous and powerful, used to cure diseases, as a love charm, or as a potent toxic substance. There is a belief, for example, that the first child born of a young woman was the strongest child because it was formed from menstrual blood. Nemecek (1958) writes:

> Among primitive peoples blood is commonly regarded as a universal charm while the menstrual flux and hymeneal blood are supposed to have a magical efficacy that cannot be surpassed. In replacement of her being rubbed over with blood the bride is frequently smeared with red clay. This procedure appears to have served as a bridge to the widely diffused importance attached to the color "red" in wedding ceremonies. [p. 31]

The psychoanalytically oriented anthropologist, George Devereux (1950), asserted that all forms of genital bleeding are unconsciously imagined to be the result of aggression, especially oral aggression. Studying Mojave puberty and menstrual rites he discerned a central unconscious fantasy in which coitus was fantasized as the means whereby the maternal body was robbed of its contents, causing intense genital bleeding. Devereux noted that defloration practices like the boastful display of the bloodstained penis were similar to the display of the scalp by the warrior. Thus, he speculated that the hymen is a kind of trophy equated with the scalp.

Peggy Reeves Sanday (1981), an anthropologist who bases many of her ideas on the work of another anthropologist, Mary Douglas (1966), discounts psychoanalytic interpretations of menstrual taboos and other taboos about pollution. These interpretations rely on such concepts as men's castration anxiety concerning blood. Instead, she makes an elaborate analysis of different types of societies in terms of their reliance on hunting (an "outer orientation") versus farming (an "inner orientation") to meet their basic needs and as a source of control over the environment. Sanday suggests that these variables determine whether a society is male or female dominated and influence attitudes and rituals about nature and blood. Menstrual blood is variously endowed with the capacity to destroy and to protect. Rituals about blood and pollution, such as menstrual taboos, give people the sense of being able to regulate their universe. She gives as illustrations various peoples' attitudes toward blood and correlates these ideas with the environmental stresses and dangers they face.

Sanday cites Douglas's notions, cited above in the section on ritual tests of virginity, that men's sense of danger is often projected onto the female body and its fluids. In general, Sanday argues, when men engage in frequent or endemic warfare, there is more need to control the sense of danger and hence there are more restrictions against menstruating women. The inhabitants of the tropical Andaman Islands in the Bay of Bengal lived where dangers from hunting game were few and warfare was nonexistent. Because the men did not fear bodily harm in the enactment of the male role, the Andamnese did not attribute danger to female reproductive functions. In contrast, the Bellacoola of the northwest coast of North America, who were constantly confronted with the real threats to survival of famine and warfare, kept more restrictions regarding menstrual blood. Dependence on salmon as the principal diet was mirrored in rigidly enforced restrictions against menstruating women going near the rivers, because of fears that their blood would pollute the fish. We find such explanations valid and interesting and not incompatible with psychoanalytic ones that focus on the individual and not on such global analyses. The psychoanalytic and anthropological explanations represent different levels of conceptualization and analysis.

In their description of the rites of menarche in various cultures, Delaney and colleagues (1988) demonstrate fantasies linking menstrual blood to hymeneal blood. During the rites for the first menarche, girls are often segregated and then "reborn" into the culture, a step into a new adult persona. Such rituals are often accompanied by a ritual defloration as well. This practice stems from the belief among such peoples that the menarche is itself a defloration. Often there is no distinction between menstrual and hymeneal blood. We find frequently that distinction is not made unconsciously by our modern-day patients, as well. In Thailand and certain African societies it was believed that a girl's first menstruation resulted from defloration by spirits. In parts of India in which there were similar beliefs, ritual defloration occurred before puberty so that the girl would not be put in danger of having her first intercourse with a deity. In other parts of the world, the newly menstruating girl was in danger not only from penetration by spirits, but by snakes. For example, in the Australian myth of the Wawilad women, the stimulus of menstrual blood was so powerful that the "great snake" was impelled to have symbolic intercourse with the women. Delaney and colleagues write, "The common association of snake and penis indicates that the taboos relating to snakes are another expression of primitive belief that the menarche is the result of a magical defloration. Eve herself gained carnal knowledge and lost her innocence to just such a creature" (p. 31). In certain places, the ritual defloration was only symbolic, but presumably expressed the same sort of beliefs. Aspects of female initiation ceremonies that involve pain, mutilation, or modification of the girl's body, especially the genitals, are symbolically linked with ritual defloration at puberty. Delaney and colleagues believe that "like defloration, bodily modification represents still another attempt by the society to control the dangerous emanations from the menarche girl" (p. 32).

Geza Roheim (1945), in his anthropological psychoanalytic study of Australian tribal culture, connects taboos against menstruation and the blood shed in initiation rites such as circumcision. For example, he suggests that in certain totemic ceremonies, men shed blood from the penis and thus are seen as taking the role of menstruating women. He states that in the circumcision ritual, the foreskin seems to represent the mother and thus the vagina. He quotes a passage from a myth from the Ooldea region in which the hymen seems to be equated with the foreskin: "After the girls' initiation they hear the boys crying out from the pain inflicted by the burning with the fire-stick. They carried their hymens in a little bag; they had been cut with a sharp flint. They threw the stone to the men who then started to use it" (Roheim, p. 78). Thus, menstruation is linked with initiation rites, which through the common element of blood, are linked to defloration. Note that in this report the explicit reference to the hymen suggests that this culture had knowledge of its existence. We wonder, however, if this was an accurate understanding or translation of the myth, since the idea of carrying hymens in a little bag seems peculiar.

The Cubeo Indians of the Amazon, in contrast, seemed to have no dread of menstruation, and menstrual taboos are minor. Menstrual blood was not human blood but was believed to be blood of the moon. The moon was an ardent hunter who came down to earth to copulate with unmarried girls and with women who were not pregnant. The moon was said to deflower the woman, causing her to bleed. The hymen, according to this belief, grew back and the moon repeated the sexual connection each month. When a woman had erotic dreams she knew that the moon would come to her (Goldman 1963). This belief about the hymen growing back reflects the wish to undo defloration, a wish we have found to underlie clinical expressions of doubting and negation about defloration, many common jokes, and literary themes such as Browning's idea of "repristination," or Molly's soliloquy from *Ulysses* (Joyce 1922) about replacing hymeneal blood with blackberry juice.

The curative powers attributed to blood from the hymen were represented in Serbia in the custom of curing syphilis by union with a virgin, but no one would "use" the woman again as antidote because she was then infected (Kemp 1935). Similarly, in Victorian pornography (Marcus 1974) the virgin appears as a cure for an epidemic of syphilis. In the African Tiv society a charm called the *akombo* protected a girl before marriage from illicit intercourse. The charm was a large snail shell worn around the neck, consecrated by an old crone who poured the blood of a chicken into the orifice of the shell. The virgin then drank the blood. Males were thought to be in danger of punishment if they threatened the girl (Abraham 1933). This is an instance of the magical power of blood upholding another taboo, that against premarital sex.

The Kanuri believed that sexual pleasure was associated with woman's blood. As one individual put it: "She knows nothing, she copulates, yes, but takes no interest in such things, there is no pleasure in it for her. When she bleeds, then she is Kamu-Kura—a mature woman—and she knows everything and will take pleasure from sexual intercourse" (Cohen 1960, p. 162).

Roheim (1945) comments that in the Aranda society, songs depicted attitudes linking sexual desire with menstruation. While menstrual blood was very dangerous to men and it was taboo to have intercourse with menstruating women, nevertheless menstruation mentioned in song always indicated sexual desire. Roheim notes an association between flowing blood, flowing urine, a flowing creek, and a surplus of sexual desire. In one song the men are so excited by menstruating women that their semen flows. But the women are also sexually excited and flowing. Menstrual blood is depicted as pouring out of the "mouth of the womb." In the song, a flowing creek is likened to the female genital, the *cunnus*. The labia are depicted as the shores of this creek. As the song continues, one woman offers another woman food, which is refused. The first woman is angry and calls her companion a *cunnus clitoris*, which evidently meant an excited genital. A virgin was a *cunnus closed*.

THRESHOLDS

In the Twi society in Africa described above, one of the ritual tests for virginity must take place at a crossroads. It is interesting how frequently defloration, which in itself is a major developmental step, is linked literally with the idea of crossroads or thresholds. Helen Diner (1965), in her study of rituals involving women, states that the practice of carrying the bride over the threshold reflects an old belief that the bride must be detached magically from her old clan so that she would be able to give birth to reincarnation of her new clan (p. 101). In the Wolof society in Africa, in another example, the successful *waXambani sheil*, or paramour, was admired and envied by the other young men. *WaXambani* means young man, while *sheil* is an abbreviation of crossroads, where witches and malevolent spirits were said to lurk at night. The successful paramour was thought very brave because in traveling from town to town on his illicit adventures he dared to pass the crossroads and other dreaded places (Ames 1953). Thus the idea of crossroads carries connotations of a forbidden step into taboo sexuality. In the Oedipus story, Oedipus fatefully meets and kills his father, Laius, at a crossroads. We wonder if the idea of a crossroads also has a concrete, anatomical symbolization of entering fantasized, dangerous female genitalia.

Philip Slater (1968), a psychoanalytically sophisticated sociologist, has explored the connection between the taboo about thresholds and fears of defloration. He stresses that the vaginal orifice has special significance because of its connection with the process of birth, and, therefore, of death. The vaginal orifice is the threshold between life and non-life, and lends itself equally well to optimistic or pessimistic fantasies. Thus, the female genitalia represent the source of life and nurturance and satisfaction or are endowed with devouring, enveloping, or entangling danger. "So long as the hymen is intact the vaginal orifice is, at the fantasy level, closed. This is perhaps the basis of the frequent use of keys and locks as symbols for the sexual act. The fear of the return to non-life is allayed by the presence of a threshold barrier" (pp. 69–70). Slater feels that such a barrier will be particularly valued by individuals who experience maternal deprivation or strong envy and hatred toward the mother. He is interested in which family constellations cross-culturally lend themselves to such developments.

Even in this brief review of the cross-cultural data we are struck by how it is not possible to separate the anthropologist's particular sets of biases or preconceptions from the data. One writer (Titiev 1971) describes how Victorian anthropologists describing the Hopi Indians changed and edited much of the language, taking out the more sexually explicit meanings and substituting their own words. For example, *mana*, the unmarried female, was translated as *virgin*, whereas the Hopi word for virgin is *kapukupu*, which means "not opened" and is more sexually evocative. In many instances, the word *defloration* may not be the word intended, or even exist, in a particular culture, but is the word used by the English translator, or the English-speaking author.

In these anthropological readings we find that "unopened" versus "unbroken" are two common images of a virgin that have different connotations. Bronislaw Malinowski, in *The Sexual Life of Savages in Northwestern Melanesia* (1929) describes a myth of a virgin birth in which the hero's mother sleeps in a grotto, or a cave, and the dripping water from the roof pierces and penetrates her hymen. In another article about this myth, by Leo Austin (1934), the language is different. The birth is described as a "hammering back of menstrual blood." Austin says that there is no word in this language for hymen and the myth is described as an opening up of the woman's tightness. He says that Malinow-

ski's word, *piercing*, is all wrong. It implies anatomical defloration, which is not intended in the myth.

Thus, anthropologists argue about whether a myth, or a given
word in a language, should be interpreted as "piercing" or "opening" and again whether or not a particular culture has knowledge of a hymen that can be penetrated and broken. The idea
of a breaking lends itself to fantasies of rape and violence, of
danger of castration, or of mutilation. As we have described, in
one African society, that of the Amhara, the picture of defloration as forceful rape was put into a dramatized ritual. In Tipipoa
(Firth 1936) a girl after her first intercourse is called "a pierced
vessel." According to Firth, the woman is described as being
"broken in her genitals" during her defloration through which
she shrieks from the pain of the hymen being perforated. In
contrast, in the Ashanti language the word for virgin, as in the
Latin, simply means a young girl prior to marriage (Rattray 1927).

It is also not clear when writers describe the hymen being
broken, or the blood from the hymen's being broken, whether
they are imposing their own understanding on the situation and
not being cognizant of, or mentioning, the fact that there may
be no accurate understanding of the anatomy in the culture they
are describing.

The deconstructionist movement (Nencel and Pels 1991) in
anthropology has been very aware of these kinds of biases. Current scholarship emphasizes the subjectivity of the observer in
gathering data and the observer's influence on the data (Hastrup
1995). Moreover, historically most of the anthropologists doing
field work have been men and thus their reports may have been
distorted by male bias (Moors 1991, p. 121).

Cross-culturally, the hymen is symbolized by images that we
have seen in classical mythology and will encounter in many
other sources as well. It appears as something breakable (a conch
shell), something consumable (food), something round (a silver bracelet), or as something that can be opened (a bud or a
container). It is also interesting how the color white has come
to signify virginity in so many societies and contexts. We think

that the more consistently these images appear, the more likely that they signify enduring and meaningful psychological and social constellations.

While it is striking that the imagery and fantasy about the hymen and defloration in this anthropological data recur regularly in psychoanalytic data and other sources, what is even more interesting is the appearance of the theme of negation. Anthropologists, like the classicists, argue about whether a given society has knowledge of the existence of the hymen or not. The field of anthropology, like many other disciplines, is questioning its methodology. That is, it is questioning the subjectivity of the anthropologist. How much of the so-called data is filtered through the observer's own biases and preconceived ideas? In this instance, the question arises as to whether or not a given society has knowledge of the hymen. While this is a legitimate and contemporary scholarly question, its repetitive occurrence in regard to the hymen seems to us to have meaning in and of itself. In future chapters we will examine this constant theme, and the possible meanings of the coupling of negation like "never" with the idea of defloration.

5

Defloration and the Hymen in Fairy Tales

Since a preponderance of fairy tales dramatize the developmental conflicts and tasks of maturing, including those of sexuality and the finding of a mate, it is no surprise that we find in them fascinating representations of various aspects of marriage. In many of these stories wedding bells ring for princes and princesses, worthy young men and women, cobblers and milkmaids alike. In her recent book *From the Beast to the Blonde: On Fairy Tales and Their Tellers*, Warner (1995) emphasizes the ways in which fairy tales describe conflicts about marriage in a social and historical context: stories of familial conflict, polygamy, arranged as well as forced marriage, intergenerational strife between mothers-in-law and daughters-in-law, death in childbirth, and second marriages that include stepchildren. Warner's thesis is that fairy tales reflect the rivalry and hatred between women that stem from these social realities. She also documents the importance of women as the original storytellers.

In addition to this sociohistorical analysis, there are multiple underlying meanings to these stories. The wishes and the anxieties of our conscious and unconscious mental life are expressed through the timeless and thus satisfying medium of fairy tales. Fairy tales, like dreams, express varieties of wish-fulfillments of important sexual and aggressive aspects of our psyches. They frequently center around forbidden sexual knowledge, such as questions about the difference between the sexes. And like dreams fairy tales employ modes of expression characteristic of unconscious mental life. Such mechanisms as displacement, reversal, condensation, and sexual symbolism are particularly prominent. Fairy tales abound with primary process thinking, which is characterized by the coexistence of contradictions, the use of concrete imagery, and an absence of the reality time-sense, all of which appear to varying degrees in symptoms, daydreams, and dreams. This, in one sense, accounts for the everlasting pleasure and fascination of children as well as adults with these fairy tales, which also seem fantastic, confused and perplexing.

It is according to psychoanalytic principles of context and contiguity that we will attribute meaning to these stories. That is, because in fairy tales marriage and weddings are the direct associative links, and because these repetitive images and cause and effect events result in marriage, we take them to be linked to the breaking of the hymen, which is an important marital event. As we will see in our clinical material, the actual virginity of the person involved is not necessary in order to evoke these ritual representations of the entire marriage/wedding constellation. Feminist writers read menstrual meanings in most blood images in fairy tales and other literature. For us, the blood in the stories seems more immediately, and certainly as plausibly, hymeneal (although we understand the unconscious links of hymeneal bleeding with menstrual blood), when its context is the preparation for or the actual wedding day.

While, as we have said, fairy tales clearly deal with marriage, embedded within them on a more symbolic level are fantasies of defloration and the breaking of the hymen. We will select a few of these stories to illustrate this set of meanings. Before we turn to specific stories, we will review the work of some other authors who have interpreted fairy tales along similar lines.

Delaney and colleagues (1988) in *The Curse: A Cultural History of Menstruation* discuss fairy tales in their chapter entitled "The Bleeding Tower: Menstrual Themes in Fairy Tales." They find in fairy tales symbols of the "eternal feminine": blood, flowers, the witch, and the moon. Although the focus of these authors is on menstruation, we feel that much of what they say has relevance for defloration. We have found repeatedly a link in people's minds between hymeneal blood, which occurs at first intercourse, and menstruation. Even the terminology of "first bleeding" used throughout Delaney's book on menstruation evokes the additional meaning of defloration.

Janice Delaney and colleagues examine another dominant image in fairy tales, that of the witch. They believe that the malicious witch and the menstruating woman are often linked. Menstrual blood produces anxieties about maternal or feminine destructiveness. These authors suggest that these anxieties are tied to "the fear that the normal order of things can be reversed, and the life-creating womb become a bloody chamber of death" (p. 163). We will show that the theme of death often emerges in fantasies about defloration.

These authors note that in these tales the color red appears most often and is the symbol of menarche and blood. The rose (or any flower) is also the dominant menstrual image in literature and fairy tales. We have found that flowers often refer to the rupture of the hymen as well. This conclusion seems warranted when the stories are about the wedding day or events specifically leading to a marriage or wedding.

Bettelheim, in his comprehensive psychoanalytic study of fairy tales, *The Uses of Enchantment* (1975), examines defloration briefly. His premise is that defloration is "an irreversible event," a forbidden or fateful threshold (p. 301).[1] He discusses

---

1. Freud (1900) reports Silberer's representation of states of falling asleep and waking up in dreams via threshold symbolism such as actually crossing a threshold, leaving one room and entering another, departures, and diving into water (p. 504). He does not link these images with defloration at this point, but he does later in 1912.

"Bluebeard" and "Fitcher's Bird" from this vantage point. In both stories, a young female is given a key and/or egg (or some other object), often by a father figure, and instructed not to enter a forbidden space or secret room. Because the girl disobeys, the objects given to the girl become irrevocably bloodied, and stand as witnesses to and evidence of the breach of the prohibition. (Note that the Hebrew word for witness, *edes*, is also the name given to the white cloth with which a virgin bride wipes herself after the first intercourse to demonstrate the presence of virginal hymeneal blood).

Bettelheim says, "The key that opens the door to a secret room suggests associations to the male sexual organ, particularly in the first intercourse when the hymen is broken and blood gets on it" (pp. 300–301). A small locked room, in psychoanalytic exploration of dream symbols, often stands for the female genitals. (See Chapter 3 for the analysis of the first dream in the case of Dora [Freud 1905] for a good example of this symbolism.)

Blood has symbolic links with both murder and defloration. Bettelheim suggests that blood means that some evil deed, often a murder, has been committed. In *Macbeth* the bloody deed of regicide leaves a stain that cannot be washed away. With her bloodstained hands, Lady Macbeth is a corrupting woman, like Eve, who urges men to evil deeds. Lady Macbeth urges her husband to perform regicide. In *Macbeth* regicide can be equated with patricide, killing the father. It is a version of the oedipal drama in which the younger usurper kills the older ruling male. Similarly, Eve urges the man to disobey the prohibitions of God, the father, and to cross a forbidden threshold, from innocence to sexual knowledge. Thus, as Bettelheim suggests, in these stories the idea of defloration is coupled with murder and death, with oedipal undertones.

Bettelheim also suggests that the egg given the heroine is a symbol of female sexuality that is to be preserved unspoiled. This idea adds another meaning to the familiar nursery rhyme "Humpty Dumpty," whose fall and cracking cannot be repaired by "all the king's horses and all the king's men." There is no earthly power potent enough to undo this irreversible act.

Another fairy tale in which Bettelheim sees the theme of defloration is "The Enchanted Pig." In this tale, three daughters venture into a forbidden room where a book "about their future marriage" is hidden. This is interpreted as the carnal knowledge that their father forbade them to acquire. Here we see an echo of the same theme as in the biblical story in which God forbade Adam and Eve to acquire fruit from the tree of knowledge. The bride of the enchanted pig has to cut off her little finger in order to become reunited with her bridegroom. She needs to build a ladder out of chicken bones in order to reach her enchanted bridegroom, but she lacks a bone for the last rung of the ladder. She takes a knife and chops off her little finger, which serves as the last rung and permits her to reach her love. Bettelheim says:

> Here we may recognize once more an allusion to the loss of the hymen, the sacrifice of a small part of the woman's body in her first experience with sex. . . . [T]he woman must relinquish the wish for a phallus of her own, and be satisfied with that of her husband. Cutting off her little finger, far from signifying symbolic self-castration, may suggest what fantasies the female must give up to be happy the way she is, so that she can be happy with her husband the way he is. [p. 323]

That is, for Bettelheim, the woman sacrifices her "phallic" masculine wishes to be happy.

This idea, intrinsic to early Freudian ideas of the girl's psychosexual development, has been challenged in contemporary psychoanalytic discourse. Bettelheim equates the sacrifice of the hymen with the renunciation of masculinity. We see this story differently. The woman is depicted as lacking a bone, or the wherewithal, to reach her love. This depiction of the woman as deficient or lacking is a common distortion of childhood, which persists in cultural expressions. What strikes us about this story, however, is the resourcefulness of the woman who sacrifices the integrity of her body to necessity.

Another story in which a female cuts off a small part of her body (which we feel symbolizes the hymen) to win a mate is one version of Cinderella, "The Ash Girl" (Grimm 1973). Here, the girl's slipper, in this version made of solid gold, becomes the object that will help the king's son choose his bride. One of the two stepsisters is attempting to fit into the shoe when her mother says, "Cut the toe off; once you're queen, you won't have to walk any more." She does so and forces her foot into the too-small shoe. The Prince is warned by two white pigeons who cry out: "Look, look! / There's blood in the shoe! / The shoe's too small. / The right bride's still at home" (p. 91). The same scene occurs with the second sister. The mother hands her a knife and tells her to cut off a piece of her heel. The king's son once again is warned and sees the blood that stains her white stockings red. As he finally tries the shoe on the Ash girl, on whom it fits, the two white pigeons point out, "No blood in the shoe! . . . He's bringing the right bride home." Here the sisters mutilate themselves at the suggestion of their mother. David Marcus (1963), in "The Cinderella Motif: Fairy Tale and Defense," sees all of the bleeding as menstrual. He interprets this story in terms of the little girl's denial of her envy of her mother's menstrual functioning.

We would say that in addition to this possible menstrual meaning, there are implications concerning virginity (Bernstein 1990). The girl who is not bleeding may represent for the nineteenth century Grimm brothers, the virtuous, intact virgin. The already-deflowered, bleeding, and sexual girls lose the prince and happiness. It is the bad mother who induces her daughters to do evil and self-hurtful acts that result in the premature, premarital loss of the hymen. Thus, the tale carries a moral that extols virginity and chastity before marriage.

In Hans Christian Andersen's "The Little Mermaid" (1926) we see another example of the voluntary loss of a body part by a female in order to marry the male.[2] In this tale, the youngest

2. Strictly speaking, some would say that this tale should not be included with other fairy tales, as it differs from other folk tales, which are distilled from oral traditions. "The Little Mermaid" is a work of

mermaid, at age 15 (the age of menarche), is allowed to swim to the top of the ocean to see the world. This occasions her falling in love with a handsome prince. Since her fish tail is considered ugly by humans, she goes to a "hateful sea-witch" for help. The sea-witch agrees to help the mermaid win the love of the prince by brewing a magic drink. The witch warns that its ingestion will cause the following to happen: "[Y]our tail will split and shrivel up into what men call nice legs; but it will hurt, mind you, for it will be like a sharp sword piercing you . . . but every step you take for a time will be to you like treading on sharp knives till the blood flows. . . . But . . . once you have a girl's form you can never become a mermaid again! You will never be able to dive down through the water to your sisters or go back to your father's palace" (pp. 41–42). The mermaid agrees to bifurcation in order to be transformed into a human girl and suffers all of this pain in hopes of winning the prince. Additional sacrifices as payment for her new anatomy (legs) are the loss of her tongue and her beautiful voice, which are added to the losses of her tail and her home. After drinking the potion, "it was as though a two-edged sword pierced through her body; she moaned with agony and lay there as one dead" (p. 43).

Here, the definitive "nevers" are paired with the idea of sacrifice for love. Menstrual and castration themes are articulated around fantasies of what makes a "human girl." That is, the mermaid's tail must be cut and she must bleed before she becomes a true human girl. Efrat Tseelon (1995) reviews interpretations of this Andersen story and says it is a story of castration. We see in this bleeding a symbol of the hymen as well as the revival of the representation of castration and menstruation as they relate to the idea of femininity. These experiences are linked together, yet the context of courtship and impending

---

literature that largely reflects its male author's imagination. Warner (1995), however, states that Andersen elaborated his story from varied strands of oral and written tales in the Eastern as well as Western tradition.

marriage emphasize the hymeneal aspect. In this tale of love and marriage, just as in Cinderella, the bad mother/witch encourages the girl to get rid of a body part, causing bleeding before marriage, and here again, she does not win her prince. He marries another. In this tale, there are allusions to premarital sex in addition to menstruation: She "dallies" and dances with the prince and her new feet bleed. (The foot as erotic symbol via fetishism is well known in the psychoanalytic literature.) She swims with the prince and lays him on the sand. She recalls how she had rested his head on her breast and kissed him. She finds that she is naked and ashamed, and wraps herself in her long hair.

Similar prohibitions against loss of virginity are found in an early French tale. "The Subtle Princess" by Marie-Jeanne L'Heritier (cited in Warner 1995) tells of three motherless sisters, Finessa, Lackadaisy, and Loquatia. Their father, the king, has to depart for a time and is advised to lock them in a castle with three magic glass distaffs. He forbids them to let anyone enter. The enchantment dictates that the distaffs, symbols of femininity and virginity, will shatter if their owners' virginity is lost. Disguised as a woman, an enemy prince gains entry to the castle, flatters Lackadaisy and Loquatia and marries them both. Their glass distaffs shatter. Finessa threatens him with an ax, and to quash him in his attempt to seduce her, she arranges for him to drop several hundred feet through the castle sewer. Prohibitions regarding sexuality for females and an irrevocable breakage of the hymeneal membrane (glass distaff) are clear.

Warner notes that in many of these tales the good or biological mothers are absent or dead and are replaced by evil stepmothers. She relates this to the serial marriages of former times based on the frequency of death in childbirth. Certainly this historical explanation is significant. But we feel that the enjoyment of these tales by generations of adults and children has more to do with their wish-fulfilling, dreamlike quality. After all, what is more overtly sad, yet unconsciously pleasurable, to the little girl in the throes of the Oedipus constellation than a story in which the mother dies and she is left either with an evil replacement or alone with her father? Other typical "motherless" favorites such as *Jane Eyre, The Secret Garden, Heidi,* and *Peter Pan* have this theme as an important and compelling component.

Another tale (Grimm 1973) with overt Christian themes, "A Child of Saint Mary," tells of the Virgin Mary who adopts and takes to heaven a little girl from a poor and starving family. The Virgin Mary gives the girl, at the age of 14 (the pubertal menarche age), the keys to thirteen doors of the Kingdom of Heaven and prohibits her from opening one of them. As we have seen in other tales, the girl is unable or unwilling to go along with the prohibition and opens the door "just a crack" in order to peek at what is inside. As a result, she is privy to the Holy Trinity sitting in fire and glory. Her finger touches the Heavenly fire and becomes all golden. "The gold, . . . stayed on her finger, no matter how much she washed it and rubbed it" (p. 9). She lies to the Virgin and refuses to confess to her sin. She is punished by the loss of her voice and must return from heaven to earth. Additional events with implicit sexual meanings are described: a king chases a deer into the thicket, pulls the bushes apart, cuts a path with his sword, and marries the girl. Eventually she is threatened with death, whereupon she desires to confess her sin and is in return granted a whole life of happiness.

The familiar themes of prohibitions which are not obeyed, seeing and knowing what one has been forbidden, a fall from Heaven as a result of disobedience, and a mark of some type which cannot be obliterated are all evident in this story. Defloration is suggested by the loss of a body part (or in this case a body function), the cutting of a path through an impenetrable barrier, and the link to marriage. In this story we find another important intrapsychic link, the notion of damage and punishment due to breaking a prohibition. Here, the stained golden finger suggests punishment for childhood masturbation, sexual curiosity, and related fantasies. There is the idea that childhood masturbation, or other experimentation, would result in the bloody rupture of the hymen (loss of virginity), and virginity can never be restored. The prohibitions to entry (crossing thresholds) when the parent/authority figure is absent may also represent worry about premature entry into unsanctioned sexuality. In many fairy tales, marriage is initiated by a kiss or by acts of courage and loyalty that free humans from enchantment as beasts. Transformations of bridegrooms, the best-known example being "Beauty and the Beast," are called by Bettelheim "animal-groom stories" and indicate for him the wish to separate the sexual from other aspects of life, in an overcoming of notions of the bestiality of sexuality. Iona and Peter Opie (1974) state: "the idea that a kiss, or the marriage bed could release a person, most often a prince, from the curse of monstrousness, was one that thrilled readers in the Middle Ages. The bewitched person was less often a young girl who had been turned into a terrifying creature or 'loathly lady'" (pp. 183–184). Through marriage or sex the bewitched, sometimes the bride, sometimes the bridegroom, are transformed, sometimes from ugly to beautiful, sometimes the reverse. The animal transformations may also allay unconscious incestuous wishes and the attendant anxieties by their exaggerated exogamous claims. Who could be intimately involved with another species?

Bettelheim (1975) sees "The Frog King," as an example of this transformation, as a representation of the first intercourse, which he feels must inevitably be painful and unpleasant. "We cannot expect our first erotic contacts to be pleasant, for they are much too difficult and fraught with anxiety" (p. 287). In this story a princess promises favors to a frog, including that of sleeping in her bed with her, in return for his finding her lost golden ball. She becomes angry with the frog and hurls it against the wall. After being thrown against the wall, the frog, who disgusts the princess initially, is transformed into a beautiful prince. In other versions of the story, it is a kiss (and all that it symbolizes) that transforms the ugly frog into the handsome man/prince. The princess and former frog are then wed. Bettelheim suggests that the frog is a phallic symbol (it is slimy, can blow itself up, and so on). We wonder if the wall against which the frog is thrown is a representation of an impenetrable barrier, a frequent idea in regard to the hymen.

In another transformation story, "The Seven Ravens" (Grimm 1973), a long-awaited baby girl is born into a family of seven boys. She is to be baptized at home. Her brothers accidentally drop the baptismal water pitcher into a well, whereupon an angry curse by the father turns them into ravens. This history is kept secret from her and it is only years later that she learns she is to blame for her brothers' enchantment and misfortune. In an attempt to break the spell, she sets off with several items, among them "a ring in memory of her parents." She visits a Morning Star who hands her a chicken bone saying, "Unless you have this bone, you can't unlock the Glass Mountain, and your brothers are in the Glass Mountain" (p. 101). Arriving at the Glass Mountain, she finds a locked gate and discovers that she has lost the bone. With no "key" to the Glass Mountain, she takes a knife, cuts off her little finger, sticks it in the gate, and manages to unlock it. Standing hidden behind a door listening, she hears her brothers wish for her presence in order to be transformed into their human forms. She steps out, makes herself known, disenchants them and is hugged, appreciated, and loved. Once again, glass, a key, a locked door, a secret, and cutting off a piece of the body are all present. Like the bride in "The Enchanted Pig," the girl in this story resourcefully sacrifices a piece of herself to reverse the bestiality of the males. A ritual baptism is the setting for the tragic events that follow. We will see that such rituals are frequently invoked as part of the constellation of wedding/hymen images in our clinical material.

One such story which has clear allusions to Christian rituals is "Lady's Glass" (Grimm 1973). It tells of a driver whose cart, heavily laden with wine, gets mired in mud. The Virgin Mary appears and asks for a glass of wine in return for getting his cart out of the mud. Since the driver has no wine glass, Mary plucks a white flower with red stripes that looks like a glass. He fills it with wine, she drinks, and at that moment the cart is freed from the mire. The flower is still called "Our Lady's Little Glass." We see here the images of glass, flower, red, white, mud, getting stuck, and the Virgin. These elements occur regularly in the underlying fantasies of defloration in our patients and also in the following folk tale.

An example of a folk tale centering around the wedding ceremony is "John Gets Married" (Grimm 1973). On the wedding day the bridegroom asks his bride, "Were you at the wedding, too?" She answers, "Of course I was there, and in full dress. My hair was powdered with snow, but then the sun came out and melted it. My dress was of spider web, but then I walked through thorn bushes and they tore it off me. My slippers were of glass; I hit against a stone, then they went clink and broke in two" (p. 307). Spider webs, something torn, something glass, and something stone are also familiar components of the fantasies about the hymen that we encounter frequently in our patients.

Bettelheim points out that in most of these tales it is a hag, witch, evil fairy, or older female who gives the idea to young girls that men are beasts. It seems once again that blame upon a mother figure is emphasized. Ortner (1991), an anthropologist, states that it is the consistently active female (for example, a mother or a witch) in these tales who is seen as wicked and is usually killed in the end. In contrast, the heroines of the stories, the little girls and princesses, rarely initiate activity. As the tales unfold, the action is moved along by bad things happening to the heroines, rather than by their initiating activity. According to Ortner (1991), the action "systematically" forces them to renounce the role of active agency. The passage to womanhood in the fairy tales almost exclusively involves the renunciation of the girl's sense of agency. With very few exceptions, girls do not achieve the mark of female adulthood as defined in these tales, that of marriage (and defloration), without such a renunciation. The idea that adult sexuality and womanhood should be equated with marriage and childbearing is a historically based one, which we personally find no longer necessarily valid.

Warner (1995) details the ways in which these tales make fun of old women's lusts and says "the aging woman emerges as the most . . . abhorrent image" (p. 43). This reflects men's defensive reaction of repulsion to the notion of an older woman as a sexual being. A depriving mother, the one whose task it is to tame the instincts and wishes of childhood, is indeed frequently portrayed and represented in the unconscious as a malevolent, harsh, threatening figure who wishes to deprive her daughters and sons by means of castration and inhibition of sexual pleasure. Moreover, the mother, because of her relative power over the helpless child, looms in the mind as a potent, powerful figure (Chasseguet-Smirgel 1976).

In the popular and familiar "Sleeping Beauty" ("Hawthorn Blossom" in Grimm 1973), the prick of a finger, foretold through a curse by an evil fairy, clearly represents first blood and thus links menstruation and hymeneal blood. Bettelheim suggests the story's meaning is that no matter what precautions parents take, sexual awakening, knowledge, and experience (including menstruation, rupture of the hymen, and/or masturbation-produced injury), ultimately and inevitably take place. In this story, a wall of impenetrable thorns that we, along with Delaney and colleagues and Bettelheim, believe to represent the hymen suddenly turns into a wall of big, beautiful flowers that "moved aside of themselves and let the fearless prince through." Thus, penetration proceeds without harm to the man. This hedge of briar roses around Sleeping Beauty had caused the death of many young men who had "remained stuck . . . [in the hawthorn bushes] . . . couldn't get free, and died miserable deaths" (p. 184). Thus, castration and death are the wages of sinful and/or premature sex. This story graphically illustrates men's fear of defloration.

The magical transformations and changes from impenetrable to penetrable, and the barrier or threshold images, are picturesque motifs that appear in many other stories. Virginity is depicted as a valued treasure, closed up in a secret, forbidden, and/

or forbidding place. In this case, the right man can gain entry to the woman with no difficulty. This wish-fulfilling fantasy assuages the terrible anxieties that accompany defloration, such as getting stuck, castrated, or killed.

Bloody themes appear clearly in the content of "Sleeping Beauty" as we know it and as it appears on the shelves of children's libraries and bookstores. Even sexual and bloodier aspects have been expunged in the revisions of the tale over the centuries. Warner (1995, pp. 220–221) traces the historical revision of Sleeping Beauty over the centuries. The Grimms' tale was similar to the earlier French tale by Perrault, "La belle au bois dormant." This tale in turn resembles a story in Basile's collection of sixty years before, and both of them rest on a tale that appears in a vast Arthurian prose romance of the fourteenth century. In Basile's version the hero, a king, is already married to someone else at the start of the story. As the king is hunting, he comes upon the sleeping beauty Talia, who has pricked her finger on a sliver of flax. When she will not wake up, he "plucked from her the fruits of love." That is, he rapes her. Twin children are fathered by the act. The king forgets this escapade, but a year later he discovers his second family. His wife, who is childless herself, and is the predecessor of the wicked stepmother in the familiar later tales, orders the twins to be butchered and fed to the king. The soft-hearted cook substitutes two goats instead. Still furious, the queen sets out to roast Talia in a cauldron. Talia stalls by taking off one of her garments at a time. In the nick of time, the king saves her and throws the queen into the fire instead. This is a story of adultery, rape, bigamy, and attempted cannibalism, infanticide, and murder. In other versions of "Sleeping Beauty" the overt sex act described in Basile's tale has become a gentle kiss. This kind of revisionism can be found in the history of many of the popular fairy tales we know today. We will see that this censorship and revision of fairy tales is paralleled by the kind of defensive negation and denial we find clinically when our patients speak of their past experiences with defloration.

"Sleeping Beauty" is one of many tales in which there is a magical opening to a place formerly sealed or impenetrable. There is a genre of stories in which a young man or prince goes through a series of perilous or difficult trials in order to find treasure. One example is from *The Arabian Nights* (Wiggin and Smith 1909). In "Ali Baba and the Forty Thieves" the magic words "Open sesame!" open the cave that hides the thieves' treasure. In many fairy tales dragons and ogres guard the treasure, moats keep strangers away, thorns protect the beauties, and so on. These represent in numerous imaginary forms the perils of defloration. For the "special" man, formerly impenetrable gates, hedges, or doors fly open to indicate that the entry is timely, smooth, welcomed, and no longer dangerous.

Bettelheim (1975) points out that according to the Bible, the "curse" (menstruation) is inherited by woman from woman. In fairy tales bleeding begins when a girl has been pricked by a male or by a self-induced event. In "Sleeping Beauty" and several tales described below, it is contact with a woman that starts the bleeding. We may be able to differentiate hymeneal from menstrual meanings of bleeding by looking at its source in the story. If the bleeding is induced after contact with a man, we may more confidently suppose it has hymeneal meanings. In either case, however, woman bleeds (via menstruation or via intercourse) because of her "naughty" actions and/or accidents in which she has been involved.

Another Grimm's tale with these now-familiar themes, and also one that includes an evil witch, is "Jorinda and Joringel." In this story, a beautiful maiden is warned by her fiancé not to go too near a castle where an evil enchantress lures prey and then cooks and eats them. The enchantress casts a spell, so if "anyone came within a hundred paces of the castle, they'd have to stop dead and couldn't move from the spot. . . . But if a pure virgin entered this magic circle, the witch would transform her into a bird" (p. 268). The young couple wanders into the forest and gets lost too close to the castle walls, whereupon Jorinda is transformed into a nightingale. She sings "My bird with the red

ringlet [or my birdie with its ring so red]/Is singing, 'Woe's me!
Woe's me! Woe's me!'/It's singing of its death to the dove,/Sing-
ing 'Woe's me, alas, alas.'" Joringel searches everywhere for
Jorinda (pp. 268–269). He has a dream of finding a "blood-red"
flower with a big beautiful pearl in the middle of it. One touch
by this flower frees whatever has been enchanted. Taking this
dream image as an omen, he looks for and finds a flower that
has a big dew drop in the middle, "as big as the finest pearl."
Joringel goes to the castle and touches the gate with the flower,
and the gate immediately opens. He enters and frees his love.
Delaney and colleagues (1988) point out that this story, with
its heroine who is a "pure virgin," clearly represents another example of symbolic defloration. Defloration, in this instance,
occurs only after a brush with the disaster of defying the lure of
the bad mother.

Another example of recurrent imagery around blood and birth
can be seen in the stories of "Snow White" and "The Juniper
Tree." Delaney and colleagues (1988) suggest that drops of blood
spilled on the snow from a mother's finger become a symbol of
menstruation and birth. "The beautiful allegory of pregnancy and
birth, encompassing the growth of life as well as the death that
always lurks within the womb, is begun by woman's blood"
(p. 168). In "Snow White" drops of blood from her pricked finger inspire the mother to wish for a child as "as white as snow"
and "as red as blood" (Grimm 1973, p. 192). We would say that
the image of blood spilled on a white surface is another allusion to the blood of defloration and the anticipation of the blood
of childbirth. In "The Juniper Tree" (Grimm 1973), a mother
cuts her finger peeling a red apple while standing in the snow
under a juniper tree. Her blood leads to a wish for a child. This
too may be a reference to hymeneal blood, which is the necessary precursor to fertilization of the womb, a first step toward
pregnancy and childbirth.

In fairy tales blood has power, and can even speak. In "The
Goose Girl" (Grimm 1973), a beautiful princess is betrothed to
a prince who lives far away. She is sent to her bridegroom with

a royal dowry. Upon her departure, the queen mother cuts her own fingers with a knife and drips three drops of blood on a white cloth, which she gives to her daughter to protect her on her wedding voyage. During the journey, the evil maid-in-waiting does not help the bride, and the blood speaks, saying that if the queen knew this was happening, her heart would break. At one point the bride bends over to drink from a stream and loses the handkerchief with the blood upon it. By losing the drops of blood she becomes weak, helpless, and under the control of the maid-in-waiting. A number of additional adventures befall them and finally she is wed to her prince. In this story, the blood on the white cloth symbolically tells the tale and assures the girl her proper place, as does the bed sheet in marriage rituals. Here once again, blood speaks, passed on from mother to daughter as protection, and its loss produces weakness. Thus, as writers such as Mary Jane Lupton (1993) suggest, blood represents feminine power, perhaps power from which men shrink.

In another bloody tale, "Lover Roland" (Grimm 1973), an evil stepmother plots to kill her lovely stepdaughter who, while hidden away, hears of the plan. She fools the evil witch into killing her own daughter by cutting off her head with an ax. The stepdaughter runs to her lover Roland who advises her to steal the witch's magic staff. In addition, she takes the dead girl's head with her, letting three drops of blood fall in various places in the house. These drops of blood speak to the evil witch as she seeks her daughter. Finally the old witch finds her child "swimming in blood" in the bed where she had been murdered (p. 208). The witch pursues the couple, who attempt to run away. The girl changes herself into a beautiful flower blooming in the middle of a hawthorn hedge, and Roland changes into a fiddler. The witch is forced to dance to the music while the "thorns tore off her clothes, pricked her until she was bloody and wounded," and finally she lies dead (p. 209). While waiting to marry Roland, the young virgin turns herself into a red stone. Several more transformations occur until she is finally reunited with Roland and they marry. Familiar colors, objects, motifs, and symbols

appear in this confused tale of marriage. Here, blood is present
as a telltale mark of a bloody deed in bed. Fear of an aggressive,
murderous castrating mother who is accompanied by phallic
appendages (the magic staff) is evident. This story's confusion
expresses the childhood fears and distortions about adult marriage and sexuality. "Bad sex" is equated with the evils of masturbation (dancing to the fiddle) and premarital sex. The girl
must "turn to stone" until she is married.

Familiar themes in these tales are the turning to stone, paralysis, and inability to move limbs, which according to some psychoanalytic interpretations represent tumescence of the penis as
well as impotence. In dreams, inability to move frequently sig-
nifies the conscience saying "no" to a guilt-ridden thought or
deed. One of the reasons that we see so many prohibitions
against looking (which means knowing) in myths and fairy tales
is that it is thought to arouse sexual and incestuous impulses
and then sexual behavior. Thus, these motifs refer to both disobedience and to the representation of longing for carnal or
fleshly pleasures. Familiar examples of failures to heed prohibitions not to look and their punishments occur in the stories
of Lot's wife, Noah's daughters, David and Bathsheba, Adam
and Eve, Medusa, Gneisha, and various of the fairy tales described above. Prohibitions and threats against sexual knowledge and exploration in childhood, as well as fear of punishment
for such curiosity, increase the salience of the infantile fears
about adult sexuality of which defloration is the hallmark.

An additional tale of the defloration-death connection occurs
in "The Robber Bridegroom" (Grimm 1973). Here, a beautiful
maiden is promised to a man whom she does not love. The bride-
to-be is forced to go to visit this man. When she does, she is
warned, "You think you're a bride-to-be and that you'll soon
celebrate your wedding, but your wedding will be with Death"
(p. 152). The fair bride-to-be finds that her bridegroom's house
is a robbers' den, and she is privy to a scene of a girl being
dragged in crying and made to drink three glasses of wine. Then
several of the robbers tear off the girl's clothes, put her on a table,

chop her beautiful body to pieces, and sprinkle salt on it. There is a gold ring on the girl's little finger that cannot be easily pulled off, so they chop off her finger with a hatchet. The frightened bride-to-be is hiding and watching this cannibalistic, murderous rape scene. We see here the familiar theme of curiosity and observing and overhearing strange and frightening events from a hiding place. Clearly, this represents a sadomasochistic primal scene in which the woman loses body parts in a bloody assault.[3] The hymen may be symbolized here by a ring that is difficult to remove.

A similar image appears in "The Girl with the Wooden Helmet" (Lang 1994), a tale from Japan, in which a wedding day feast and celebration is described. A girl whose beauty is hidden beneath a wooden helmet is about to have her hair styled. She is unable to divest herself of her helmet, which had been given to her by her mother in order to protect her as "it was more difficult for a beautiful woman to pass unheeded than for others" (p. 176). As word of her beauty spreads, many "impudent" men appear and try to lift or remove the helmet. She rejects all suitors until a special man appears who seeks to marry her. In a dream her mother appears and tells her to marry him. To prepare her hair for the wedding, her maids attempt to lift the helmet off her head but find that "the harder they pulled, the faster it seemed to be, til the poor girl yelled with pain" (p. 178). Thus, she has to be married with the helmet on. As the ceremonial cup of wine is emptied, the helmet suddenly bursts with a loud noise, and falls in pieces on the ground. The floor is covered with precious stones that have fallen out of the helmet. All, of

---

3· The term *primal scene* refers to the experiences, fantasies, and distortions that children have surrounding the secret sexual life and sexual behaviors of their parents, which frequently look strange and violent to children. The primal scene, and hence intercourse, is often comprehended through the child's distorting lens of very primitive fantasies. For example, in this story the scene of defloration is represented in orally aggressive imagery.

course, live happily ever after. The helmet acts as a protection, a kind of chastity belt, and is a representation of the hymen, which bursts on the consummation of the wedding. All of the jewels (of sexuality) fall out to earth. Again, we see the romantic idea that only one man is destined to be the bridegroom and to receive the treasure of the girl's virginity.

We will end our discussion with a tale that appears to embody many of the images and themes that we have seen surrounding defloration. In "The Elf Maiden," a very confusing yet revealing tale from Lapland (Lang 1994), a young man stranded on an island hides from a boat load of people "from another world" who seem "strange." Two young and beautiful girls discover him, and one pinches him in her curiosity to see what "he is made of." She pricks her hand, screams, and bleeds because he had a pin sticking in the sleeve of his jacket. The others leave the island quickly. Left behind is a bundle of keys, the girl whom the pin had pricked, and the young man. "You will have to make me your wife," she says, "for you have drawn my blood, and I belong to you" (p. 172). They breakfast on wild cherries and go off to visit her parents. After much celebration as the couple prepares to leave her parents' home, the new wife whispers, "Take care to jump over the threshold as quick as you can, or it will be the worse for you" (p. 173). The groom listens to her and springs over the threshold, as his father-in-law throws a great hammer at him, which just misses him and would have broken his legs. As they are on the road to their home his wife warns him that he must not look back no matter what he hears or sees. The couple lives happily from that point on, except that from time to time, the girl vanishes. When finally the hero complains, she tells him that she is compelled to go against her will and that the only way he can stop her is to drive a nail into the threshold so she cannot pass in or out.

This tale, which must have idiosyncratic historic elements related to the Lapland experience, also has an abundance of the themes and images that we have seen throughout our study. Thus, curiosity, being pricked and bleeding, thresholds, castration and its connection to oedipal configurations, the inevitability of certain events, specific objects like keys and cherries, prohibitions, and so on abound. The repetition of these images and their relationship via intrapsychic representations to the introduction to active sexual life for females and its impact on males is an indication of their strength and capacity to affect our lives. We will trace these themes throughout our different sources and later speculate about their dynamic meanings in our patients.

6

Thresholds in Beatrix Potter and Edith Wharton

*T*wo eminent women writers whose difficulties with marriage and sexuality, and specifically anxieties about defloration, are evidenced in their writings are Beatrix Potter and Edith Wharton. Autobiographical and biographical materials and their journals provide additional evidence of their concerns. Both women, although of widely different backgrounds, literary talents and interests, and personal styles, had one major circumstance in common: they both remained virginal or unawakened sexually until they were in their forties. Additionally, both were child-less. Both wrote about the unhappy childhood homes they wanted to leave behind. The two suffered serious traumatic ill-nesses or rheumatic or typhoid fever during childhood or ado-lescence. They both had cold, forbidding mothers, felt closer to their nannies and governesses, and closely identified with their fathers. Both exceptionally intelligent women commented on the lack of sexual enlightenment and education in their back-grounds. Both evidenced precocious visual sensitivity and artistic ability. Even the names they gave the beloved country homes they created for themselves were similar: The Hill Top and The Mount.

BEATRIX POTTER

We draw on Alexander Grinstein's careful biography of Beatrix Potter (1995), the author and illustrator of children's literature, including the popular *Tale of Peter Rabbit* (1902). Beatrix, the daughter of well-to-do middle-class parents, grew up in a large house in Kensington, England in the latter part of the nineteenth century. As was customary for children of her class and circumstances, she was looked after by a nanny and a large staff of servants. During her youth, Potter suffered from depression and low self-esteem, aggravated by episodes of illness. Early on, she showed feelings of conflict and confusion about marriage and the role of women. In 1885, during her late adolescence, she wrote a discourse on her cousin's engagement that was critical of her choice. Better lonely than an unhappy marriage, she asserted. As for herself, she on one occasion said that marriage would be "stupid"; on another, she contradicted herself and stated that a happy marriage would be the "crown of a woman's life."

Potter's mixed feelings about marriage apparently were connected to her strained and conflicted relationship with her mother. Her strong negative feelings toward her mother were barely concealed in her journals and were personified in the many negatively pictured mothers who appear in her tales. Grinstein interprets the story *The Tale of Two Bad Mice* (1904), in which frustrated and hungry mice destroy the interior of a doll's house, as revealing Potter's feelings of anger and deprivation at the hand of maternal figures. In her journal there are many more positive references to her father, whose artistic interests she shared. Apparently, Potter spent much of her life struggling against her conflicted emotional and economic dependence on her parents, a situation not uncommon for unmarried women in the early part of the twentieth century in England. Grinstein surmises from the repetitive themes in her stories of children's curiosity and her own early interest in biology expressed in detailed drawings of nature and microscopic observations that Potter had very little in the way of sexual enlightenment (p. 63).

Belatedly, at age 37, Potter began to develop a close professional relationship with Norman Warne, a publisher, with whom she gradually fell in love. For the first time she was seriously considering marriage. Her mother, however, took a strong dislike to Warne, whom she saw as beneath the family's status. In this matter, Mrs. Potter remained disapproving, implacable, and remote, as apparently was her typical character (Grinstein p. 88). In 1903, during this period of struggling against her parent's disapproval of her relationship with Warne, Potter wrote *The Tale of Mrs. Tiggy-Winkle*. In it, a little girl named Lucie meets a hedgehog named Mrs. Tiggy-Winkle, supposedly modeled after a real person in Potter's childhood, a washerwoman with whom she spent time. While Mrs. Tiggy-Winkle is ironing, the girl plies her with questions. Child analysts tell us that a child's insistent questions frequently express sexual curiosity and represent other underlying questions that go unanswered by the parents. One of the pieces of ironing is a damask tablecloth stained with currant wine, which Mrs. Tiggy-Winkle says could not be washed out. As she is walking along a steep path, looking for a lost handkerchief, Lucie hears Mrs. Tiggy-Winkle singing: "Lily white and clean, oh! / With little frills between, oh! / Smooth and hot-red rusty spot / Never here be seen, oh!" (Potter 1905, p. 18). Lucie, standing on a little doorstep, knocks twice and interrupts the song.

Grinstein tells us that Potter provides a specific association to this spot in a letter written in 1905 to Warne. Potter wrote, "She [Mrs. Tiggy-Winkle] is supposed to be exorcising spots and iron stains, same as Lady Macbeth, the verb is imperative and apparently it is not reasonable to use 'no' with a vocative noun. It is a contradiction to address 'no spot!' I am afraid this is rather muddled." Indeed, this passage is muddled, partially because of Potter's obsessive pondering about the use of negatives: "it is *not* reasonable to use *no*" (Taylor 1989, p. 120).

Mrs. Tiggy-Winkle has the dangerous and aggressive qualities of Lady Macbeth and those attributed to Potter's mother. The story was written when conflicts with her mother may have run especially high. At the time she was writing *The Tale of Mrs. Tiggy-Winkle*, Potter had begun to fall in love with Warne and must have hoped that Warne would propose to her. It is likely that she was preoccupied with the fantasy of being married and having a family of her own, a fantasy that now might become a reality. Such thoughts probably engendered tremendous anxiety in her about her mother's disapproval and antagonistic attitude, as we can discern from her characterization of Mrs.Tiggy-Winkle as being potentially dangerous, a hedgehog with prickles. As her friendship with Norman developed and as it gradually took the form of a love relationship, her mother's openly antagonistic attitude about it served to mobilize Beatrix Potter's anxieties about her mother's antagonism even further (Grinstein 1995, pp.100–101). We would stress that what the prospect of marriage might mobilize especially are anxieties related to oedipal competition.

In her journal, Potter associated the red stain with Lady Macbeth. Grinstein sees this association of Mrs. Tiggy-Winkle with Lady Macbeth as evidence of Potter's fear of the dangerous and aggressive qualities of her mother (p. 99). We think the image of the red stain also reveals some guilt over an "evil" deed. Lady Macbeth, in trying to wash the memory of the blood from her hands cries, "What's done cannot be undone" (5.1.75). Lady Macbeth urges her husband to perform the forbidden and evil act of regicide. With the killing of the king she becomes queen. In this way she assumes the role of oedipal victor, as does Macbeth.

This concern about blood may allude to Potter's guilty fantasies and fears about losing her virginity in an anticipated marriage with a man whom she was beginning to love. A bloody, evil deed of oedipal murder that cannot be undone is Potter's direct association to stains, which lead us to defloration. "Smooth and hot-red spot" on a white cloth is certainly evocative of hymeneal blood, especially in the context of marriage. Note in the rhyme "never here be seen" and, in the passage from the letter, the string of negatives, of *no*'s. We have found that whenever thoughts about the hymen and defloration appear clinically, they are inevitably introduced with such negations. Most women who hear of a rusty red spot on a white cloth would also think immediately of menstrual stains. We have seen the conflation of menstrual blood and hymeneal blood in other sources and will address the reasons for this in later chapters.

In 1905 Norman Warne proposed to Beatrix Potter, who intended to accept, in spite of her parents' opposition. One month after his letter of proposal, Warne died at the age of 37. The death was a terrible shock and loss to her. She received little sympathy from her parents in her grief. It was years later that Potter met William Heelis, a local solicitor. He proposed to her in the winter of 1912. Significantly, it was in this period of the courtship with Heelis that she took up writing, or rewriting, fairy tales, with their themes of romance and marriage. Grinstein believes this turn in her writing reflected her renewed interest in relations between men and women, following a long dry and unhappy spell after the death of Warne. It is particularly interesting to us that Potter chose to rewrite these particular fairy tales because of their references to blood and defloration, as for example, "Blue Beard" and "Sister Anne." In these tales, the conception of marriage and sexuality was that the woman would be beaten, eaten, and/or tortured by the man. These themes provide familiar instances of the sadomasochistically interpreted primal scene between the parents as a scary, violent battle. We saw these sadomasochistic themes in Chapter 5 on fairy tales.

At this time Potter was saying in her personal correspondence that she herself was quite tired of being "goody good and nice." That is, she was tired of living a life so constrained by the wishes, demands, and critical opposition of her parents. She wanted to be free, to be married in spite of their opposition. So, despite her parents' disapproval, she accepted Heelis and was married in the fall of 1913. She was 47; he was 42.

The story that came out of this period is *The Tale of Pigling Bland* (Potter 1913). In a letter Potter wrote at this time, she said: "I think I shall put *myself* in the next book, it will be about pigs" (Taylor 1989, p. 173). Thus, we may be safer than usual in reading personal significance in this tale. *The Tale of Pigling Bland* is the story of two pigs who set out on their own on a journey to market. Aunt Pettitoes gives the two little pigs instructions. Beatrix Potter adds her personal comment in her own voice: "If you once cross the county boundary, you cannot come back. . . . Here are two licenses permitting two pigs to go to market" (1913, pp. 22–23). She includes an illustration of herself giving a license to one of the pigs. We are struck with the clear allusion to her upcoming marriage with the inclusion of (marriage) licenses, and efforts at independence. The two pigs need a license, and Pigling Bland expresses the wish to cultivate his own garden and not work for others. So, too, there are more hidden allusions to a child's fantasized dangers of marriage and sex. The pigs are after all in danger of ending up at a slaughter house themselves. Here, once again, in this story is the idea of the crossing over a threshold or boundary, the county boundary, from which one cannot return. We find this idea is frequently associated with loss of virginity and of the breaking of the hymen. As Potter was once again anticipating marriage and the marriage bed, she writes of the irrevocability of crossing boundaries and thresholds. She had written about blood stains ten years before when she was engaged for the first time.

Potter had a particularly difficult time leaving her parents and getting married. We can only speculate about the reasons for this. It is not unreasonable to assume that, among other factors, sexual inhibitions may have gotten in the way of her marriage and sexual fulfillment. Grinstein elucidates how the theme of a child's sexual curiosity and search for enlightenment runs through Potter's writings. One such example is *The Tale of Squirrel Nutkin* (Potter 1903), in which a series of riddles is posed by Squirrel Nutkin to Old Brown, who does not answer but remains aloof and contemptuous. Riddles frequently represent disguised questions about the facts of life, according to psychoanalytic interpretations. Riddles can pose the child's underlying question, "Where do babies come from?" Such questions must often be disguised because they are forbidden in a particular historical and social setting and family, such as Potter's. In *The Tale of Squirrel Nutkin*, Nutkin provokes Old Brown with a riddle that concerns Humpty Dumpty. One psychoanalytic interpretation of this nursery rhyme based on a clinical case (Petty 1953), centers on sibling rivalry: Humpty Dumpty falls from being the favored only child after the birth of a younger sibling. Our associations to the fallen Humpty Dumpty go in another direction, to something broken, the hymen, and lost forever. We have found in our clinical material that the idea of "cracking" is commonly associated unconsciously with the rupture of the hymen, and a vulgar term for the female genital is *crack*.

In Potter's first version of this story, the squirrels bring Old Brown a basket of newly laid eggs. In the final version the gift is a pie with twenty-four blackbirds. Grinstein says both pie and basket serve as hatching places and represent the womb. The Opies (1974) interpret the children's poem "Four and Twenty Blackbirds," to which the pie in Potter's tale alludes, as a representation of the process of fertilization. The first riddle in the tale concerns a "Little Wee man in a coat, a staff in his hand and a stone in his throat." The solution is a cherry. Potter had discarded an original, unpublished version of the riddle, which was similar: "We lie picked and plucked and put in a pie." Here the solution is currants. Thus, we have a link to the cloth stained by currants in *Mrs. Tiggy-Winkle*. That a very common image for the hymen is the cherry provides another associative link to the stained cloth. A red stain that cannot be washed out, sexual riddles, currants, and cherries all suggest defloration.

Potter consciously kept waiting for her parents' permission to marry. Another possible source for Potter's struggle to break away from her parents was her unconscious oedipally based attachment to her father. A journal entry when she was 28 describes a photographic trip with her father to a Scottish castle. She comments on the heat during the journey and describes the castle, saying she "never saw a more romantically silent spot for a castle" (Taylor 1966, p. 341). She also quotes a poem, "The Red Etain of Ireland," which is about an ogre who steals a king's daughter and sadistically beats her. This castle served as the model for her novella *Sister Anne*, a variant on "Bluebeard." Although she expresses overt irritation with her father on this day, we see allusions to erotic ties to him in this material: the romantic spot, the poem with its oedipal themes, and the links to the tale of *Sister Anne*. Potter's conception of her father, and of men in general at certain times must have been similar to descriptions of the loud, fearsome ogre, the Red Etain. Grinstein concludes, in regard to Potter's feelings about her father, "The context of the material strongly suggests that, like many girls, Beatrix Potter did have such fantasies about him at one time" (p. 278). We will see these same dynamics in Edith Wharton.

WHARTON

Edith Wharton was born in 1862 into a socially prominent New York family, the Joneses. The stultifying atmosphere was one in which behavior had to be proper and was constantly under scrutiny. There were two brothers, twelve and sixteen years older than Edith. Her father, a good-looking man of leisure and inherited wealth, had strong intellectual interests. His extensive library provided his only daughter her sole education. Edith educated herself in literature, philosophy, religion, and major European languages, and she acquired a taste for European culture and architecture. She was never drawn to fairy tales, though she loved mythology. She derived much pleasure from reading, from pure words. She had a passion for making up stories from the age of 6 and during her adolescence had poetry published. At 15 she wrote *Fast and Loose*, a novella about an English girl who throws over a teenage boyfriend and marries an aging lord.

The family moved to Europe when Edith was four and returned to America when she was 10. Wharton was a frightened neurotic child with many phobias and severe anxiety attacks. Later she became very psychosomatic. A biographer quotes a letter in which Wharton described the agonies she had suffered as a child: "for *twelve* years I seldom knew what it was to be, for more than an hour or two of the twenty-four, without an intense feeling of nausea, and such unutterable fatigue that when I got up I was always more tired than when I lay down. This form of neurasthenia consumed the best years of my youth, and left, in some sort, an irreparable shade on my life. . . . I worked through it, and came out on the other side" (Wolff 1978, p. 52). Note the idea in this quote of a crossing or threshold in coming out on the other side.

In Wharton's journals and autobiographies, her mother emerges as a cold, aloof, prudish woman who adored clothes. She spent her time in social affairs. A warmer maternal surrogate was an Irish nursemaid. In *Life and I*, a long autobiographical manuscript, which was probably written in 1920 and served as a first draft of her published autobiography, *A Backward Glance* (1933), Wharton describes how her mother responded to her early sexual curiosity with "You're too little to understand" and "It's not nice to ask about such things." As Wharton wrote in her memoirs,

> Once when I was 7 or 8 an older cousin had told me that babies were not found in flowers but in people. This information had been given unsought, but as I had been told by MaMa that it was not Nice to inquire into such matters, I had a vague sense of contamination, and went immediately to confess my involuntary offense. I received a severe scolding and was left with a penetrating sense of "not niceness" which effectually kept me

from pursuing my investigation farther; and this was literally all I knew of the processes of generation till I had been married several weeks. [Wharton 1920, pp. 33–34]

This description echoes Potter's depiction of Old Brown who was aloof and unresponsive to little Nutkin's questions. Of course, this purposeful attempt to keep young girls ignorant did not solely characterize Wharton's or Potter's mothers, but was a far-reaching societal practice and norm. We saw this idea that girls must be kept ignorant of sex represented in fairy tales such as "Fitcher's Bird" or "Virgin Mary's Child." In her biography of Wharton, *Feast of Words: The Triumph of Edith Wharton* (1978), Cynthia Griffin Wolff paints a picture of the society in which Edith struggled to come of age: "The code of 'niceness' was proclaimed throughout the land. Young ladies were kept 'pure' for their husbands—and purity entailed a kind of systematic assumption of their total ignorance. Society assumed that they need be told nothing before they became wives and mothers" (p. 36).

In adolescence Wharton was possessed by nameless terrors which she was convinced were lying in wait for her. These haunting fears had their origins in her convalescence at age 9 after typhoid fever in Germany. Lenore Terr (1987), in her psychoanalytic study of the effect of early trauma on creativity, suggests that Wharton's illness, with its accompanying feelings of entrapment and posttraumatic hallucination, made a long-lasting mark on her psyche in the fear of ghost stories and night terrors. Typhoid would have meant that the child would have been confined and isolated in her room with no one but doctors allowed to see her.

Later, when someone put in her hands a tale of robbers and ghosts, she became victim to a relapse of the fever and another affliction, an intense fear:

This illness formed the dividing line between my little childhood, and the next stage . . . and when I came to myself, it was to enter a world haunted by formless horrors . . . now I lived in a state of chronic fear. Fear of what? I cannot say—and even at the time, I was never able to formulate my terror. It was like some dark undefinable menace, forever dogging my steps, lurking, and threatening; I was conscious of it wherever I went by day, and at night it made sleep impossible, unless a light and a nurse-maid were in the room. But whatever it was, it was most formidable and pressing when I was returning from my daily walk (which I always took with a maid or governess, or with my father). During the last few yards, and while I waited on the door-step for the door to be opened, I could feel it behind me, upon me; and if there was any delay in the opening of the door I was seized by a choking agony of terror. It did not matter who was with me, for no one could protect me, but, oh, the rapture of relief if my companion had a latch-key, and we could get in at once, before It caught me! [Wharton 1933, pp. 16–18]

Terr (1987) has postulated that the ghostlike image that haunted Edith is an heir of the traumatic time of her sickness when she was isolated and the white-clothed doctors hovered at her threshold.

Five years later she was still having acute recurring apprehension of "some dark indefinable menace forever dogging my steps, lurking and threatening" (Wharton 1920, p. 17). Thus, the fear was worse when she came back at the end of her daily walk at dusk. There, on the threshold of the house, she was sure the horror was preparing to spring upon her and no one, not even her father, could protect her. This phobia we will call a phobia of thresholds. In describing her fear of tangible thresholds, she refers to yet another threshold, the dividing line between childhood and the next stage.

At age 25, she met Teddy Wharton, who came from the same social stratum that Wharton did. At 33, he was a passive, non-intellectual man with whom she shared few interests. He was taken up with the sports of fishing and riding. Wolff (1978) states that the marriage was not consummated for three weeks and always thereafter the physical relationship between the pair (such as it was) was agonized. R. W. B. Lewis (1985) speculates that it soon became nonexistent and that as soon as she had to share a bedroom with Teddy, Edith suffered asthma. Others have stated that the marriage was virtually sexless. Certainly the marriage was unhappy, as Wharton perceived her parents' marriage to be. Its unhappiness was mirrored repeatedly in the descriptions of unhappy marriages that Wharton created in her writings.

In 1908 Edith met a dashing newsman, recently divorced, named Fullerton. For the first time in her life, Edith fell deeply in love and entered into a passionate love affair, about which she wrote rapturously in poems and letters. Whether or not she was physically a virgin, this was her sexual awakening. The affair lasted for three years and broke up because Fullerton's interest turned to other women and because Wharton had to return to America. Shortly after they broke up Wharton divorced Teddy, whose many blatant sexual affairs and financial mismanagement, including embezzlement of her funds, she could no longer tolerate. Wharton never again had a passionate affair nor did she remarry. In spite of her disappointment with Fullerton's somewhat caddish behavior toward her, she remained on friendly terms with him and never regretted the affair. She wrote him, "whatever those months were to you, to me they were a great gift, a wonderful enrichment; and still I rejoice and give thanks for them! You woke me from a great lethargy." As Gloria Erlich (1992), who quotes this letter, concludes, "Edith Wharton was determined to complete her human experience by pursuing at whatever age and at whatever cost her long-deferred sexual education" (p. 105).

It is our thesis that Edith Wharton's threshold phobia can be traced to her sexual conflicts and inhibitions and, more specifically, reflects fears and fantasies about losing her virginity and being deflowered. As with Potter, it is not enough to utilize social mores of the time to explain the sexual inhibitions and ignorance that Wharton suffered around the idea of the wedding night. While these are important influences, we will look to added intrapsychic, unconscious meanings.

Wolff (1978) postulates that the origins of the threshold fears could be traced to Wharton's conflicts with her mother. Wolff speculates that unconsciously the girl conjured up the image of her mother waiting ominously inside the house ready to scold and to humiliate her. While these arguments are indeed plausible and convincing, Wharton's description of the last long moment of phobic fear is immensely suggestive of other meanings. The most intense moment of agony always occurred when she "waited on the doorstep for the door to be opened." This last fear pursued her into adolescence. "I was a young lady with long skirts and my hair up before my heart ceased to beat fear if I had to stand for half a minute on a doorstep" (Wharton 1920, p. 18).

Wharton's phobic fears were concentrated on the *crossing* of the threshold itself. She was not afraid while she was outside or inside, but during the crossing from outside to inside, that is, in the penetration of the doorway from the outside to the inside. Thus, the threshold phobia suggests a fear of penetration, both of penetrating and/or of being penetrated. There is a great deal of evidence that this fear of penetration, or crossing over a threshold, was a sexual fear for Wharton.

Certainly, Wharton took special interest in thresholds. In her book on architecture she devoted a whole chapter to doors and another to entrances and vestibules. "It should be borne in mind of entrances in general that, while the main purpose of a door is to admit, its secondary purpose is to exclude. The outer door, which separates the hall or vestibule from the street, should clearly proclaim itself an effectual barrier" (Wharton and Codman 1902, p. 103). As shown in the previous chapters, we have been struck with the repetitive symbolism and linkage of thresholds and barriers to images of the hymen and defloration.

Many authors have commented on the motif of thresholds that runs through Wharton's works and its connection to themes and conflicts of oedipal rivalries, sexual conflicts, and incest. Wolff (1978) feels that *Ethan Frome* (Wharton 1911), the first significant novel Wharton wrote after her affair with Fullerton, is essentially about transition, a juncture between the worlds of immaturity and adulthood. The story begins with two men who make their way from the front door down a darkened hall to stop on the threshold of an inner room. They are poised on the threshold, the door beginning to swing open, as the narrator begins his tale. The architectural details, characteristic in Wharton's works, are striking. As Wolff points out, there are two threshold scenes with Zeena and Mattie, Ethan's wife and his illicit love, in the book. These are the only two significant passages preserved from an earlier version of the novel. Wolff infers that Wharton chose these because they were especially meaningful to her. The narrator continually pictures Ethan at the juncture of two worlds, echoing his psychological dilemma. Wolff suggests that the character of Ethan is caught up in a conflict between childhood and adulthood, a conflict with which Wharton herself struggled. Wolff continues,

> We know what thresholds meant to Edith Wharton long ago, and though we need not have this knowledge to understand the novel, it greatly enriches our reading of it. The threshold of Lucretia's (Edith's mother) house was a place of transition for the adolescent girl; at this juncture, the opposing demands of two distinct worlds were visited upon her—the world of adulthood, independence, freedom, and sexual maturity; and the world of childhood, obedience, limitation, and emotional starvation." [p. 173]

Several authors have taken up the threshold themes in the novella *Summer*, published in 1917. It chronicles the relationship between an adolescent girl and her adopted father and is the most overtly erotic and manifestly incestuous story of Wharton's published fiction. Charity is the informally adopted daughter of Lawyer Royall and his wife. With the death of his wife, Royall becomes interested in Charity, who has become a young woman. Charity is disgusted and frightened by his sexual interest. Royall asks her to marry him, but she falls in love with a handsome young stranger. During the summer her passionate relationship with this young man develops and results in Charity's pregnancy. In the end, after many twists and turns in the plot, Charity finally marries Royall. Erlich (1992) is struck by how thresholds are linked with incestuous, oedipal conflicts in the novel: "Throughout the novel, Lawyer Royall's image falls between the lovers—in doorways, at moments of embrace—always he is aware of her sexual activities and contaminates them. He looms over the threshold and outside windows, haunting the girl with his unceasing vigilance" (p. 128). In another scene, Charity, awaiting her lover, becomes "aware that a shadow had flitted across the glory-flooded room. . . . The door opened and [in] Mr. Royall walked." (Wharton 1917, pp. 203–204). That is, the father on whom the girl is fixed in the oedipal complex comes in the way of her sexual life with other men.

Wolff (1978) also sees *Summer* as a drama of thresholds. She points out that the story explores the implications of the passage through adolescence, from childhood to sexual maturity and independence. It begins, in fact, on the threshold of the girl's journey to self-discovery: "A girl came out of Lawyer Royall's house . . . and stood on the doorstep. It was the beginning of a June afternoon" (Wharton 1917, p. 7). For Wolff, growth has a strong sexual component. As she puts it, growth leads to the delights and fears of being penetrated, and intercourse leads to pregnancy. Wolff notes that Wharton has "plunged back to her old crisis of the threshold once again" by representing a liaison between a daughter and father figure and resurrecting the oedipal dilemma of love for the father, which conflicts with the need for the mother. (Wolff saw Edith's phobia essentially in terms of a fear of her mother.) Both the first sexual encounter which occurred on the threshold of the girl's bedroom and the sexual conclusion when she reenters the guardian's house, are essentially incestuous scenarios (Wolff 1978, pp. 306–307). When Charity is 17, Royall "violates her innocence" by trying to enter her bedroom:

> when she saw him in the doorway, a ray from the autumn moon falling on his discomposed face, she understood. . . . [A]s he put

his foot across the threshold, she stretched out her arm and
stopped him. . . . "Charity let me in—I'm a lonesome man." . . .
Her heart gave a startled plunge. . . . "This ain't your wife's room."
[Wharton 1917, pp. 28–30]

The young girl's fears of sexual intercourse may mirror similar
fears of the young Wharton herself. A Wharton scholar (White
1991) emphasizes in Wharton's works the theme of the intrusion of the "coarse masculine" into an idyllic female world. A
good example can be found in *Summer* in the scene in which
the heroine's communion with nature is interrupted by a man's
muddy boots trampling some frail white flowers.

Later in the novel the girl stands outside a window and
watches her young flame, Lucius. She is compelled to acknowledge the sexual implication of crossing this threshold: "She
suddenly understood what would happen if she went in . . .
the melting of palm into palm and mouth on mouth, and the
long flame burning her from head to foot" (Wharton 1917,
pp. 105–106). When she has sex with Lucius, she goes to a
halfway house on a mountain, and they cross the threshold
before having sex.

These scenes make explicit the connection with forbidden,
or adult, sexuality and the crossing of a threshold. Thus, such
unconscious connections may have been at play in Edith's mind
when she became fearful of crossing thresholds as a child. Wolff
(1978) puts it well: "The longing from which the girl had run—
against which she had deployed regression as a defense—is a
flaming, consuming love for the father, a fear of penetration that
is inextricable from a desperate yearning for it" (p. 307). We
think that there is even more to this fear than an oedipal longing for the father. We will return to this idea later.

An explicitly sexual and incestuous story left by Wharton
among her papers, unpublishable because of its pornographic
quality, was "Beatrice Palmato" (Lewis 1985, pp. 544–548). This
was handwritten and details the incestuous encounter of
Beatrice with her father. It includes such phrases as:

. . . with a deeper thrill she felt his lips pressed upon that quivering invisible bud, and then the delicate firm thrust of his tongue, so full and yet so infinitely subtle, pressing apart the close petals, and forcing itself in deeper and deeper. . . .

"My little girl," he breathed, sinking down beside her, his muscular trunk bare, and the third hand quivering and thrusting upward between them, a drop of moisture pearling at its tip.

. . . and at last, sinking backward into new abysses of bliss, felt it descend on her, press open the secret gates, and plunge into the deepest depths of her thirsting body. . . . [Lewis 1985, p. 548]

We have come to recognize many of these images as familiar ones, representing the female genital, the hymen, and defloration. Remember, for example, "Jorinda and Joringel" with the pearl in the petals of a red flower, or the secret gates and depths mirrored in many fairy tales such as "Blue Beard."

In the Palmato fragment, this lusty interlude occurred after a previous defloration. "'I was—remembering—last week'—she faltered, below her breath. 'Yes, darling. That experience is a cruel one—but it has to come once in all women's lives. Now we shall reap its fruit'" (Lewis 1985, p. 548). We feel that this sequence echoes the events in Wharton's own life—an early, painful defloration with Teddy, followed years later by a passionate sexual awakening with the forbidden and probably unconsciously incestuous figure of Fullerton.

Erlich, in her insightful book, *The Sexual Education of Edith Wharton* (1992), sheds much light on these ideas. A chapter entitled "On the Threshold" is followed by one called "The Passion Experience." This sequence highlights the meaning to Erlich of the threshold anxiety and panic attacks that were so eloquently and explicitly described by Wharton. That is, the threshold phobia had to be dissolved before the passion experience could occur. In "On the Threshold" Erlich draws out the theme of sexual ignorance and the search for enlightenment in Wharton's works, which is similar to the one we have seen in Potter's writings. *The House of Mirth* (1905) tells of Lily Bart, an impoverished, beautiful, young orphaned woman who seeks security through marriage. As Erlich points out, Lily approaches marriage "in ignorance of its personal and sexual dimension" (p. 58). This ignorance parallels Edith's anxiety-ridden questioning of her mother prior to her marriage. In the short story "The Old Maid" Wharton writes of the sexual instruction and information that passes between a mother and a daughter on the eve of marriage.

The character Lily from *The House of Mirth* (1905) feels compelled to marry Rosedale, a suitor about whom she had serious misgivings because of his "race." Rosedale, a "Levantine," that is, a Jew, is both attractive and repulsive to Lily, and resembles the Levantine father in Wharton's "Beatrice Palmato." The exogamous, sexual object is the recipient of projected and demeaned sexual impulses, just as the animal groom in fairy tales accomplishes this psychological compromise. Lily thinks, "there were certain things not good to think of, certain midnight images that must at any cost be exorcised—and one of these was the image of herself as Rosedale's wife" (p. 400). Here the ghostly, frightening images of Wharton's phobias emerge in a clearly sexual context. In a seduction scene, Lily reacts to the somatic evidence of sexual arousal with terror. Her fear is displaced and is focused on the man's hand, which "grew formidable" (p. 235). The hand appears as an important motif for the expression of childhood's oedipal longings in Edith's first and earliest memories described in her autobiography and journals: her small hand held in her father's palm, a first kiss from a boy while their hands touch, and the name *Palmato*, or palm.

In the chapter called "The Passion Experience," Erlich (1992) details Wharton's passionate sexual affair at age 45 with the 42-year-old bisexual, divorced Fullerton. He had just ended a long affair with an older woman and was engaged to his adoptive sister. Clearly he had oedipal issues of his own to match those of Wharton. Although he was characterized by Wharton's admirers as a scoundrel and a "middle-aged Lothario," Fullerton's magnetism was apparent. He was an expatriate Harvard graduate who was friend to such luminaries as Bernard Berenson, Oscar Wilde, George Santayana, and Henry James. Wharton returned or destroyed his letters to her and requested he do the same. Luckily for posterity, he did not and hundreds of her love letters are available to us.

Louise Kaplan (1991) has characterized this relationship as a masochistic perversion on Wharton's part; however, Wharton, who overcame inhibitions regarding her unsatisfactory and essentially celibate marriage and was able to engage in the adulterous liaison, wrote: "I felt for the first time that indescribable current of communication flowing between myself & some one wise—felt it, I mean uninterruptedly securely, so that it penetrated every sense & every thought . . . & said to myself: 'This must be what happy women feel.'" She wrote also: "I have drunk of the wine of life at last, I have known the thing best worth knowing. I have been warmed through and through, never to grow quite cold again till the end" (cited in Erlich, p. 75). Here again is a "never," not related to the actual rupture of the hymen but referring to the first sexual passion. The experience made Wharton into an awakened Sleeping Beauty. Could anyone have put the joys of sexual awakening any better? Thus, the pleasureful oedipal connotations of the affair and not just the negatively tinged masochistic ones strike us. We see in the affair with Fullerton a thinly displaced oedipal and incestuous, yet adaptive, deflowering relationship from which Wharton was able to grow and take pleasure.

Through the awakening with Fullerton, or perhaps before it, Wharton was able to work through her sexual inhibitions and earlier phobias about thresholds. It is illustrative to look at Wharton's writings before and after the affair to see evidence of this process. During the height of the affair, Wharton was consumed with it and was unable to turn her attention to writing. Soon, however, she began to write poetry, the first since her adolescent efforts that was published. It included the long and beautiful poem "Terminus." The name was chosen to describe an experience that occurred in a station hotel and marked a temporary end to their relationship. "Wonderful was the long secret night you gave me, my Lover, / Palm to palm, breast to breast in the gloom" (Lewis 1985, p. 259). Note the reference to palms, evocative of the first memory of putting her hand in her father's palm, and the Beatrice Palmato fragment. In another sonnet, one of a series in "The Mortal Lease," she puts into words a theme of loss of virginity. Lewis tells us that the words are her image of herself, ready to cross over the threshold into the wilds of sexual experience:

> the nun entranced
> Who nightlong held her Bridegroom in her soul.
> And I would meet your passion as the first
> Wild woodland woman met her patron's craft,
> Or as the Greek whose fearless beauty laughed,
> And doffed her raiment by the Attic flood.
>
> [cited in Lewis, 1985, p. 235]

At the end of the affair, Wharton, for the first time in her life, wrote a series of ghost tales. Remember that her phobia of thresholds had begun, according to her, when she was frightened by a ghost story given to her when she was recovering from a childhood illness at age 9. Thus, the affair may have freed her from both her fear of thresholds and her aversion to ghost stories. The first of these stories she wrote was called, perhaps significantly, "The Bolted Door" (Wharton 1910). This is a strange and rambling story about a man, Hubert Granice, who attempts to convince a series of people that he has murdered his uncle in a crime covered over so carefully that it is perfect. Once again the tale begins on a threshold: "In exactly three minutes Mr. Peter Ascham, of the eminent legal firm of Ascham and Pettilow, would have his punctual hand on the doorbell of the flat. . . . And the sound of the door bell would be the beginning of the end—after that there'd be no going back, by God— no going back!" (p. 3). One of the many oddities of the story is what on the surface seems like the gratuitous inclusion of idiosyncratic details. The murder of the uncle was motivated by the old man's cruel dismissal of a gardener. The protagonist had visited his uncle to find him contemplating a huge melon in front of him. "Look at it, look at it, did you ever see such a beauty? Such firmness—roundness—such delicious smoothness to the touch. It was as if he had said she instead of it, and when he put out his senile hand and touched the melon I positively had to look the other way" (p. 12). The Italian undergardener, specially recommended for the melon houses, had been assigned to the care of the melon. "And that very morning he had been ordered to pick the melon, which was to be shown the next day at the county fair, and to bring it in for Mr. Lenman to gaze on its blonde virginity." But in picking it, the gardener had the misfortune to "drop it crash on the spout of a watering pot, so that it received a deep gash in its firm pale rotundity, and was henceforth but a bruised, ruined, fallen melon. . . . The old man's rage was fearful in its impotence" (p. 12). This passage seems ridiculous, except if viewed as a description, perhaps a mocking one, of a defloration, with the father's reaction to the spoiling of the daughter. How else could one interpret a melon dropped on the spout of a watering pot, receiving a deep gash (slang for female genital), or a melon, described as "blonde virginity?"

A few years later, in 1912, came *The Reef*, Wharton's novel of a woman who, like Edith herself, in mid-life longs to circumvent sexual inhibitions. According to Erlich, an "'unexpected obstacle,' the sharp first words of the novel, foreshadow the reef of inhibitions hidden beneath the flood of Anna Leath's rising passion" (1992, p. 106). The thinly veiled theme of incest in the novel appears in the tangled web of relationships among the main characters. As we have said, Wharton's choice of Fullerton had incestuous shadings.

It would appear that for Edith Wharton, sexual urges were too heavily tied unconsciously with forbidden incestuous impulses. Adeline Tintner (1980) is one of many scholars who have been struck by the incestuous themes in Wharton's works. She chronicles the struggle between mother and daughter in Wharton's late novels in terms of competition for the father. *The Mother's Recompense* (1925), for example, depicts the horror of a woman who learns that her daughter is to marry the young man with whom she herself has been in love. Erlich (1992) postulates that the denial and sacrifice of Wharton's sexuality for some years was attributable to her atonement for a strong oedipal rivalry with her mother for her adored and handsome father (p. 125).*

We would agree, but we see in the phobia another side of the oedipal configuration. On the one hand, the fear of crossing over the threshold expresses the young girl's fear of crossing over into forbidden sexual territory, the oedipal rivalry with the mother for the father, and with it the highly charged, yet frightening wish to be penetrated by him. On the other, it also expresses the girl's fear of, and wish for, being the penetrator herself. Remember that Edith was most frightened of entering from the outside into the house when she returned from a walk, of crossing over the threshold herself. Edith struggled to ward off her unconscious wishes to take on the role of, and identifications with, the opposite sex. Wharton's masculine identifications, which began with her beloved father, were adaptively put to life on the pages of her novels in her wonderful portrayals of men, as in the central character in *Ethan Frome*, and Vance Weston in *Hudson River Bracketed* (1929), for example.

An erotic fantasy derived from the clinical situation, which dynamically parallels what we feel is the structure of Edith Wharton's threshold phobia, can be found in Person's psychoanalytic study of fantasy (1995). Person describes the case of a young woman who could only have an orgasm during intercourse

---

*It has been postulated that Wharton was the victim of early childhood sexual abuse (White 1991), although there is no verifiable evidence for this. Whether or not it is true, the presence of sexual abuse does not affect our argument.

if she fantasized walking through the door of a pale yellow Victorian house, a fantasy that first occurred during early adolescence as a masturbatory fantasy. Psychoanalysis revealed that the color yellow referred symbolically to her preference for Asian men as sexual partners. This preference could be traced to her history in which her father had been stationed in Vietnam, so that she unconsciously associated Asian men with her father. Beneath this oedipal fixation lay another conflict. The patient revealed that she was deeply ashamed of being with the Asian men, whom she viewed as effeminate. Seeing her partner as feminine allowed her to maintain an underlying fantasy that she was the partner with the penis. Thus her orgasm was tied to the moment that she, in the phallic position, traversed the doorway of the yellow house. "The underlying wish in the Victorian house fantasy is to posit herself as the active, penetrating participant during sex, and to deny any sense of being passive and penetrated; it is she who crossed the threshold, not a man who enters her. . . . The fantasy, then, encompasses a kind of cross-gender identification—though a minimal one (that is, she never consciously wanted to be male, never consciously hated being female)" (pp. 79–80). These words, we believe, could be applied to Wharton, with her minimal cross-gender identification. Her threshold phobia defended against and masked a conflicted wish to be the active penetrator of the woman in the sexual act.

For Wharton, the loss of her virginity and initiation into sexual pleasure were an intrinsic part of her psychological and creative life. As Erlich (1992) points out, the library became a place of secret initiation for the young Edith:

> But this increase of knowledge was as naught compared to the sensuous rapture produced by the sound and sight of the words. . . . [T]hey sang to me so bewitchingly that they almost lured me from the wholesome noonday air of childhood into the strange supernatural region where the normal pleasures of my age seem as insipid as the fruits of the earth to Persephone after she had eaten of the Pomegranate seed. [Wharton 1920, p. 10]

The pomegranate plays a central role in the story of Persephone, which we have seen as a powerful metaphor for the loss of virginity. It is the pomegranate, and not the apple, that is thought by many to be the fruit that tempted Eve in the Garden of Eden. The pomegranate, traditionally seen as a symbol of female fertility, clearly held some significance for Wharton. It is the title of one of her short stories as well as the title of a poem. Erlich suggests that the tale of Persephone resonated for Wharton because she, too, was reluctant to accept the prescribed female destiny of marriage and the role of mother. Persephone acquired a special sexual knowledge that set her apart from her mother, yet, unlike Demeter, she was barren. In the poem "Pomegranate Seed" written in 1912, a few years after the end of her affair with Fullerton, Wharton expresses how she, too, was separated from her mother because of "her failure to participate in the chain of generation" (Erlich, p. 44).

In "The House of the Dead Hand," published in 1904, several of these important motifs come together. The Lombard family lives in Italy. Over a threshold a female hand, carved in marble, is the emblem of "some evil mystery within the house" (Wharton 1904, p. 509). The father dominates the daughter's sexuality and fortune. He controls access to a painting purchased with her dowry money. This sensuous painting, the daughter's property, is kept hidden in the depths of the house, shrouded from light by a curtain. From a vantage point marked by a pomegranate bud in the carpet, he allows chosen visitors to view it on condition that they never reproduce it.

According to Erlich, "the story reeks with erotic symbolism such as dark corridors, the parting of velvet folds to reveal hidden treasure, a female image that can be contemplated but must never be reproduced. The hand symbol, however awkwardly presented, forms the center of an image constellation that is characteristic of Wharton's imagination—father–daughter relationships, fearful thresholds, lust for knowledge, and the often-recurring pomegranate" (1992, p. 42). To this constellation of images we add the theme of defloration.

In summary, much has been written about the lives of Beatrix Potter and Edith Wharton suggesting that issues of virginity and defloration might be integral to understanding their literary works. For both of these writers, the combination of a precocious intellect with a zealous conscience, evidenced in their feelings of the "not niceness" of their sexual interests, certainly led to sexual conflicts and inhibitions. We find evidence that the physical reality of defloration and the breaking of the hymen are represented as important dynamics in their psychic lives. The motif of thresholds in their writings testifies to the centrality of this dynamic.

CHAPTER

7

❧

Images of Defloration and the Hymen in Literary Works by Men

 The loss of virginity has stirred writers and poets from all over the world to write about it in their poetry and prose. In the previous chapter, we have shown how conflicts about defloration and crossing thresholds played important roles in the lives and the creative work of two famous women writers. With these writers we found that the subject became an underlying or unconscious motif in their work; with other writers it is an explicitly and manifestly described event. In studying Potter and Wharton we used autobiographical and biographical material in connection with their writing. In this chapter we will not focus on the life experiences of the various authors we chose but rather will discuss the explicit and conscious expressions of themes of defloration in literature.

Our search through literature revealed striking parallels to what we have found so far in other sources and in our clinical material. We will examine how insights gleaned from psychoanalysis unfold in literary contexts. Specific imagery, fantasies, and themes concerning defloration and the hymen appeared repeatedly and consistently.

We found differences in the conflicts and feelings about this topic in the writings of men and women writers. In general, these differences paralleled the differences we have seen in our men and women patients. Men are most often concerned with competition with their fathers and other men for the prize of the virgin; their quest is to be first to conquer her. In this search they experience hardships, danger, and the fear of castration or death. They are obsessed with ideas of the alluring siren, on the one hand, and the pure, unapproachable and untouched maiden, on the other. Thus, literature written by or about men's experiences with defloration is colored with fear and bravado.

For women, concerns center on feelings of loss and regret. They are preoccupied with the sadness of being torn from their homes and their mothers. They reproach their mothers for not protecting them or preparing them for their lives of adult sexuality. They cry out in sadness, disappointment, and anger because the men who take their virginity abandon them or do not love them. The idea of loss of virginity as an irreversible threshold is drawn the most poignantly by women. These feelings and conflicts of fear, loss, and regret often predominate over descriptions of sexual pleasure. A commonality, however, is that the language of negation and undoing runs through every literary work about defloration that we have read, be it by men or women.

We have chosen several examples from such writing in order to illustrate these consistencies in the themes and imagery about defloration and the hymen that seem to us to have significant psychological meanings. These works are from many genres, from varied parts of the world, and of differing qualities. Given this melange, it is all the more striking that the same imagery and themes appear repeatedly. By no means do we wish to imply that these works of literature can be reduced to these meanings, but only that they are illustrative of one line of interpretation. Nor is our intention to make a textual or literary critique or to provide a full contextual frame for the presentation of these excerpts, for which we feel others are far better qualified. For the sake of discussion, we have organized our examples from literary works by men in terms of interrelated themes of psychoanalytic significance. These are oedipal conflicts; castration anxiety; sadomasochism; painful passages and thresholds; separation from, loss of, and anger at the mother; and the meaning of blood.

OEDIPAL THEMES

Defloration as a Trophy or Gift

A central dynamic in the oedipal drama for men is the desire to win the love of a virgin over all competitors. One of the earliest pieces of Western literature, *The Romance of the Rose* (1275), a thirteenth-century French poem written by de Lorris and de Meun, employs a central metaphor of defloration. An allegory in the form of a dream, the tale has been interpreted as an ironic treatise on the dimensions of love. In it, love and social and religious institutions are ironically satirized. The plot concerns a lover attempting to win his love. The lover is attracted to a rosebud, representing the lady's love and encircled by a walled garden. He tries to pluck it, but Cupid stops him and tells him the requirements of courtly love. He must overcome the characters of Jealousy, Shame, Fear, and Danger to obtain his rose. Hymen and Juno are invoked as the gods of weddings. The assault and the winning of the Rose clearly symbolize the defloration of a virgin. The following are several examples of the sexual imagery conveyed in part by the use of double entendre. The protagonist is making his final assault on the fortification surrounding the rose.

> I had to assail it vigorously, throw myself against it often, often fail. . . . [Y]ou would have been reminded of Hercules when he wanted to dismember Cacus. I had worked so hard that I was covered with the sweat of anguish when I did not immediately break the paling, and I was indeed, believe it, as worn out as Hercules, or even more. Nevertheless, I attacked so much that

I discovered a narrow passage by which I thought I might pass beyond, but to do so I had to break the paling. . . . I broke down the paling with my staff and gained a place in the aperture. . . . I would have relaxed for nothing until the entire staff had entered, so I pressed it through with no delay. But the sack, with its pounding hammers, remained hanging outside; the passage was so narrow that I became greatly distressed, for I had not freed any wide space. Indeed, if I knew the state of the passage, no one had ever passed there; I was absolutely the first. The place was still not common enough to collect tolls. I don't know if, since then, it has done as much for others as it did for me, but I tell you indeed that I loved it so much that I could hardly believe, even if it were true, that the same favors had been given to others. No one lightly disbelieves what he loves, so dishonored would it be; but I still do not believe it. At least I know for certain that at that time it was not a well-worn, beaten path. [p. 352]

The imagery is deliberately used to convey humorously sexual meanings. For example, the staff and the sack used by the religious pilgrim reappear in thin disguise as the penis and the scrotum. The negations—"no one had passed there" or "no one disbelieves"—in the passages are noteworthy. The portrayal, beautifully and humorously characterized from the two male authors' vantage points, is of defloration as a storming of a barrier or paling, a symbol of the hymen.

Here is the idea of wanting to be the first to storm the paling, or to capture the rose. As we have described earlier, Freud suggested this was a central wish for men, representing conflicted sexual desires for their mothers. Even in the face of the reality of the presence of virginity and the intact hymen, there is still obsessive doubting about being the first. The doubting alternates between the conflicted oedipal wish to be the first and the fear of retribution for the realization of that wish. In the above passage, the loved woman is idealized and elevated, yet degrading thoughts about her slip in with the reference to prostitution and the collecting of tolls. The doubts will be quashed but may return. Nevertheless, the pleasure for the lover is worth the difficulties: "Before I stirred from that place where I should wish to remain forever, I plucked, with great delight, the flower from the leaves of the rosebush, and thus I have my red rose" (p. 354). Defloration in this medieval romance is depicted as the gathering of roses.

Vivid and poetic images of defloration and men's concerns with possession and competition can be found throughout the works of Shakespeare. Shakespeare depicts defloration through multiple images of plucking flowers, giving gifts, winning trophies, or aggressive assaults. We will use excerpts from four of his dramas—a tragic-comedic romance, a tragedy, and two comedies—as examples of this theme: *Pericles, Hamlet, The Tempest*, and *Measure for Measure*.

In a comical scene from *Pericles* that takes place in a brothel, Lysimachus asks the price of a virgin. (The cost for a virgin is more than that of a woman who has been already "paced" or tamed.) Boult answers, "For flesh and blood, sir, white and red, you shall see a rose." Bawd then cries, "Here comes that which grows to the stalk; never plucked yet, I can assure you. Is she not a fair creature?" (4.6.37–46).

The virgin Marina is led before Lysimachus but her virtuousness disarms him and he declines to take her. Lysimachus says to Boult, "Boult, take her away. Use her at thy pleasure. Crack the glass of her virginity and make the rest malleable." Once she is "cracked," the woman is portrayed as subjugated, moldable, and compliant, a picture that forms the core of many works, such as Shakespeare's *Taming of the Shrew* or Shaw's *Pygmalion*.

Ophelia is spurned by Hamlet in his mad rage about the murder of his father, the king, by his uncle, who then marries his mother. In the famous passage, he cries out to "the fair Ophelia" to "Get thee to a nunnery" [can mean brothel in slang]. Ophelia goes mad with sorrow and in her delirium sings of the faithlessness of men who steal the virginity from maids:

By Gis and by Saint Charity,
Alack, and fie for shame!
Young men will do't, if they come to't;
By cock, they are to blame.
Quoth she, before you tumbled me,
You promised me to wed.
So would I ha' done, by yonder sun,
An thou hadst not come to my bed. [4.5.59–66]

Out of the context of the plot, one would think that Ophelia herself has been betrayed, that she has given up her virginity to Hamlet who has used and left her. Ophelia's rage and sadness do not come from losing her virginity but from being spurned inexplicably and suddenly by a man whose expected love has turned to derision.

She drowns herself, a virgin forever. Shakespeare's poetry describing her death is replete with symbolism of virginity—flowers and maids:

There is a willow grows aslant a brook,
That shows his hoar leaves in the glassy stream;
There with fantastic garlands did she come
Of crow-flowers, nettles, daisies, and long purples
That liberal shepherds give a grosser name,
But our cold maids do dead men's fingers call them:
There, on the pendent boughs her coronet weeds
Clambering to hang, an envious sliver broke;
When down her weedy trophies and herself
Fell in the weeping brook. Her clothes spread wide;
And, mermaid-like, awhile they bore her up. [4.7.167–177]

The language is ambiguous and paradoxical. Ophelia dies a virgin and yet the imagery reeks with sexual innuendo. In her betrayal and in her death, it is as though she has given up her virginity. She lies on the long purple flowers that are shaped like penises, her clothes are spread wide, and the broken sliver alludes to a broken heart and suggests broken virginity.

The image of the mermaid in the last line is very interesting and compelling. (See the section on "The Little Mermaid" in

Chapter 5.) The mermaid is a composite, half woman and half fish. The virgin of the sea, the mermaid is a siren and a lure. The beautiful top half is often seen as alluring, the bottom as ugly and strange. In the male's view, the woman's castrated state is denied and she is given a phallic long tail. At the same time she is literally castrated in the sense that her female genital is obliterated and her sexuality is cut off.

In *The Tempest* Prospero gives Miranda to Ferdinand in marriage with this warning:

> Then, as my gift and thine own acquisition
> Worthily purchased, take my daughter: but
> If thou dost break her virgin-knot before
> All sanctimonious ceremonies may
> With full and holy rite be minister'd,
> No sweet aspersion shall the heavens let fall
> To make this contract grow; but barren hate,
> Sour-eyed disdain and discord shall bestrew
> The union of your bed with weeds so loathly
> That you shall hate it both: therefore take heed,
> As Hymen's lamps shall light you. [4.1.13–23]

Here is the idea of virginity as a valued commodity, bartered between men and given by maidens to them. This warning against premarital sex and its ruination of a future marriage is issued just before Prospero presents a masque for the lovers. The masque takes the form of the traditional epithalamic celebration, a nuptial song in praise of the bride and bridegroom.

The warning against the dangers of premarital sex is also found in another Shakespearean play, *Measure for Measure*. It is a play about hypocrisy and morality surrounding sexuality and lust. The rigid and supposedly moral deputy, Angelo, has decreed that Claudio is to be put to death for the offense of begetting an illegitimate child. Angelo announces to the beautiful and chaste Isabella, Claudio's sister, that if she will yield her virginity to him he will spare her brother's life. He muses:

Shall we desire to raze the sanctuary
And pitch our evils there? O fie, fie, fie! [2.2.171–172]

Later, he enjoins her:

You must lay down the treasures of your body
To this supposed, or else to let him suffer. [2.4.96–97]

The imagery, like that of *The Romance of the Rose*, is of defloration as a razing or storming of a barrier and of a treasure to be
surrendered. Isabella, of course, will not yield, even under the
threat of death for her or her beloved brother. For Isabella, as
for many other literary heroines, no fate is worse than the shame
of loss of virginity.

Unspoiled Nature

As illustrated above, a manifestation of the oedipal drama and
conflict for men is their desire to keep the image of mother as
pure. They do not wish the father or any other competitor to
possess her. Thus, the virgin is idealized. The wish for untouched
virginity can be discerned in dreams of unspoiled nature and
untouched virgin territory. Perhaps nowhere is this idea more
clearly expressed than in the works of the male romantic poets.
Lord Byron, Percy Shelley, John Keats, and William Wordsworth
wrote lyrically about untouched nature, a metaphor for virginity. They also depict a ravished nature to demonstrate that virginity can be spoiled and lost.

Wordsworth's poem "Nutting" (1799–1800a) was inspired by
memories of feelings and experiences he had as a boy. He describes going hunting for nuts in a rugged, deep woods. His
forced penetration into the untouched scenery and subsequent
exultant pleasure clearly suggests a sexual experience:

Through beds of matted fern, and tangled thickets,
Forcing my way, I came to one dear nook
Unvisited, where not a broken bough
Drooped with its withered leaves, ungracious sign

Of devastation; but the hazels rose
Tall and erect, with tempting clusters hung,
A virgin scene!—A little while I stood,
Breathing with such suppression of the heart
As joy delights in; and, with wise restraint
Voluptuous, fearless of a rival, eyed
The banquet;—or beneath the trees I sate
Among the flowers, and with the flowers I played;

. . . Then up I rose,
And dragged to earth both branch and bough, with crash
And merciless ravage: and the shady nook
Of hazels, and the green and mossy bower,
Deformed and sullied, patiently gave up
Their quiet being: and unless I now
Confound my present feelings with the past,
Ere from the mutilated bower I turned
Exulting. . . .

Then, dearest Maiden, move along these shades
In gentleness of heart; with gentle hand
Touch—for there is a spirit in the woods.

The reference to "fearless of a rival" is reminiscent of Freud's ideas of man's oedipally based fear (in this case, disavowed) of being the first to deflower a virgin. Significantly, from our vantage point, the next published poem Wordsworth wrote in the same time frame and place as "Nutting," was named "Strange Fits of Passion Have I Known" (1799–1800b) and was about his dreams of a young love; thus, the depiction of a penetration on a virgin nature is followed temporally by a portrayal of a fit of passion. In "Nutting" there is the other side of idealized unspoiled nature, that of being spoiled and ravaged. It can be understood as a male's guilt-ridden fantasy of what has happened to the virgin as a result of his assault and aggression.

Another romantic poet, William Blake, believed that human beings have to open themselves to everything and not to draw back from bodily experience. His long poem, "The Book of Thel" (1789), becomes a myth of human self-consciousness. A disembodied soul, represented as a virginal girl, laments her knowledge of her inevitable death and of the fragility of her beauty. Terrified of mortality and sexuality, the soul refuses to enter embodiment. She asks the flowers, clouds, earth, and creatures around her why they do not cry, as she does. She looks into the "couches of the dead" and hears a voice of sorrow, which asks, "Why cannot the Ear be closed to its own destruction? . . . Why a tender curb upon the youthful burning boy? Why a little curtain of flesh on the bed of our desire?" As far as we know, this last, rather curious, line is one of the very few poetic references to the hymen, for what else can "a little curtain of flesh on the bed of our desire" be?

The Fallen Woman

Defloration as an act of conquest, and the woman's consequent shame and degradation, is a very common motif taken up in many works of literature. One of the most sensitive accounts of defloration from the woman's vantage point was written by a man, the great nineteenth-century novelist, Thomas Hardy. In the tragedy *Tess of the D'Urbervilles* (1891), Hardy describes the shattering of Tess's innocence. In the chapter, "The Maiden," the setting foretells Tess's loss of virginity, which is to come. The event of defloration follows a May-Day dance, which takes place in a historic fertile vale. The women who participate dress in white gowns and carry peeled willow wands and bunches of white flowers. The only woman who stands out is Tess, who wears a red ribbon in her hair. The red ribbon foretells the defloration to come. Hardy goes on to say, "Tess at this time of her life was a mere vessel of emotion untinctured by experience" (p. 51).

Tess has left home to work for a rich family and to better herself. Her mother has high hopes for a marriage between the son, Alec, and Tess. On a Saturday night off, Tess goes to a fair and market in a near-by village. A group of drunken peasant women begin to hurl insults at her and a fight looms. She is rescued by Alec, who offers to take her home in the fog on the back of his horse. With sexual designs on her, he rides off the track into the woods and then actually becomes lost. She waits in the woods while he supposedly rides ahead to find their way. Hardy describes her as she lies asleep, unaware she is about to lose her virginity. When Alec returns

> he could see absolutely nothing but a pale nebulousness at his feet, which represented the white muslin figure he had left on the dead leaves. . . . Why it was that upon this beautiful feminine tissue, sensitive as gossamer, and practically blank as snow as yet, there should have been traced such a coarse pattern as it was doomed to receive; why so often the coarse appropriates the finer thus, the wrong man the woman, the wrong woman the man, many thousand years of analytical philosophy have failed to explain to our sense of order. . . . An immeasurable social chasm was to divide our heroine's personality thereafter from that previous self of hers who stepped from her mother's door to try her fortune at Trantridge poultry-farm. [pp. 118–119]

This lovely imagery of whiteness and nebulousness appears frequently in anthropology, myth, and fairy tales to represent virginity. The hymen is vividly represented as beautiful feminine tissue, sensitive as gossamer, clean as snow, on which is traced a course, masculine pattern. Here again, as well, the loss of virginity is associated with a fateful, irrevocable step.

After the seduction, Tess cries out: "I wish I had never been born—there or anywhere else!" and "I didn't understand your meaning till it was too late." (Notice the string of negatives here.) Alec, who deflowered her, responds, "That's what every woman says." Tess replies, "How can you dare to use such words! . . . My God! I could knock you out of the gig! Did it never strike your mind that what every woman says some women may feel?" (pp. 124–125).

In the next chapter, "Maiden No More," Tess returns home several weeks later. Her mother asks if she has returned to get married. When Tess tells her what happened, her mother reproves her for not having been more careful or for not getting the man to marry her:

"O mother, my mother!" cried the agonized girl, turning passion-
ately upon her parent as if her poor heart would break. "How
could I be expected to know? I was a child when I left this house
four months ago. Why didn't you tell me there was danger in men-
folk? Why didn't you warn me? Ladies know what to fend hands
against, because they read novels that tell them of these tricks;
but I never had the chance o' learning in that way, and you did
not help me!" [pp.130–131]

Conquest and the subsequent loss and shame suffered by the
woman is portrayed very differently in *Sister Carrie*, (1900), a
novel from the American school of realism by Theodore Dreiser.
His language is not poetic and laden with the imagery of nature
as is Hardy's, but is down-to-earth in its pictures of the modern
industrial society. In this story Dreiser creates a character, a
"fallen woman," who defies the social conventions of the times.
She leaves home to live under another family's care, takes up
with a man, loses her virginity, and is never married. Since she
is not punished for her loss of virtue, and since her seducers
are not brought down for their wrongdoing, the book was mor-
ally alarming to the public. The defloration scene is not actually described in the narrative. Just as in *Tess of the D'Urbervilles*,
however, it and its significance are foretold by a dream. Carrie's
sister Minnie dreams that Carrie is falling into a black pit in an
old coal mine. After Carrie has succumbed to Drouet, the man
thinks, "how delicious is my conquest" and "'Ah,' thought Carrie, with mournful misgivings, 'what is it I have lost?'" (p. 90).

The Need to be First

In James Joyce's great novel, *Ulysses* (1922), several passages
represent defloration through a series of images and literary
allusions. Philosophizing, jesting, and boozing, a group of men
tease young Stephen. One of the men, Lenahan, says he had
heard of "those nefarious deeds and how . . . he [Stephen] had
besmirched the lily virtue of a confiding female" (p. 392).
Stephen denies this,

for he was the eternal son and ever virgin. Thereat . . . they re-
hearsed to him his curious rite of wedlock for the disrobing and
deflowering of spouses, as the priests use in Madagascar island,
she to be in guise of white and saffron, her groom in white and
grain with burning of nard and tapers, on a bridebed while clerks
sung kyries and the anthem *Ut novetur sexus omnis corporis mys-
terium* till she was there unmaided. He gave them then a much
admirable hymen mimim[1] by those delicate poets Master John
Fletcher and Master Francis Beaumont[2] that is in their *Maid's
Tragedy* that was writ for a like twining of lovers: *To bed, to bed*,
was the burden of it to be played with accompanable concent
upon the virginals. [p. 393]

Later, another character, Dixon, quips that the poets Fletcher
and Beaumont would better be named Beau Mount and Lecher.
In this sophisticated word play, Joyce both glorifies and mocks
the rites of, and the attitudes, toward virginity.

In Molly Bloom's soliloquy, which comes in the last part of
the novel, after talking of "something wrong with us 5 days every
3 or 4 weeks" she continues

I bet the cat itself is better off than us have we too much blood
up in us or what O patience above its pouring out of me like the
sea anyhow he didn't make me pregnant as big as he is I dont
want to ruin the clean sheets the clean linen I wore brought it
on too damn it damn it and they always want to see a stain on
the bed to know you're a virgin for them all that's troubling them
they're such fools too you could be a widow or divorced 40 times
over a daub of red ink would do or blackberry juice no that's too
purply. . . . [p. 769]

Note the combining of menstrual and hymeneal blood in this
sequence. Molly is making fun of men's obsessions with virginity and their need for proving it. Joyce puts into Molly's words
his own worries and obsessions about fidelity and purity.

---

1. Mimim is an ecclesiastical song.
2. These are Elizabethan dramatists who collaborated on plays and
who were said to have shared the same women.

In a letter to Nora Barnacle, Joyce writes on August 7, 1909,

Is Georgie my son? The first night I slept with you in Zurich was
October 11th and he was born July 27th. That is nine months
and 16 days. I remember that there was very little blood that
night. Were you fucked by anyone before you came to me? . . . I
have been a fool. I thought that all the time you gave yourself
only to me and you were dividing your body between me and
another. . . . If I could forget my books and my children and forget that the girl I loved was false to me and remember her only
as I saw her with the eyes of my boyish love I would go out of
life content. How old and miserable I feel! [Ellmann 1975,
pp. 158–159]

Joyce refers to Nora as "my little wild-flower of the hedge" in
his obsessive brooding about her virginity. "When that person
whose heart I long to stop with the click of a revolver put his
hand or hands under your skirts did he only tickle you outside
or did he put his finger or fingers up into you? If he did, did
they go up far enough to touch that little cock at the end of your
cunt? . . . I know I was the first man that blocked you but did
any man ever frig you?" (Ellmann, pp. 182–183).[3] This is another example of how a man's knowing he is the first to deflower
a woman does not remove the neurotic doubting about it, which
here is displaced to a question about "frigging." The conflict
about being the first remains. The attribution of a phallic "little
cock" onto the female genital calms castration anxieties. We will
discuss this defensive maneuver in Chapter 10.

CASTRATION ANXIETIES

Oedipal competition brings related fears of castration. In many
of the great novels in the English language men's concerns about
competition, wishes to be the first with the desired women, and

---

3. *Blocked* means intercourse and *frig* refers to digital manipulation.

their guilts and fears of punishment for these wishes are drawn powerfully. In *Wartime Lies* (Begley 1991), a historical novel depicting a Jewish boy's struggle for survival in Europe during World War II, boys talk about women and sex, illustrating such guilts and fears:

> [T]hey explained how one could shove it in between a girl's legs so she would bleed or into her rear end. In either case, it had to hurt. Women bled every month anyway. They used paper to stop it, but sometimes they couldn't. The blood was called kurwa. The worst insult was to call somebody "kurwamac" . . . . That was mother or son of that blood. You could shove it into a woman when she was bleeding and women liked it, but it was a very dirty thing to do. The boys wanted to know if I had already shoved it into Irena. . . . They thought I should try, when she was asleep. All I had to worry about was the blood that her mother would see in the morning. [pp. 35–36]

The boys adapted a song to each boy and to the girl he liked and marched up and down the alley singing: "I will shove in my two-meter, you will bleed a whole liter. She cries it's hard, it's hard, but this just makes him fart. She cries now I bleed, but he pays no heed" (p. 36).

The themes of aggression and the confusion of menstrual and hymeneal blood are part of this memory of a boy's adolescence. The boys are confused and conflicted about which orifice to penetrate. They have a cloacal fantasy, that is, a child's confused view of female anatomy that women have one big internal cavity. Pain and blood color their anxious brooding about sex and their sexual performance. The song attempts to make light of their anxiety over penetration and inflicting pain. Singing with bravado about a two-meter penis counteracts castration anxiety and narcissistic worries. The idea of deflowering Irena while she sleeps takes us back to the romantic tale of "Sleeping Beauty," but betrays the boys' fears of women. The several references to mother and blood in the midst of the boys' talk suggest their oedipal preoccupations.

SADOMASOCHISM

Rape is the ultimate in conquest and assertion of sexual power over women. In the ancient Greek myth of Persephone, as we have seen, the virgin was deflowered through an act of abduction and rape. Without the mediation of integrated defenses, conscience, or opposing societal norms, the conflicted sadism noted in many of the above works of literature unfortunately becomes translated into real violence.

The *droit du seigneur* was a medieval custom giving the feudal overlord the right to the virginity of his vassals' daughters on their wedding night. The *droit du seigneur*, according to Francis Litvak (1984), may or may not have been a sociological and historical fact. Nevertheless, it makes its appearance in countless works of literature, drama, and music, including Shakespeare, Voltaire, and perhaps most familiarly in the opera *The Marriage of Figaro*. Litvak has collected and described countless examples from European and American literature from the seventeenth through the twentieth century. Frequently the subject is treated comically and the literature portrays how the bride and groom trick the lord and prevent him from exercising his "rights." The action is not always comic, however, and the girls do not always escape. Especially in Italy and France, where feudalism had a strong foothold for long years, the *droit du seigneur* was accepted as a horrible fact of life and portrayed as such. In eighteenth- and nineteenth-century literature the *droit du seigneur* is the subject of the most scathing and biting invective against the acts of a licentious and brutalizing nobility. Such atrocities were pictured as backdrops and reasons for the great revolt of the peasants in France, the Jacquerie, in 1358. In the novel *The Jacquerie* (1841), by the English novelist and historical writer George James, a noble invokes his right. A young bride is dragged up to the castle in terror, and when her bridegroom tries to rescue her, he is killed. The bride does not return for several days and is found dead. The *droit* is also used broadly in pornographic literature of the era, in which the torture of young virgins is described in lascivious and horrific detail. The *droit* is the epitome of the notion of defloration as a trophy awarded to the man, while the girl is an object or chattel. There is a whole literary tradition that depicts blood sacrifice of virgins such as Iphigenia, Polyxena, Chryseis, and Cassandra. This is another link of virginity with death.

While clearly an outrage of a previous era, the *droit du seigneur* may have served hidden psychological purposes beyond satisfying the lord's appetite. It also parallels the practice of a substitute initiator of the bride seen in many cultures, which we have detailed in Chapter 4. This practice defends against oedipal guilt about being the first to deflower the woman.

In pornographic literature, defloration of virgins reaches the extremes of abuse and sadism. Steven Marcus (1974) presents a comprehensive study of pornography in Victorian England. This body of writings was authored by men, and thus represents male fantasies as well as sexual attitudes of the time. In such fantasies, the idea of ravishing a virgin and subjecting her to numerous detailed and lascivious ordeals gives special delectation. Citing an anonymously authored work of eleven volumes called *My Secret Life*, Marcus (1974) points out that sadistic impulses are most saliently described and enacted when the protagonist deflowers young girls who have been purchased by him from prostitutes. Marcus quotes such a passage, one of the more tame excerpts: "[M]y lust grew fierce, her cry of pain gave me inexpressible pleasure; and saying I would not hurt, yet wishing to hurt her and glorying in it, I thrust with all the violence my buttocks could give, till my prick seemed to bend and pained me" (p. 176). In another passage, hard to stomach, a young virgin is raped: "Her tears ran down. If I had not committed a rape, it looked uncommonly like one. I got off her, saw for an instant her legs wide open, cunt and thighs wet and bloody, she crying, sobbing, rubbing her eyes" (p. 137).

Marcus suggests that all pornography, given its male authorship and phallocentric point of view, concentrates upon the phallus. Indeed the male protagonists become equated with the phallus, and the women are transformed into objects upon which the penis works its destructive or exciting effects. "Pornography is, after all, nothing more than a representation of the fantasies of infantile sexual life, as these fantasies are edited and reorganized in the masturbatory daydreams of adolescence" (p. 286). We concur with Marcus's understanding of pornography.

In summary, men writers concentrate on oedipal themes, castration concerns, and sadomasochistic fantasies in their depictions of defloration. Hardy is an exception who approaches the event from the point of view of the woman and portrays the experiences sensitively and subtly. We will turn now to works by women writers.

8

Images of Defloration and the Hymen in Literary Works by Women

*I*n contrast to the more violent or adventurous tales of conquest and assault of outer worlds written by men, the tales of women writers seem to concentrate on the inner worlds of disappointment and loss, on the closer fears of separation from the security of home and mother, as opposed to the terrifying confrontation of facing the larger world alone.

THRESHOLDS AND PASSAGES

Women writers have described defloration as a painful rite of passage for the girl, marked by intense feelings of pain and disappointment in the sexual experience itself and in the men who often leave them. Their works include many coming of age novels. Among the female writers who have dealt poignantly with the subject is Edna O'Brien in the first two novels of *The Country Girls Trilogy and Epilogue* (1960). O'Brien portrays the adventures of Kate, a young, unmarried Catholic girl who loses her virginity to a non-Catholic man who is separated from his wife and somewhat older than she. He has bought her a wedding ring to pretend to the world that they are married. Guiltily, she feels "as if people were going to accuse me of my sin in public" (p. 314). Kate remembers the defloration scene:

"I could eat you . . . like an ice cream," and later when we were home in bed, he resaid it, as he turned to make love to me. . . .
   "That ring has to last you a long time," he said.
   "How long?"
   "As long as you keep your girlish laughter."
   I noticed with momentary regret that he never used dangerous words like "forever and ever."
   "Knock, knock, let me in," he said, coaxing his way gently into my body.
   "I am not afraid, I am not afraid," I said. For days he had told me to say this to myself, to persuade myself that I was not afraid. The first thrust pained, but the pain inspired me, and I lay there astonished with myself, as I licked his bare shoulder. . . . I knew that I had now passed inescapably into womanhood.
   I felt no pleasure, just some strange satisfaction that I had done what I was born to do. My mind dwelt on foolish, incidental things, I thought to myself, So this is it; the secret I dreaded and longed for. . . . All the perfume, and sighs, and purple brassieres, and curling pins in bed and gin-and-it, and necklaces had all been for this. I saw it as something comic and beautiful. . . ."
   "You're a ruined woman now," he said, after some time. . . .
   I felt different from Baba now and from every other girl I knew. . . . I thought of Mama and of how she used to blow on hot soup before she gave it to me. . . . [pp. 315–317]

Guilt colors this whole interaction: the guilt of premarital sex for a Catholic girl, the guilt of rebellion from family for an adolescent, and underneath, the guilt about childhood oedipal wishes. To disguise her unacceptable oedipal wishes from herself, she selects, on the one hand, a partner who is older and like her father and, on the other hand, an exogamous figure, outside of her religious and ethnic group, and thus seemingly unlike her father. In this way, the man can be consciously experienced as a safe, nonoedipal choice.

As with many girls' first sexual intercourse, Kate experiences the loss of her virginity as somewhat of a letdown. She thinks wistfully of her dead mother at this point with the unvoiced little girl's wish for protection and care. Also, the mother comes to mind because the girl is on the verge of achieving a childhood wish of taking the rival's place. She voices the sense of having taken the "inescapable step into womanhood."

The oral imagery—ice cream and hot soup—speaks to unconscious links between orality and sexuality, which we have seen repeatedly in our study of defloration. Just why this may be so is open to question. One answer is that in the unconscious, food is often equated with love and/or sex. An additional reason for the oral imagery is that the vagina is frequently symbolized by a mouth, which has lips and receives. This orality may in itself carry oral fixations and modalities or it may express later developmental issues.

Again we note that negatives—"I am not afraid"—are scattered throughout the description of the defloration.

In *The Beggar Maid* by Alice Munro (1977) there is another poignant scene of this rite of passage. The heroine, Rose, meets a young man at college who pursues her, although she does not feel the same ardor for him. She loses her virginity with "an unpracticed counterfeit of passion. . . . She was pleased when it was accomplished; she did not have to counterfeit that. They had done what others did, they had done what lovers did. She thought of celebration. What occurred to her was something delicious to eat, a sundae at Boomers, apple pie with hot cinnamon sauce" (p. 84). Here, as in the passage from O'Brien, we see that the idea of food is associated with defloration. In these few words, Munro captures the girl's experience of defloration as not truly sexually satisfying, but rather an event traversed, with the anxiety finally behind her. Here the heroine wants a celebration after sex. Ritual, in some form, is a frequent association to defloration.

What intensifies the pain of defloration can be the man's insensitivity to and distortion of the girl's experience. In her book *Albion's Story* (1994), Kate Grenville describes the wedding night from the male protagonist's vantage point.

> We were married in the rain and my bride's hair smelled of orange water and rain when I deflowered her. Her pleasure in me was so great she writhed and arched beneath me like a hooked fish. "Albion! Ah!" she cried, and I heard amazement in her voice, and the lust of every woman, for she had been hollow and now she was filled with my bursting passion.
>
> Tears are the ultimate smile: Norah shed them on her wedding night, ah, such tears, and as fast as I licked them off her face she produced more. I would have liked to say, "Norah, how well your tears become you!" but modest maid as she was, she covered her face with her hands, or turned away from me, so I had to grasp her wrists and force her arms down to her sides, and then I could approach my face to her, and feel her tears cool on my own cheek, feel them salt on my tongue. [p. 96]

Grenville, a woman, depicts the man's sadism toward his wife by showing us his thoughts. The language—"hooked fish" and "tears are the ultimate smile"—betrays the narcissistic, sadistic, and uncomprehendingly self-deceptive character of this man's deflowering of the woman. It also shows the familiar themes of the girl's pain and discomfort and the man's need for conquest.

A sense of loss, regret, and pain permeates the experience of defloration in the poem "The Wedding Night" by Anne Sexton (1964). The poem is a lamentation for lost love and for the precocious giving up of one's virginity. Sexton uses flowers as a rich metaphor for the fleeting nature of youth and of virginity:

> There was this time in Boston
> and then it was over.
> I walked down Marlborough Street the day you left me
> under branches as tedious as leather,
> under branches as stiff as drivers' gloves.

I said, (but only because you were gone)
"Magnolia blossoms have rather a southern sound,
so unlike Boston anyhow,"
and whatever it was that happened, all that pink,
and for so short a time,
was unbelievable, was pinned on.

The magnolias had sat once, each in a pink dress,
looking, of course, at the ceiling.
For weeks the buds had been as sure-bodied
as the twelve-year-old flower girl I was
at Aunt Edna's wedding.
Will they bend, I had asked,
as I walked under them toward you,
bend two to a branch,
cheek, forehead, shoulder to the floor?
I could see that none were clumsy.
I could see that each was tight and firm.
Not one of them had trickled blood—
waiting as polished as gull beaks, as closed as all that.

I stood under them for nights, hesitation,
and then drove away in my car.
Yet one night in the April night
someone (someone!) kicked each bud open—
to disprove, to mock, to puncture!
The next day they were all hot-colored,
moist, not flawed in fact . . .
Then they no longer huddled.
They forgot how to hide.
Tense as they had been,
they were flags, gaudy, chafing in the wind.
There was such abandonment in all that!
Such entertainment
in their flaring up.

After that, well—
like faces in a parade,
I could not tell the difference between losing you
and losing them.

They dropped separately after the celebration,
handpicked,
one after the other like artichoke leaves.
After that I walked to my car awkwardly
over the painful bare remains on the brick sidewalk,
knowing that someone had, in one night,
passed roughly through,
and before it was time.

The speaker recalls a short celebration, a wedding. She links
her own painful loss of virginity with this event. "Then it was
over" and she was left behind, abandoned. She equates losing
the love object with the loss of the unopened buds, with their
short-lived color. She links the magnolia buds to the memory of
herself, a prepubescent flower girl at a wedding, in a pink dress,
sure-bodied. The magnolias, as well, can be interpreted as images of the female genitals. With the description of the unopened
buds having not yet "trickled blood," there is a clear allusion to
the breaking of the hymen and to violence. The buds were
opened rudely and violently. Defloration and its aftermath are
a ruined memory, colored by loss.

An underlying subtext of this poem brings to mind ideas discussed regarding the Cinderella tales in Chapter 5. These tales
carry a cautionary message that premature or premarital sex
means that the man will be lost to the errant girl. Only the virtuous, unopened, and unbloodied girl gets the prince.

Another female poet who explicitly exploits the idea of defloration as a rite of passage is H. D. in a group of poems entitled
Hymen (Doolittle 1983). The governing metaphor of these poems
is a nuptial ceremony that expresses the female poet's spiritual
quest, an unfolding of destiny often involving pain. Throughout
the volume of poetry we see a collage of images of the flowers
and colors passing before us in a dreamlike procession evoking
the experiences and moods of defloration. Virgins from mythology carry the flowers that are caught in their moment of comple-
tion at the point of expiring. Here we find the hymen used as a
liminal concept between the living and the dead.

SEPARATION FROM MOTHER AND
ANGER ABOUT SEXUAL IGNORANCE

Part of the pain of the passage from childhood into adult sexuality for the young girl stems from the actual or symbolic separation from the mother. This pain is vividly expressed in a short story called "My Daughter's Wedding Day," by Punyakante Wijenaike, a woman writer from Ceylon (1963). It is written from the point of view of the mother of the bride, as she worries and waits to get the proof of her daughter's chastity after the wedding night. Although she keeps telling herself that she is confident of her daughter's innocence, and she tries to put on a calm exterior for her family and the new in-laws, she is terrified and in turmoil. In the story is a poignant passage that describes both the mother's and daughter's sadness at the separation that the marriage brings. The parting forever is one of the meanings of the concept of "never," or "nevermore," which we see so often in descriptions of defloration.

> And now the time has come for my daughter to leave the house. She comes to me crying and it is strange that I do not see her as she is, tall and comely in her wedding saree, but as a tiny toddler who is tumbling about our compound, dirty and unwashed. My hands tremble as they receive her and our tears mingle tasting like bitter salt in our mouths. Aiyo! how fast a daughter grows up and now I will be left alone with only the men folk in the house. How hard is a mother's fate! A hand pulls and we are parted, for ever. [pp. 123–124]
> I embrace my daughter for the last time and her nails dig into my arms in her agony. She does not want me to go for she is frightened now like a little child abandoned in the dark. . . . I turn my head away and wail loudly. . . . I feel near to fainting myself. [pp. 125–126]

Later, after the ceremony, the mother's tension mounts. How will she bear the shame if her daughter is not a virgin? Her thoughts also turn to an empathic wish to help the girl:

My daughter's marriage bed keeps appearing ceaselessly in my thoughts. It is a moment each woman has to face in her own way and I had prepared my daughter for it as best I could. Yet I know the terror she must be undergoing at this very moment. What woman does not fear such a moment, especially if she was chaste? A newly acquired aunt on her husband's side would no doubt instruct and advise her before she retired. That is the custom but could this woman offer the same comfort as a mother? My poor daughter! How she must be crying out for me! [p. 126]

The night stretches onward. The mother waits anxiously for the messenger from the bridegroom's house, who will bring a tray of fresh red flowers, a symbol of the daughter's chastity (and of spilled hymeneal blood). The mother cannot hide her joy when they arrive with "this proud testimony of her daughter's chastity" (p. 128).

It is interesting how often the mother leaps into the picture at a girl's initiation into sexuality. We do not think that boys have their fathers consciously present in their minds during their first sexual experiences to such a degree. Witness the following passage from the novel *The Lover* (1985) by Marguerite Duras. The scene of a girl's loss of virginity is described. The sequence shifts to her memory of her mother in darned stockings, "a mother who never knew pleasure." Then the scene shifts back to the present: "I didn't know you bled. He asks me if it hurt, I say no, he says he's glad. He wipes the blood away, washes me. I watch him. Little by little he comes back, becomes desirable again. I wonder how I had the strength to go against my mother's prohibition. So calmly, with such determination" (p. 39). As the girl steps into the world of adult sexuality for the first time, thoughts about her mother's prohibitions against sex come to mind, perhaps because of her uneasiness about taking on the role of adult woman and oedipal competitor and losing the mother's protection.

In *The Lover*, the girl compares her sexual experience with her belief about her mother's lack of pleasure. In the short story from Ceylon, the mother speaks of how she tried to prepare her daughter for her wedding night, but could not soften the girl's seemingly inevitable terror. In *Tess of the D'Urbervilles*, the girl complains bitterly that her mother did not prepare her for her first sexual experience. Young girls frequently hurl charges against their mothers that they ill-prepared them for adult sexuality and for their experience of sexual initiation and defloration. We have encountered this feeling in our clinical material as well as in anthropology, myths, and fairy tales.

BLOOD AND DEATH

In her autobiographical novel *The Bell Jar*, Sylvia Plath describes a crucial six months in a troubled young woman's life. During this period Esther Greenwood attempts suicide, becomes hospitalized, and loses her virginity. The defloration is described once more as a fateful crossing of a boundary—a painful passage. On a furlough from the sanitarium, she deliberately decides to dispose of her virginity. Earlier in the novel she had mused to herself about virginity:

> When I was nineteen, pureness was the great issue. Instead of the world being divided up into Catholics and Protestants or Republicans and Democrats or white men and black men or even men and women, I saw the world divided into people who had slept with somebody and people who hadn't, and this seemed the only really significant difference between one person and another. I thought a spectacular change would come over me the day I crossed the boundary line. [1972, p. 66]

After outfitting herself with a diaphragm, Esther deliberately and consciously sets out to find herself a man. She meets a suitable one coming out of the Harvard library. "I was standing at the top of the long flight, overlooking the red brick buildings that walled the snow-lined quad and preparing to catch the trolley back to the asylum, when a tall young man with a rather ugly and bespectacled, but intelligent face, came up and said, 'Could you please tell me the time?'" (p. 184). The imagery, the colors of red and snow, the marking of the passage of time, are familiar backdrops to scenes of defloration. The choice of "a random stranger" as the agent of defloration for the girl, which we see here and repeatedly throughout literature and in clinical examples, disguises the choice of an oedipal object. The stranger is reassuringly not the father and can be the focus of unconsciously projected erotic fantasies.

The defloration for Esther does not produce the major change she had expected; instead it was painful: "It hurts. Is it supposed to hurt?" (p. 184). Upon returning to her friend Joan's apartment, Esther begins to bleed badly, to hemorrhage in fact. Joan helps her and rides with her to the emergency room. After being "fixed" by a young male resident on call, Esther returns to the asylum, but Joan is missing. A few days later Esther finds out that Joan has hanged herself. In this juxtaposition of events, Plath seemingly comments on the plight of women: women are imprisoned as in a bell jar, but their escape into heterosexual roles is no escape. It promises only pain, blood, and death.

In Christina Rossetti's poem "The Convent Threshold" (1862), the speaker on the doorstep of the convent feels caught between sexuality and chastity. Choosing to become a nun because there is mysterious, unspecified "blood" between her lover and herself, she looks down to see her lily feet "soiled with mud, / With scarlet mud which tells a tale." Again, we see the association between crossing over a threshold from which one cannot return and a forbidden love.

The ritual custom of displaying the stained white bridal sheets is the centerpiece of a short story by Isak Dinesen (1983) called "The Blank Page." The nuns in a convent make the bloodied sheets of the royal houses of Portugal into objects as sacred as altar cloths and read the stains as if they were hieroglyphs. In Susan Gubar's (1981) reading of this text, she makes the point that in Western culture, as represented by its literature, the female is portrayed as the ground on which the male's creativity expresses itself. The female is the text; man's creative force constructs art, indeed woman herself, out of the woman's blankness and passivity. Women's forms of self-expression and creativity have been limited so that they avail themselves of whatever they have at hand. "Not an ejaculation of pleasure but a reaction to rending, the blood on the royal marriage sheets seems to imply that women's paint and ink are produced through a painful wounding, a literal influence of male authority" (p. 20). In Dinesen's tale, the virginal nuns create art from their labors in the fields as well as the bloodied sheets:

> [T]hey grow the finest flax and manufacture the most exquisite linen of Portugal.
> The long field below the convent is plowed with gentle-eyed, milk-white bullocks, and the seed is skillfully sown out by labor-hardened virginal hands. . . . At the time when the flax field flowers, the whole valley becomes air-blue, the very color of the apron which the blessed virgin put on to go out and collect eggs within St. Anne's poultry yard, the moment before the Archangel Gabriel in mighty wing-strokes lowered himself onto the threshold of the house, and while high high up a dove, neck-feathers raised and wings vibrating, stood like a small clear silver star in the sky. [p. 101]

The act of creation is expressed beautifully in metaphoric language describing a sexual defloration and impregnation.

In appreciation for the excellent quality of the linen, the convent receives "that central piece of the snow-white sheet which bore witness to the honor of a royal bride" (p. 103). The sheets are placed in heavy, gilt frames and hung in a special gallery. Thus, Dinesen implies that the fact of blood must be taken into account before we can understand the nature of female art. We believe that the intrapsychic representations of blood and its many connections must be taken into account before we can understand sexual fantasies of women and men.

In all these writings by men and women about defloration, guilt and anxiety, disappointment and loss, and violence and death intrude on the pleasurable sexual experience. Perhaps left with these unhappy images of defloration, we can be consoled by the sensuous, beautiful love verses from the *Old Testament*, "The Song of Songs":

> Behold thou art fair, my love; behold thou art fair;
> Thine eyes are as doves behind thy veil. (4.1)
> Thy temples are like a pomegranate split open
> Behind thy veil. (4.3)
> A garden shut up is my sister, my bride;
> A spring shut up, a fountain sealed.
> Thy shoots are a park of pomegranates
> With precious fruits (4.12)
> Let my beloved come into his garden
> And eat his precious fruits. (4.16)
> I sleep, but my heart waketh;
> Hark! My beloved knocketh:
> Open to me, my sister, my love, my dove, my undefiled. . . . (5.2)
> My beloved put in his hand by the hole of the door,
> And my heart was moved for him.
> I rose up to open to my beloved. (5.4)

Defloration and the Hymen in the Psychoanalytic Process

*I*n the following three chapters we will describe the relevance and meanings of the hymen and the loss of virginity as they appear in clinical material. We will illustrate how the themes of defloration and the hymen—important for both male and female patients in their sexual and mental lives—are expressed in many different ways. These phenomena have been noticeably absent in clinical reports and largely ignored by clinicians. We believe that recognizing these contents and their meanings can help therapists to understand and deal with important resistances and enactments. The denials and negations that we have been tracing throughout this work result not only from patient resistances but also from countertransference blind spots in the therapist/analyst. In addition, recognizing these meanings can aid empathic and interpretive understanding as well as further a working alliance that contributes to successful therapeutic outcomes. We will also demonstrate that defloration can represent a metaphor for the entire psychotherapeutic process. Appreciation of its meaning can enhance the understanding of the therapeutic endeavor.

The process of psychoanalysis or a psychoanalytically oriented psychotherapy is often represented by metaphor. At times the whole of the treatment is experienced in terms of a central organizing metaphor that may reflect a focal unconscious fantasy of the patient (Arlow 1979). A patient may experience the analysis as a process of anal extraction, a metaphor that also expresses his or her approach to people and life. For example, on the eve of his beginning analysis, a patient dreamed that he was about to be given a huge "sigmoid," to which he associated "Sigmund" [Freud]. We have found that in some of our cases the entire psychoanalytic treatment is perceived as a process of defloration. The analytic process can be experienced, like a defloration, as an opening up, a sadomasochistic invasion, a prelude to a love relationship, a stripping of defenses, or a power struggle. Erotization of the analytic process may accompany these experiences. In other instances, certain phases of the analysis, such as its beginning, the conversion from psychotherapy to psychoanalysis, or certain persistent resistances, become expressed as a defloration or a penetration. Both men and women use the metaphor of defloration, although as we will see later, the specific conflicts and affects concerning defloration and the hymen expressed by men and woman differ. In most of our clinical examples, the material about defloration and the hymen emerged spontaneously. In only a few instances did the analyst question the patient directly when the material seemed clearly derivative or representative of defloration, although not specifically named or acknowledged.

The following cases in this and the next two chapters come from our own practices or were provided by colleagues. We have taken care to disguise material for the sake of confidentiality. Because fragments of analyses and analytic processes have been selected, there is an obvious truncation of material. Our intention is to demonstrate the underlying meanings and fantasies pertaining to defloration. Thus, we may give the impression that in the clinical situation we do not pay attention to patients' resistances and to problems of technique. The emphasis on unconscious fantasy is an artifact and does not reflect the actuality of our everyday work with patients.

In all of the cases the use of negations and denials is evident, and it may be useful to distinguish denial from negation. *Denial* is a means by which some or all of the meanings of an event are repudiated unconsciously. Sometimes this is called disavowal. Denial usually refers to an external reality. For example, a patient who is a physician denies ever reading about, seeing, or even hearing about a hymen. This symptom functions to efface reality. *Negation* permits the repressed into consciousness, but in the negative form. For example, a patient who introduces the topic of defloration will then insist that her words did not mean anything.

OPENING PHASE

The metaphor of defloration comes up in our experience most often in the beginning of an analysis rather than in other phases of the process. We have selected several examples to highlight the ways in which beginning treatment was experienced as a defloration. Others of these examples will be scattered throughout the other sections of the chapter.

> A young man who desired to marry, but had trouble in his relationships with women, began psychoanalysis with a female analyst. In one of the first sessions he reported a dream in which he was running. His foot was caught in a wire cover over a hole with alligators below. Being acquainted with psychoanalytic jargon, he laughed and said, "This is 'vagina alligatoria' instead of 'vagina dentata.' I never thought I'd have such a transparent dream." Upon further questioning, he said, "The foot is my penis caught in the covering over the vagina. Maybe I think you're a virgin when it comes to doing analyses. The wire behind the pubic hair is the hymen, a dangerous thing to traverse." He associated to the word "transparent" as "being able

to see through the hymen like a porthole in a ship. Then I could see if there was anything in there."

This material graphically reflected the anxieties and wishes that had been aroused by beginning the analysis. He hoped that the analyst was competent and would be able to help him to accomplish what he wanted, yet he feared she was inexperienced, like a virgin. He wished to be able to see what was ahead so as to avoid unpleasant surprises, that is, to see through an imaginary membrane, like a hymen, into the mysteries beyond. His sexual feelings, aroused by being in the presence of the female analyst, were projected onto her, making her appear dangerous. He wished to penetrate the analyst sexually, but was afraid of getting caught in her clutches, concretely imagined in terms of her dangerous genitals. He saw her as a biting, castrating menace, an alligator. This man experienced beginning analysis as his deflowering the analyst with all of its dangers and excitements. The hymen was represented as the translucent porthole, a narrow window into the excitements and dangers of a woman, as experienced from the vantage point of a young, confused boy. These early conflicts were immediately stimulated by the transference and probably were repeated in his difficulties with women. This might be viewed as an early sexualization of the analytic process.

Another young man, just beginning his analysis after having left another treatment prematurely, reported the following dream. He is riding in a car in the back seat with a woman in the driver's seat in front. A curtain between them is tied back and begins to loosen. He becomes anxious because he can't see ahead as the curtain covers more and more of his view of the windshield. They're going so fast on the highway that he is sure that they will crash through the windshield. He says, "It's awful to think of the cracking glass and all those sharp edges sticking out." Among his associations is a statement that "crack and crash remind me of the female genital and breaking through the hymen. I only had one such experience."

Here, understanding the defloration theme helped the female analyst to comprehend the patient's intense anxieties about beginning the analysis. The reversal of the perceived balance of power and gender roles by lying down and not being able to see the analyst is depicted in the dream by not being in the driver's seat. He is afraid of dangers that he cannot see. These include the threat from the female analyst about whom he knows little, sexual fantasies and fears, proceeding "too fast," and anxieties about the unknown road ahead, the analytic treatment. The communicated interpretation of this early dream helped to allay the patient's anxieties and allow him to proceed in treatment.

A young woman in the opening phases of her analysis started a session by saying she had been thinking about her analysis and what she had been talking about. She spoke of feeling absolutely blocked recently. When asked about being blocked, she thought about being invaded with "boundary violations." She began to talk about rubbing suntan lotion on her little boy. She mused, "Is that too stimulating?" She reported watching a movie in which a man physically abused his wife. She thought again of her own "blocks," her silences, and being forced to talk. She reflected that young women feel forced into getting married, a kind of sexual invasion, in her opinion. She recalled the night of her wedding and what a painful and long process it was for her hymen to be broken. It took many days to get comfortable with sex and several days of bleeding. She told her girlfriend, who was going to get married, "Don't tell anyone sex is fun. It's not what it's cracked up to be. It hurts a lot." Her older married sister had told her about the hymen. Her mother had told her the first time would hurt but afterwards it's OK. She concluded, "Intellectually, I knew about the anatomy of the hymen, but I didn't know it as an actual sensual perception. I was totally unprepared. My mother told me nothing about my period, which I had first at age 10. I thought something had broken inside of me. I was bleeding. No one told me about the bleeding or that menstruation would happen every month."

The analyst interpreted to the patient that she was afraid of what the analysis would be like for her, that she feared that she would be forced to talk as she had felt forced to be married, and that she also feared that she would be invaded and hurt. For this woman, the memories of the pain of rupture of the hymen were invoked as she experienced her therapy as a similar painful invasion. She also expressed the fear, reexperienced in the beginnings of the transference, that the analyst, like her mother and other female figures, would be of no help to her in this process. They would supply intellectual information, but to no avail; the painful affects would be hers to struggle with alone. In her associations, this woman clearly demonstrated the common linkage of feelings about defloration with those about menstruation.

CONVERSION FROM PSYCHOTHERAPY TO PSYCHOANALYSIS

In the following case the utilization of the couch and the change to psychoanalysis provoked a defloration fantasy.

A 50-year-old widowed woman who had been in psychoanalytic psychotherapy for two years was converting to psychoanalysis by increasing the frequency of sessions and using the couch. She reported at the beginning of one of the first hours on the couch that she had taken an antihistamine the day before and had slept well, but now felt odd: "There is something between me and my brain, like a thin veil." When the analyst asked her about the thin veil, she replied, "The only thing that comes to mind is literary—a hymen—Hawthorne's *Scarlet Letter*." She thought of the shame of committing adultery. "The hymen, that's a membrane which according to mythology is intact in a virgin. All women are supposed to be pure, virginal, and this is equated with everything good—noble character, cold, and pure." She thought of another association to a veil: "to disguise the identity in order for trickery; something between the reality, the protection, and the illusion." She asked herself, "What has this to do with myself? Obviously I think of the way I felt as a developing woman. I remember what we thought of girls who 'fooled around.' We didn't say 'slept with someone' or 'got themselves laid.' The girls I knew weren't like that. I really had a conventional attitude." She went on to associate that an unbroken hymen was supposed to be evident to the bridegroom and to all society by blood on the sheets. She thought of Lorca, the Spanish playwright: "his terrifying plays, one of which was *The House of*— something. I can't remember the name. Repression, lost love, and terrible things happened."

This is a reference to the tragedy, *The House of Bernarda Alba* (García Lorca 1941). In the play, a house of unwed sisters is presided over by a tyrannical mother. Tragedy erupts when one of the sisters becomes involved with a man whom another sister wants. Much is made of the theme of virginity. The play ends as the mother cries that her daughter died a virgin. Another famous play by García Lorca that the patient may have had in mind is *Blood Wedding* (1941). In this play a bloody murder ends the wedding.

The patient continued, "That's not part of my world—I didn't have a lot of ideas—I had no boyfriend and I really wanted to have one. (Note the negations and the idea of namelessness.) I remember my girlfriends and I talking about some girl and guy, occasionally a pregnancy or a forced marriage. I remember jokes about the hymen, like athletic girls might not have one intact. One couldn't tell. I remember having the hymen pierced was supposed to hurt, like the wedding night was supposed to be painful. To me, everything was a mystery. I knew very little about my body. I never looked or dreamed of looking." When asked why not, she replied, "There were layers and layers of prohibitions, my own perhaps. I don't remember my first vaginal exam by a doctor; I have no memory of it. My mother didn't talk about such things. The girls I knew didn't talk to me about such things. I had a friend whose mother talked to her about menstruation. It was not a time or a culture for specific talk about the body." The patient then thought of the word *hymeneal*— "a word I'm not sure of or how to pronounce"—and *lamia* (meaning epithalamia)—"another word I'm not sure of, but it's a poem written for someone on their wedding night." She thought the veil referred to the uncovering of her deepest thoughts and her concern that maybe she really didn't have any "deepest thoughts." She continued, "So I had a hymen and I never knew when it got broken. I remember, you know. I don't remember a terrible pain. I do remember . . ." When asked what she remembered, she described the unromantic setting of her first intercourse, which was disappointing. Nevertheless, she had decided to go ahead based on an ultimatum by the boy: either go to bed or he wouldn't see her anymore. "I did not have any feelings of a romantic kind. I don't think I was terribly aroused. I am sure he had an orgasm. I really think so. I don't remember for sure. I doubt I had a clear idea of what an orgasm was supposed to be. I really was not very knowledgeable. I wouldn't say that I was aware, but not letting yourself be totally aware of what you are doing is particularly what it's about. What it's about is that you're not actually sure of what's going to happen because I didn't think that what we were going to do was a good thing to do. I just completely—well, not completely—I wanted to be a virgin on my wedding night, I'm sure."

The analyst interpreted to her how this veil between herself and her brain was a metaphor expressing how she was feeling in the analysis. The patient's immediate response was that maybe she would be stopping the treatment. When asked why, she replied that maybe she had already found out all that she could. And "removal of the veil leaves one naked, or that I would know a lot of bad things about myself." The analyst pointed out that the patient was the one who was using the label of bad and was worried that the process of understanding herself would be shameful or painful. The patient said, "I feel I have such a mountain to break through—like the hymen—it seems so difficult—layers—such a thickness—I'm no longer young." The analyst asked why it was that the patient wished to remain an intellectual virgin. What else was her concern? The patient replied, "Maybe it would be like the Emperor has no clothes. You break through and there is nothing." To the analyst's question "Nothing?" the patient replied, "Nothing—not a perfect brain—very pedestrian—not a perfect sensibility. What if I find everything I'm hiding from myself? To a degree I don't know what there is I'm going to find out—so how do I start?" (The patient's reply of "nothing" may allude to "no thing," that is to say, no phallus. Bertram Lewin [1948] and Joseph Slap [1979] both have discussed and demonstrated clinically the idea that the female genital is phallocentrically perceived as castrated, as nothing.)

The conversion to psychoanalysis was experienced as a total new beginning of treatment, as if the patient had not been in therapy to that point. It also became an uncovering likened to a breaking through of the hymen. Her denials, negations, and protests represent, isomorphically, the hymen.* The patient was frightened of the difficulties to come: pain, fear of what she would find beneath the veil, "badness" or disappointment that there would be nothing, that she would be revealed to be bodily, emotionally, and intellectually deficient. The idea of getting on the couch aroused memories of her original defloration and the ultimatum either to have intercourse or be rejected. It seems as if she experienced the conversion to psychoanalysis as an ultimatum by the analyst. She feared that like the boyfriend the analyst would not see her any more unless she conformed to the analyst's desires. She had the impulse to flee the analysis in order to escape her fears and perhaps to leave the analyst before the analyst left her. Throughout the session, the repeated expressions of doubts, negations, and undoing are remarkable. The negations reflect her anxious ambivalence about proceeding with what to her was a sexualized and frightening experience.

Some weeks later the same patient reported that she had had a dream, which, when she woke up, seemed to continue for a few minutes. "I am not sure if I was still sleeping or—really I think I was awake. I, or the protagonist, was a man. All the characters were men. It had to do with something I described to you last time, being powerless and pursued by not-nice men, maybe Indians, intent on doing me bodily harm. I go upstairs and sneak out over the roof." When asked about being a man she replied, "That's an old thought, wishing that I had been born a man. Male means being independent, free, strong, and unafraid. I know that many men aren't. But that's a big thing, actual physical strength. Men were strong, physically powerful and stronger than I. I don't remember my father spanking me." The idea of bodily harm brought a thought of war and a sense of evil, fear, and pain. She associated pain with child-

---

*Our thanks to Dale Boesky, M.D., for this insightful understanding.

birth. "I have always made a big thing of having a high threshold of pain and I've been proud of that. Dentists, for example, it's painful what they do in your mouth." She went on to recall a TV show in which a daughter had accused her stepfather of molesting her. The patient wondered, "How could a man invade, do that to his own child? Invasion—the threshold is gone over and once you invade, it's torn. Really the body, the vagina . . . I think of blood, pain and horror. If you were a man, maybe I would have to do such things. That's different than if you're a woman."

These last two sentences are ambiguous. In saying "you were a man" it is not clear whether the patient is referring to the analyst or to herself. On the one hand, there is the allusion to her experiencing of the analyst as a sadistic male who was invading her privacy. On the other hand, in this phrase as well as in the dream she may be defending against being a feminine victim by assuming a masculine role or identification.

When associating to the roof she thought of the phrase "falling off the roof," meaning menstruation. "I didn't know a lot about it. Just had these little hints about it. My mother didn't say anything, and when she discovered blood in the bathroom she left me a Kotex pad and a belt. I do know that it was my father that I would get some sympathy from. I was embarrassed when I first began to menstruate. I didn't want people to know it happened to me. That's a significant reaction. I don't want people ever to know how I feel—like something is wrong with me." She was silent. Her thoughts wandered again to Indians, of scalping, setting on fire, and raping. This association is reminiscent of the anthropological studies that suggest that scalps symbolically represented the hymen to certain tribes (Devereux, 1950).

The dream elaborates the patient's feeling of deficiency, of a sense of femininity as a kind of castration, as "nothing." For her, being female is experienced as being in the victim's position. She wished to be a man to correct these feelings of deficiency and vulnerability. Entering treatment evoked concerns about humiliating herself and exposing fantasized deficiencies and vulnerabilities to the analyst. The analyst was experienced as a man who invades her and molests her. Again we see the link between menstruation and defloration. With the reference to the threshold, the entire analysis is foretold in hymeneal terms.

RESISTANCES

A woman in the middle phase of her analysis was experiencing difficulties in talking, which led to long silences. She noted that she felt forced to talk, although the analyst had waited through the silences.

"It felt that way at the moment. [that is, being forced] But I want to talk, of course, although I am feeling blocked." When asked, "What about being blocked?" she recalled feeling that way before and began talking about being intruded upon. "And I was thinking about, and I blocked talking about, something about sex." When the analyst asked her what that was, she replied that now the analyst was trying to force her to talk. She said, "Well, what am I going to do in order to avoid talking about sex? Do I have to? I don't think I have to. Now, exploring the inner space, the private space, for reasons . . . That's my sense of being in analysis. You help yourself by allowing someone to invade your space. Sometimes that's painful." The analyst said, "I think you are telling us about what's going on here between you and me in which you feel invaded and worried that I do hurt you."

The patient replied, "True. I was thinking about my tennis teacher who I have a crush on. My girlfriend said I better talk to you about it, but I have not wanted to. Really, I do have many romantic fantasies about him. Must be romantic, not sexual. And I am head over heels for this man! It doesn't feel right. I don't know. How would you know? You don't know what it feels like when I talk about certain things. You understand the theoretical, but not the feelings, perhaps. So, some of my feelings . . . A man irks me when he does certain things, yet I just can't stay away from him. Can't find another one that's better. There is something in this man. I went away from him but then I came back, and I don't know. Is it him, or is it his skill?" After a pause, she began to talk about how the tennis teacher reminded her of the first boy with whom she had sex. He insisted on having intercourse, to which she reluctantly submitted and experienced as painful.

In this case, the ongoing resistance, of being "blocked" and feeling forced to talk is experienced as a defloration with the analyst as the perpetrator and the patient as the victim/virgin. To the extent that the patient gets the analyst to probe (for example, when the analyst asked what it was that the patient was thinking about, rather than exploring the reason for the resistance) the interaction between them becomes a scene of deflowering.

In association to a dream, a male patient talked about "something that was used." His thoughts went to a "used woman."

> That means not a virgin. It was very difficult for me to visualize my mother having sex. I wanted love. Love with women, not necessarily sex. Virginity is really something that doesn't exist. I've never really known a virgin. Every woman I've known has been something else. Although the first time I had sex, it was with a woman who said that she was a virgin. I was 19 and she was 16. But I'm not sure she was a virgin. Maybe it's not real. It's a cultural myth. I've never met a virgin. I think of Virgin Mary. A fallen woman is a used woman. All women are used, and when they're used they become a woman.

The words like "fallen," "used," and "filthy" came to the patient's mind as associations. When he thought of "fallen," he remembered that he had read earlier that there was something with a woman bleeding the first time—a membrane or a hymen—but he had never had sex when he was younger. He said that he had "a mental block. I very clearly do not remember with any woman a block like a hymen or a membrane." He had read of different ways of penetrating. "The gradual way is not necessarily the best. Don't be soft in it. It's less painful if you just do it."

The mental block the patient was experiencing in remembering and in processing the meaning of his thoughts was represented by the block, the membrane that blocked the vaginal passage. The remarkable juxtaposition of "clearly" and not remembering indicates conflict. The conflicted use of negations— he never met a virgin; virginity does not exist, and so on—is especially striking. Here, content and process are both of a "block." Moreover, he is identified with a woman; he has a block, a hymen.

In another instance, the defloration experience of analysis was masked until the analyst changed slightly from her usual attitude during the sessions. The patient was a woman whose mother was described as intrusive and controlling. Typically, this analyst tended to be rather direct and forthright in her comments. At one point, however, the analyst couched her intervention in more tentative language, beginning with a phrase, "Perhaps, this might mean. . . ." Following this intervention, the patient remembered an experience that had apparently been repressed and that she had never reported before. When she was 5 years old, her mother had set out to massage her hymen, with the explanation that it would make it easier for the girl later. This had been experienced as very traumatic by the girl. What the analyst made of this communication was that the patient had been in the throes of an underlying transference in which the analyst's assertiveness was experienced as the mother's intrusiveness. The analyst's departure from her usual mode of talking allowed the resistance to lift and gave the patient enough reassurance to remember and to tell her about the traumatic incident in her childhood. In the patient's associations following the telling of the memory it became clear that the analyst's departure from her usual mode of intervention meant to the patient that the analyst was very different from the mother. We speculate that the disparity between the reality of the analyst's tentative intervention and the patient's unconscious image of her as her intrusive mother allowed her to feel free to remember and to relate this material. In the transference the analyst had been perceived as the intrusive mother, deflowering the patient for her own good.

A woman patient, coming to new material in her analysis, recalled her wedding night. She was a virgin and bled profusely. Feeling deeply embarrassed and ashamed, she spent much time that night trying to wash out the blood stains from the sheets on the hotel bed because she was afraid that the maid would find them the next morning. (We are reminded of Lady Macbeth and Potter's Mrs. Tiggy-Winkle from Chapter 6.) Retrospectively, the patient figured that she must have felt guilty, as if she were caught at something bad. She speculated that in spite of the fact that she was legitimately married, she must have felt as if she were caught doing something she was not supposed to be doing, like masturbating or having illicit sex. The memory communicated her fear that the analyst would find her thoughts dirty, unacceptable, and illicit. It also helped the analyst understand and address the nature of the resistance at that time.

Examples of material in which the theme of defloration is bypassed are frequent. For example, a young female analyst in the opening phases of treating a young woman reported the following: The patient began to talk spontaneously of having been prescribed the pill for regulating her period from about age 18. Then she stated emphatically, "I didn't become sexually active until years later." There was no further inquiry about the communication of this event and why it came up at that time. The reference to this milestone of defloration was not recognized by the therapist as having possible implications for the patient's experience of the treatment and its significance in and of itself.

A male analyst in supervision presented dream material from a female patient. In the dream, the patient was being attacked and her dress was being ripped in front. She went on to describe some of her sexual experiences. She linked the dress's being ripped in the front with the hymen's being ripped in defloration. However, the analyst interpreted this image as a castration experience and did not investigate it further. Thus, possible allusions to how the patient was experiencing the treatment and the therapist in terms of the kinds of defloration themes we have illustrated above were not explored. This common and sometimes automatic processing of material into phallic or castration terms is both limiting and incomplete. A mutually collusive silence about exploring fully the meanings of this material can occur and can contribute to problems in establishing a therapeutic alliance in the opening phases of treatment. Important events to the patient are either misconstrued or diminished in their importance. In these cases both female and male analysts contributed to resistances by not recognizing the themes of defloration as important communications of the patients' experience of the process. In one of Freud's now-famous dreams, defloration themes were evident, but unrecognized. Freud's dream of July, 1895, "Irma's Injection," as it has come to be called, can be viewed as a defloration dream. In his self-analyis, which formed the basis for his developing theories of the mind, Freud relied heavily on his own dreams. He presented the revolutionary idea that dreams are disguised, unconscious wish fulfillments. By tracing each element of the manifest content of a dream such as that of "Irma's Injection" Freud demonstrates what he calls a detailed, but by no means complete, analysis of the dream. This particular dream has given rise to a least eighteen important articles that take up different aspects and interpretations of the dream content and Freud's associations. These writers also utilize additional biographical material to augment Freud's own associations about the context in which the dream occurred. There is little disagreement among the many interpretations that the dream has important sexual meanings, though these were not explicitly delineated by Freud (Efron 1977, Erikson 1954, Hartman 1983, Lupton 1993, Mautner 1991, Schur 1966, Swan 1974.)

The dream consists of a large hall with numerous guests, among whom was a woman named Irma. Freud takes her aside and reproaches her for not accepting his "solution." She reports pains in her throat, stomach, and abdomen. Freud is alarmed and takes her over to a window and looks down her throat. She seems "recalcitrant." Then she opens her mouth and he finds a "big white patch" and "whitish grey scabs upon some remarkable curly structures modeled on the turbinal bones of the nose" (Freud 1900, p. 107). A friend percusses her through her bodice. She had been given an injection of "propyl, propyls . . . proprionic acid . . . trimethylamin." In the dream Freud comments that one should not thoughtlessly give injections like that and thought that the syringe had "not been clean" (pp. 117–118).

Among the many plausible interpretations of this dream, we would suggest that reading it as a defloration scene with reference to the hymen seems justifiable, and we will summarize the arguments of those authors whose hypotheses point to such a reading. Anzieu (1986) sees the dream explicitly in terms of a defloration. He writes, "the examination of the nose and throat is a gynecological examination in disguise, a substitute for it" (p. 145). According to Anzieu, looking into cavities in the dream represents sexual curiosity about the female genitalia. The element *propyl* relates to *preopylaea*, which in Greek architecture represents an entrance. These architectual structures are common symbols of the body in dreams. For example, the Labia Majora can be considered the entrance to the female room, the vagina. Anzieu uses Freud's associations to the Irma dream to back up his arguments. In the context of discussing the Irma dream, Freud tells a story of "the man who was charged by one of his neighbors with having given him back a borrowed kettle in a damaged condition. The defendant asserted first, that he had given it back undamaged; secondly, that the kettle had a hole in it when he borrowed it; and thirdly, that he had never borrowed a kettle from his neighbor at all" (Freud 1900, p. 120). This comical story, which is Freud's association to his dream, demonstrates the unconscious mechanisms of denial and undoing, that is, certain realities are distorted due to anxiety and guilt about the idea of inflicting damage to a borrowed object. Anzieu sees sexual and deflowering images in this story. For example, he suggests that the kettle represents a woman's belly or body, which is damaged or has a hole in it. Another reference to deflowering stems from the idea of an examination. Anzieu asks, "When someone is the first to examine a new subject does he not deflower it?" (p. 147). The entire dream, when looked at from a perspective of bodily representation, seems to be a symbolic exploration of a woman. Along similar lines, Anzieu interprets Freud's (1899) analysis of a screen memory of two boys who snatch flowers from a girl. Anzieu links this to possible sex play during early childhood by Freud and his nephew

John. It is, Anzieu says, "an easy picture puzzle to solve": they deflower her (p. 304). Thus, for Anzieu, defloration becomes a general metaphor for Freud's pioneering efforts in understanding the inner workings of the mind.

Max Schur (1966) furnishes biographical background for the dream that was recorded in Freud's unpublished letters to his friend the physician, Wilhelm Fliess. Fliess frequently discussed his theory with Freud that the turbinal bones in the nose were connected to the female sexual organs. Freud had been treating a young woman named Emma Eckstein for hysterical anxiety and symptoms of pain and bloody secretions from her nose. According to many researchers, Irma in the dream stood for Emma and probably several other figures as well. Freud himself said that the figure in the dream is a composite. According to Schur, Freud asked Fliess to examine Emma to determine whether there was a somatic origin in her nose for her symptoms. Fliess recommended surgery and operated on her. She continued to have pain and extensive hemorrhaging, and a fetid odor now emanated from her nose. Ultimately it was found that Fliess had left iodoform gauze in the cavity. The patient went into shock when this gauze was removed. Needless to say, this incident was cause for much dismay and soul searching for Freud and probably gave rise to the theme of guilt in the Irma dream.

Thus, we can see that blood and hemorrhaging are parts of the latent associational material related to Freud's Irma dream. The guilt-ridden idea of causing pain to a woman by invading an orifice of her body that is seen as related to the genitals is an intrinsic part of this dream. Lupton (1993) wrote that at the heart of the mystery of the dream lies the phenomenon of menstruation. She ascribes Freud's surprising inability to follow the clues that lead from the turbinate bones to menstruation, and abdominal pains to dysmenorrhea, as evidence of anxiety about this topic. This inability was all the more significant, she argues, given how well acquainted Freud was with Fliess's idea that the nose, the female genitals, and the menstrual process were con-

nected, and to what a degree Fliess hovered in the background
of the dream.

One clue to such a meaning was the reference in the dream
to Irma's not feeling well. Mahoney (1977) points out that feeling unwell is the German euphemism for a menstruating woman.
Another prominent element in the dream refers to the reddish-
violet turbinal bones, which Freud examined after Irma's "re-
calcitrance" at "opening her mouth properly." The color red is a
familiar one in our material about defloration. "Whitish grey
scabs" appear as another element in the dream. In one of our
clinical examples we discovered that a "scab" appeared as a representation of the hymen. Freud associates the "white patch"
with mucous membranes and with a "diphtheritic membrane"
of his oldest daughter, Mathilde. According to an account by
Ernest Jones (1953) of Mathilde's childhood bout with diph-
theria, she swallowed a piece of fruit, began to cough intensely,
and dislodged the "obstructive membrane." We note that hymen
means a membrane. Freud had discussed trimethylamin, another element in the dream, with Fliess, who, in addition to his
linkage of the turbinal bones with the female sexual organs,
believed that this was one of the products of sexual metabolism
(Freud 1900, p. 116).

Freud's own words about his reactions to the dream are suggestive of the possible underlying, but not recognized, meanings about defloration. In a letter to Fliess, Freud speaks of
"unveiling" the mystery of the dream (Erikson 1954, p. 7). Freud
writes, "I will not pretend that I have completely uncovered the
meaning of this dream or that its interpretation is without a gap"
(Freud 1900, pp. 120–121). At another point Freud states in
his associations to the dream, "Frankly, I had no desire to penetrate more deeply at this point." Freud observes his unusual
phrasing in the dream when he reports "a portion of the skin
was infiltrated" (p. 113). He follows this observation by speaking about shifting the blame for causing pain, which we have
found to be a common anxious response in men for guilt about
deflowering and "violating " women. Alan Elms (1980), in his

essay on the sexual meanings in the dream of "Irma's Injection," points out that a primary definition of the verb "to infiltrate" is to penetrate the interstices of a tissue of substance. Elms writes that Freud seemed to have an anxiety neurosis that involved fears about the sexual act as physically damaging to women. We believe that breaking or ripping the hymen is a kernel of reality around which such fears coalesce.

TERMINATION

The patient was a middle-aged woman who had begun psychoanalysis shortly after the breakup of her marriage, which had been sexless for years. She was phobic and inhibited and considered herself to be frigid. After four years in analysis, she had broken free from her inhibitions and had begun to date some men and enjoy sex for the first time in her life. She was feeling very positive about herself as a female and experiencing intense pleasure sexually. Yet there were traces still of a primary fear that if she let go of the hold she had on herself she would go wild sexually. In the transference the image of analyst had changed from what at first had been a controlling, forbidding parent to that of a wizard or witch who initiated and lured the patient into her new sexual ways. She began a session by reporting she had had a long dream:

> I only remember some scenes from it and they were all interspersed with a man. How it was going with him was rocky. In one scene people were facing an antique curio chest with glass doors, filled with all this stuff: china figurines, plates. . . . I had taken out a plate and was trying to put it back. It was hard to put it back. Some kind of big deal, trying to get it back. The plate had a picture of a person on it—Josephine Baker. In the next scene I am outside . . . And suddenly the lawn is covered with flowers. The color of the flowers was a kind of a coral/shrimp color, but pale, not vibrant. The man is acting like a stranger, but I had a sexual relationship with him, which I had forgotten.

She continued associating to the dream:

Actually, I was watching a movie on TV last night about Josephine
Baker. I found her daring. She made something of herself, although she had trouble with intimacy. But she pulled off a lot of
important things. She was in the Resistance; she adopted all
those kids. She did change her life dramatically. I guess that
equals my attempts to change my life. The rest of the stuff in
the chest was ugly and uninteresting. I rearranged the shelf when
I took out the plate, and I couldn't get it back the same way. The
stuff inside it was not of value any more. Joe [the first boyfriend
with whom she had sex after the divorce] had a cabinet like that.
One of the people who was watching may have been my mother.
I don't know. So it's change in me. The old things in me that are
important to her that I have now changed. I put the plate back
in front of the other things. The flowers, they were in all different stages of growth. I like flowers. If I were a princess, I'd always
have cut flowers around. And lots of flowers in gardens. The
house in the dream had a big porch, and steps going down. It
had been around a long time. Probably that's me. I've been
around a long time. I don't know who the man was. Tim? [a man
with whom she recently had had a passionate affair, but whose
business took him out of town constantly]. Or Joe? Or Pat?
[new man on the scene]. But in any case I didn't get anything
established.

She went on to talk about a girlfriend's problems with men and
concluded that men have problems with intimacy and ambivalence. She and the friend had read *Prince of Tides* and had found
the sexual relationship between the male character and female
psychiatrist upsetting and threatening. She continued, "I'm in
turmoil about Tim coming into town. In the dream I don't seem
to get into a relationship. The changes in me that aren't changes
yet is what it seems to be about. Because I would like to move
toward termination, but I am not in a committed relationship
yet. Like the flowers are uneven, not fully developed. Maybe
they have to be of equal growth."

The analyst asked, "That's what you think?" "Well that's all
I've come up with. Actually when you ask that, it makes me think

that I've been deflowered. That's something sexual. But there's no prince . . . yet. And, somehow, my relationships have been troubled." The analyst remarked, "Like Josephine Baker." "Yes, look how far I've come. But look how far I haven't come. I feel so free, but I haven't been able to find a relationship . . . Joe, Tim . . . Is there some guarantee that you'll get what you want in the end? I want to get this show on the road!"

This hour foreshadowed the termination that was to come within the next year and ushered in the termination phase itself. In the session the patient spoke of the changes already made within herself, changes that at this point are not yet consolidated or comfortable. She depicted this process of change as flowers in different stages of growth. Her old ways were those with which her mother would approve—the old stuff in the cabinet—but they were no longer available or desirable to the patient. The mother was looking on to the whole scene, reminiscent of what we have seen throughout our survey of literature in which the mother seems to be present in girls' minds so frequently during their sexual initiations. The new self, Josephine Baker, of which she was proud, was shoved with difficulty in front of the old stuff. Furthermore, the new daring and sexual self was frightening. The guilt she still felt about her sexuality was projected onto the analyst, the initiator, and her ambivalence about intimacy, onto men. The patient felt frightened about her sexuality; now that it was out of the curio cabinet, it could not be put back in, just like the contents of Pandora's Box.

The metaphor for this change and the initiation into the termination phase is one of defloration. The cabinet with the glass doors has an anatomical allusion to the female genitals, with the glass—the hymen—in front. In this case, however, it is not loss, but opening up that is the dominant feeling. There is the sense of a threshold crossed and of irreversibility, with accompanying anxiety, but also positive excitement: "Let's get this show on the road!" The patient's associations to the mass of flowers in the front yard is to deflowering, with the sense of abundance, a longed-for fertility (Josephine Baker's many children), and sexual passion.

It is interesting that a male colleague who heard this material felt that the flowers were penises, and that the patient was dealing with penis envy and feelings of castration (cut flowers). While this is a possible reading of this material, we feel it misses the affective tone and the more joyously feminine aspects of the current state of the patient's life, a sexual/emotional rebirth. The reddish color of the flowers, "coral" or "shrimp," is one we have found often associated with loss of virginity. Yet they are pale and not vibrant. We understand this as the patient's defense against the intensity of her sexual feelings, an attempt to mute them. "Antique" has many determinants. It refers to old childhood feelings, old feelings about herself and her body as "ugly and uninteresting." These feelings are reawakened in the transference. On the one hand the analyst is seen, in contrast to the previous image of the mother, as reassuring and not disapproving, and, on the other hand, as luring her into sexual excess. The idea of resistance, for this patient, who was well acquainted with psychoanalytic terms, signaled her recognition of her own resistance. Like Josephine Baker she had made many changes and yet was frightened about them. Josephine Baker was seen as a female able to transcend her background and feelings about herself as a female. The patient often identified with figures such as Josephine Baker whom she perceived as being disadvantaged or oppressed. In the transference, she also often pictured the analyst as an exotic figure from a different cultural or ethnic background than herself.

As we have seen, defloration and representations of the hymen have come up in the opening, middle, and termination phases of analytic treatment, including resistances at specific points. We will now turn our attention to the analyses of men and women to explicate the similarities and differences that emerge.

10
౨ఌ

Defloration and the Hymen in Male Patients

*W*ords such as *never*, negations, denials, reversals, and doubting predominate when patients speak of the hymen. In addition, bisexual imagery appears with regularity in the clinical material of both males and females. The content, feelings, and conflicts about the hymen and defloration, however, differ between men and women. It is understandable that these differences appear as the experience—psychologically, physically, and socially— of defloration in a heterosexual relationship is naturally quite different for men and women. With our male patients, the material can be organized around three major themes: oedipal conflicts, castration anxiety in multiple forms, and sadomasochism. With our female patients, the material can be organized around several different themes: genital anxieties, damage, and vulnerability; protection and thresholds; guilt about masturbation; menstruation, blood, and childbirth; and the role of mother. Of course, all of these themes are entwined, but we will highlight each for the purposes of our discussion.

As stated above, we have found many bisexual images and
fantasies in our clinical material in which defloration and the
hymen appear. Since bisexuality is a term that has been used
and defined differently in the psychoanalytic literature, it is
important that we explain what we mean by it. Freud's concept
of bisexuality was a bio-psychological one. He proposed that
people are born with both male and female dispositions. Although he warned against equating masculinity with activity and
aggression and femininity with passivity and masochism, in his
writing he often slipped into making this equation. For example,
he wrote, "The suppression of women's aggressiveness, which
is prescribed for them constitutionally and imposed on them
socially, favors the development of powerful masochistic impulses, which succeed, as we know, in binding erotically the
destructive trends which have been diverted inwards. Thus
masochism, as people say, is truly feminine." (Freud 1933,
p. 116). He went on to assert that this is true when it occurs in
men as well as women. This is not the sense in which we are
using the concept of bisexuality. In our material, bisexual imagery has a different meaning. Often we see a composite bisexual
image of the genitals and of the hymen in particular. For example, the hymen in a patient's fantasy or dream may be represented by what that patient defines as encompassing masculine
and feminine aspects: a cork covering a female-like container,
which at the same time is phallic shaped. Such an image seems
to reflect a child's confused view of his or her body and genital
apparatus, a view carried over into the adult's mental life. At
times such images appear to be compensatory defensive con-
structions that serve to repair perceived deficits. Such images
may reflect a common wish to have both genitals or to be both
sexes, a wish that comes out of narcissistic concerns and strivings
(Kubie 1974). Bisexuality has another central determinant. Our
use of the idea of bisexuality comes in the context of an appreciation of object relations and the role of identification in development. Children, of course, identify with both sexes, with
both parents. They take both sexes into their internal worlds of

self and objects. Thus, in our material we see individuals struggling or oscillating between feminine and masculine identifications in their fantasies about defloration. Often this switching serves the purpose of defending against conflicted aspects of one role versus the other—deflowerer or deflowered, penetrator or penetrated. We would like to emphasize that we have tried to avoid any *a priori* definitions of "feminine" or "masculine" and instead have taken the meanings the patients themselves have ascribed to their thoughts and behaviors.

The following are typical examples of material about the hymen and defloration derived from male patients.

THE HYMEN AND POSITIVE OEDIPAL THEMES

A 40-year-old married male, several years into his analysis, was beginning to experience intensely erotized feelings for his female analyst. He reported a dream in which he was standing at a big desk. It looked like a rare and beautiful cherry desk he had once owned. Someone "older and bigger" was getting many gifts. He associated to the analyst's desk which had cherry-wood crossbars. Cherry reminded him of virginity, purity, a great gift: "first prize because it means I'm the first. A cherry was something I never encountered. ["Cherry" is a term commonly used for the hymen.] I'm supposed to have sex with my wife and never anyone else." Of their early premarital sex life, he said, "She did not have a hymen that I was aware of." He speculated that "Someone older and bigger must be my father."

The dream represented his desire to be the first with his mother. He wished to possess a virginal mother, who would present him with the gift of her cherry intact. This material was followed by another dream, of a child with a hole in its forehead "where I put in a needle and fluid spurts out. Someone had already drilled the hole." His associations went to adolescent talk of drilling girls, drilling through the hymen. "I never had a virgin. I would not like to have been the first and cause the pain." This dream and the one above are two sides of the same coin; the first expresses the oedipal wish to be the first with the mother/analyst, and the latter, the undoing of that wish out of anxiety.

Anxiety connected to incestual wishes characterizes the next example, as well. A 20-year-old man reported a dream about a dead-end street, which he associated with birth, death, and the female genitalia. He said, "Beautiful ladies are a trap." His first thoughts went to Sharon Stone, the dangerous blonde in the movie *Basic Instinct*. He recalled a scene in which she takes a shower and the shower doors steam up. "People can't see in." Sharon Stone reminded him of his mother. He then remembered the famous scene from the movie *Psycho* in which a woman is murdered in the shower by a male killer dressed as a female. The patient described how he masturbated while looking through a half-open window at older women passing by his apartment. People could not see in but he could see out.

He thought of "something that is a little opened and half covered—like a slit, or where a cavity is covered." When the analyst asked about a covered cavity, he said, "I never found one, never found a hymen." He was taking a course on human sexuality in which this topic had been discussed. He claimed he had had at least three virgins, but none had a hymen that he could detect. "I forgot that hymens exist because I never encountered one." He said that a hymen should be "an opaque, thin membrane through which one couldn't really see, like the shower door." Earlier he had told the analyst of how as a little boy he had peeked at his mother through the shower door. In another memory his mother and father hugged as she stepped out of the shower (probably a condensed "screen memory"). The stimulating and frightening view of his nude mother, associated with the memory of her with his father, was an important organizing factor in his development and the underlying source of castration anxiety. The complaint that he could never find a hymen may also imply that he was searching for the mother's hidden penis.

He mused, "A girl who has a hymen has a nice gift for someone, a certification that you are the first." He did not talk about it with his first girlfriend. He felt he might have ruptured the hymen digitally although he did not remember feeling it. Other girls said that he was the first but there was no evidence of the hymen, difficulties in penetrating, or blood. "It was not an experience I've had," he concluded.

Here the hymen is viewed as a gift, as the covering of a dangerous and exciting trap, and as a barrier that obscures vision and entry. Note the striking reoccurrence of negations, which are attempts to mediate the underlying anxiety throughout this material. The wish to be first and the sexual interest in women who reminded him of his mother illustrate his heightened incestuous conflicts.

One defense against this forbidden desire for his mother is captured by the transvestite figure from *Psycho*, a man dressed as a woman. The patient projects his sadistic killing impulses onto a "dangerous" woman, and at the same time, he defuses this terrifying image by conjuring up a disguised killer. There is an unconscious identification with the woman as well. The transference to an older woman analyst revived these anxieties and defenses.

As in this case, the boy's need to be first with the woman does not always carry only the oedipal meaning of replacing the father. A yearning to be first, or special, may reflect rivalries with siblings or other figures important to the mother.

The idea of cherry as hymen occurred in association to this patient's dream. The cherry may have had similar meanings in another male patient's dream, but was not recognized as such. Herman Nunberg (1947) reported a patient's dream that came toward the termination of the analysis. According to Nunberg, bisexual ideas dominated this patient's intrapsychic life, probably connected to the fact that the patient had been traumatized by a circumcision at age 5. The patient had formed the idea the prepuce was the female part of a man.

The dream was as follows:

Ann's navel protruded in three shapes: first, it protruded like a dog's penis with a sort of head stretching out, but more like a dog's penis protruding from a sheath; it was long, red and looked like the neck of a clam; the whole thing was flesh-coloured. I got great satisfaction from taking the navel in my mouth, sucking it. Secondly, the sheath disappeared. The head remained like the pistil of a flower, without the shank. Third, the navel protruded in the form of a cone, the point of the cone touching the belly. In the opening of the cone was a white, cheese-like-tasting substance. I ate it. The pistil looked like a cherry. I buried my mouth and nose in it and ate it and had its taste in my mouth and its smell in my nose. At the end of the dream I had the feeling of having completely satisfied myself. [p. 158]

In his interpretation of the dream, Nunberg asserts that the cherry like cone with the cheesy substance represents the patient's penis and mother's nipples condensed into one image. While the patient's associations are not available, we think that an equally plausible additional interpretation is that the cherry may represent the hymen. Bisexual conflicts and wishes are equally expressed by imagery combining pistil with cherry as a nipple, as well as cherry as a hymen. Moreover, this man had linked the prepuce as a female part. We have found in several of our cases that the prepuce, or foreskin, was equated with hymen.

THE HYMEN AND CASTRATION ANXIETY

As in the above examples, castration anxiety often accompanies oedipal strivings. The image of a dangerous trap, seen in one of the preceding cases, reoccurred in the material of a divorced 50-year-old male. He was in treatment for the first time, that is to say, it was a virginal experience for him. In his opening dream, which reflected anxieties about starting an analysis with a woman, he reported being in an office with a girl whose pants are suddenly down and her legs open. "Over her vagina is a black wire. I was able to penetrate through the hole and had a super-large penis." He said the black wire was like the covering over a champagne bottle, which "when you open it can surprise you—explode and spurt out." The wire reminded him of a cage, a trap. The office looked like the analyst's. The new experience of lying down led to pleasurable memories of lying in bed with his mother.

The imagery of a covering was not linked directly to the hymen and was not elucidated until several years later. At this point in the analysis, oedipal longings toward his mother in the transference were emerging in a clearer and more workable form. The patient recalled an image of his mother sitting on a screened porch, which was all wire. He was reminded of the kind of wire on a champagne bottle "covering the hole." He said, "Popping the cork is like an ejaculation." He recalled his opening dream and thought of the covering of part of the woman's body like a trap, the wire covering over the hole. "Wire mesh is like a screen." In response to the analyst's query for clarification, he replied, "It's like with a virgin—there is a covering. What's hidden in there, who knows? I never had sexual intercourse with a woman who was a virgin, where there was a hymen. For some reason I did not want to. I never chose to. I did not think it was important. My thought was that the girl wanted to save it until marriage." He reported recently being fascinated by reading about the abuse of women and the ritual removal of the clitoris. Abuse reminded him of some sort of bondage, and a "covering" or wire could produce abuse. "When you break and enter, then there is something bloody."

The bisexual imagery of "something popping out" from behind the screen or wire expresses an important dynamic in this case. The image of the bottle with "something popping out" represents the wished-for and feared phallic mother. In this fantasy a woman is imbued with a phallus, hidden behind the wire perceived as hymen, and therefore is no longer perceived as castrated. In another sense, the hymen that the patient "never encountered" may be equated unconsciously with the phallus the patient wishes/fears to find inside the woman's body. One fear of castration stems from retribution for sexual and sadistic impulses projected onto the analyst. It also reflects the patient's identification with a virginal female, a victim of the penetrating analyst. He often remarked how impressed he was by the analyst's "penetrating" comments.

In another case a man had a dream in which a plant was "half covering the doorway to the analyst's office." He said, "The tree is taking over and it's like a trap. This was like a man-eating tree or bush. A tree can be protection." As he mused about a man-eating trap he said, "I'm not totally convinced that a woman's vagina has the capacity to snare a man's penis." His thoughts went to an overgrown bush that covered the doorway to the analyst's office. It reminded him of the female genitals and pubic hair and of his confusions about the female genitals. He thought of his mother and remembered that she was not particularly discreet about nudity. He recalled how many times he saw her breasts or saw her in her underwear. He remembered getting into bed with her as a child and generally being stimulated by all of this.

He recalled a previous dream in which he had to clear out a drain trap filled with hair on the floor of the shower. He thought of his penis being caught and an empty hole and his losing his penis. One understanding of the dream of the bush's taking over the doorway is that it demonstrates the patient's feeling that any sexual attraction to the analyst might be a trap for him. The "bush half covering the doorway" recalls similar images of a slit, a half-opened cavity, a partially opened window, and so on, which all referred to the hymen. Remember that the hymen anatomically has been described as a crescent. The image here is a frightening and confused one of a hidden trap. Again, the oedipal longings toward mother and being stimulated by her, now revived in the transference, bring fantasies of being punished by castration.

Castration fears, confusions about female genitals, and oedipal conflicts mixed with ideas about defloration all occur in the following case. A man reported a dream that he had wanted to tell his analyst but "forgot." Such ambivalence is yet another example of the anxiety about the hymen and defloration that produces defensive negations. The patient was a twice-married man, struggling with scoptophilic impulses revived in the transference, who reported the following dream:

> There was a suitcase on its side that opened up, which looked like a photo album with leaves. The outside of the suitcase was translucent or transparent, and of a strange material. After the second leaf was lifted there was a squished white snake in there with a big round head, like a king cobra. It raised itself halfway in a serpentine S. There was a dangerous dark animal with us, a mongoose. There was an element of danger. That phallic-like snake emerging was supposed to be reassuring, but then it was not. I didn't know if the mongoose would swallow the snake, or if the snake would swallow the mongoose. The translucent or transparent aspect reminds me of the wedding; I meant to say first communion.

Here the patient caught his own slip of the tongue. He had recently attended his niece's first communion. As he associated to his slip—"wedding"—he said, "The wedding makes me think of the beginning of the sexual relationship. In reality someone gave my niece something which was translucent. Something that looked like a vase or a purse. Translucent also reminds me of women's nightgowns." He noted

> the stark contrast throughout all the dream. The contrast of blacks and whites. Darks and lights. My experience is I don't know who is who, and what is what. A mongoose animal—I do not know what it looks like, but it was dark. Yes. *Mons* plus *goose*. A goose has a long neck which you can break. Even the skin on the snake was milky-white. It was half-erect, and I wonder whether the skin had been shed? The important thing is that the skin was also very thin and translucent, like a membrane. . . . All of this must have to do with male and female genitals.

When the analyst asked what came to mind about a translucent membrane, the patient said that he couldn't think of anything. Because of the slips, thoughts of weddings, and the beginning of a sexual relationship, the analyst asked, "What about a hymen?"

He replied, "I don't know anything about a hymen. My wife told me that I was the first. But I can't remember. Did she or didn't she bleed? I think there was bleeding, but I don't remember. Maybe no woman can be believed."

After a long silence, the patient continued, "I know I was the first. I don't like the idea because it has the idea of hurt in it." Then he returned to the idea of a vase or purse as a container. He thought of flowers in the vase, which might wilt. The analyst remarked that wilting could fit in with the notion of deflowering.

"I remember how my wife looked at the wedding. Oops, I mean communion." Calling the communion a wedding, he made the same slip again. "If we are talking about body parts, what I think of is light skin and dark pubic hair." At that moment he had a memory of seeing his mother naked. "And I think I saw her vagina." The analyst asked, "Do you mean vagina?" He said, "No, not exactly vagina." But the thought is that he saw her bleeding. "Maybe she was cleaning herself up. I remember the blood trickling down her leg." The patient became very nervous and uncomfortable and said that he was embarrassed "to talk about body parts, or anything about that." Confused, he added "Maybe it wasn't at that time."

This dream contains what many would recognize as elements of the primal scene: the dark and light shifts, the confusing images, the conscious thoughts of genitals. The shadowy bodies suggest the confused, frightened child's perceptions of the sexual scene between adults. The confusion of whether the snake would swallow the mongooses or vice versa reveals confused fantasies that sexual intercourse involves pain and hurt and the devouring of one or both parties. The thought of pain leads the patient to the idea of wilting flowers, a frightening chain of thoughts for him. The two slips of tongue from one ritualized ceremony to another, a first communion to a wedding, signal a possible link to unconscious thoughts about virginity and defloration. In the patient's words, "a wedding is a beginning of a sexual relationship." The string of obsessive questions reveals strong anxieties: he reported an image of a bloody vagina and then equivocated. He wondered if he really saw it or not. He questioned whether or not he was "the first." He wondered who would swallow whom in the dream. He worried whether or not he could believe any woman. Beneath these questions may lie another: Who would swallow or hurt whom first in the analytic situation? Finally, here again is a defensive and confused attribution of genital bisexuality in the image of a mongoose (mons plus long-necked goose).

Castration fears abound in this material. The patient stated that the goose had a long neck that could be broken. The half-raised, squished milky snake evokes an image of a post-coital penis, perceived from a frightened child's vantage point. The analyst interpreted the wilting of the flower as defloration, but it could also be seen as a representation of castration. The point is, however, that castration and defloration are connected for this man.

THE HYMEN AND SADOMASOCHISM

The act of penetration in defloration and the reality of breaking through the hymen often seem to evoke in men fears about their sadistic impulses and their store of sadomasochistic fantasies. For example, a young man spoke of a girlfriend who had suffered dyspareunia. He reported a dream in which there was a group of men who were wandering around:

> They came to an area like an arena, but not exactly. All these people, several hundred, were all in couples. There was going to be a ritual, a ritual tribal murder of some type. All around this area was a little white wooden fence. These couples were sitting in a position where it looked like loving care. The head of one person was lying in the lap of the other. Then at the signal of something, one person in every couple would stick something

in the ear of the other, and then there would be a cracking
through the ear. Everything would show on a big TV screen and
it showed it happening to a young girl.

Thoughts of the white fence led to memories of a crib. The
ear reminded him of something similar to a vagina. The cracking brought thoughts of a potato chip and the slang term for
vagina, crack. Cracking also was "like ripping through something
like the hymen of a young girl. A membrane needs to be ripped
or torn. I never thought of that any more," he asserted. "I never
thought that was so great. That never grabbed me. As a teen-
ager we talked about the first time we made love with girls."

The dyspareunia of this young man's girlfriend evoked anxieties that seem to have originated in experiences of the primal
scene. The idea of the primal scene is suggested by much of
the manifest content of the dream: an arena, strange sounds,
an exhibition of a scene, couples in unusual positions such as
one's head in the other's lap, the slats of a crib through which a
toddler might peer out, the vantage point of the child, and so
on. Much previous work in the analysis had indeed linked primal scene events with the patient's forbidden sexual fantasies
of his mother. The intercourse of the adults seemed to be interpreted as a painful ritual "murder" of sorts. The hymen ripping
added to and lent credence to the anxiety-provoking infantile
notions of intercourse. The hymen here is likened to the ear-
drum, a membrane that is cracked, or to a potato chip. The
patient's statement, "That never grabbed me," indicates an additional sadistic attribute to the female genital.

Early in his analysis, another young male patient was struggling with fears of being hurt by the analyst. He reported a
dream that followed his having intercourse with his girlfriend
who was "bleeding," that is, menstruating. In the dream a man
was being operated on and his ribs were exposed, "but it looks
kind of dry, not bleeding." In the dream two men gestured with
their arms as if in a sword fight. Ribs evoked associations to
Adam and Eve. When asked about the words, "not bleeding,"

he responded, "The only time anyone bleeds is if there is a period or if something is terribly wrong." This led the analyst to ask, "What about the first intercourse?" He said, "Oh, I never thought about that, I never remembered that. I forgot that. That's when the hymen is broken." He then recalled another portion of the dream in which a woman surgeon inserted a long knife and the wound was gushing.

We think that the patient experienced the analytic process as a rupturing of the hymen by a penetrating analyst. He, like many patients beginning analysis and confronted with a new relationship with the analyst, fantasized being like an exposed, opened virgin. Anticipation of intimacy and closeness can become defensively sexualized. Thus, a major transference–countertransference paradigm in the case was the image of the analyst as the castrating, penetrating surgeon and the patient as feminine victim. Also, the analyst was associated to Eve, the seductress who lured man into evil. In saying "anyone bleeds," the patient blurred over the gender distinction and betrayed his unconscious identification with the female. Here again, the fantasy of bisexuality is prominent. The above material demonstrates that conflicted sadomasochistic fantasies around defloration and penetration lead to the negation and denial of such events.

Such is the case with yet another male patient who reported a dream of "hair coming out in patches. The hair looked like pubic hair." He recalled seeing the genitals of a 5-year-old girl when he was about 10. Her genital area appeared to him like the skin that "covers the balls—only nothing is there." He compared the male and female genitals. "If one is a Jew, you circumcise although now there is a wave of anti-circumcision feeling. A piece of skin is not necessary, or is it? The hymen in women reminds me of such a piece of skin. Circumcision makes a man like a woman. A piece is removed." In the previous weeks, anti-Semitic material had been expressed with embarrassment. The patient was fighting a feared wave, not only of anti-circumcision, but also his own anti-Semitism in retribution against the Jewish analyst. Anti-circumcision came out of his castration anxiety; anti-Semitism reflected his fear of the analyst as castrating and castrated. Here we see an equation of foreskin and hymen in the service of maintaining the fantasy of bisexuality and denying the difference between the sexes. The only other person we have found who has made this equation was Roheim (1945). In the following case the sadomasochistic imagery and fantasies are especially striking. A male patient had a history of overstimulation in childhood and reactive symptoms of exhibitionism. Being excited and frightened by the analyst's attempts to understand his provocative use of what he considered dirty words, he had thoughts of exposing himself to her. He said, "My girlfriend told me the name of a certain type of flower, which I forgot. I remember the book *My Secret Garden*, which told all about a woman's sexual fantasies. The cover is a picture of a woman with a flower in her pubic region. It's a very pretty picture." He thought of *deflower* but he did not have any words to put to it. Spontaneously, he added, "The hymen is not something that I consciously thought about. I don't think I knew anything about the hymen."*

This material occurred in the context of the patient's being stimulated by barely repressed sexual fantasies about his girlfriend's teenage daughter whom he fantasized to be a virgin. He asserted, "Young girls are the instigators. They set up pursuit, and then they keep boys at arm's length." In the transference, he perceived the analyst as the dangerous instigator as well.

As his thoughts returned to the desire to expose himself to the analyst, an image of an eagle claw came to mind. A bird of prey "picks up prey and rips it into pieces and feeds it to the

---

*A male homosexual whose anxieties about the female genitals had not yet emerged clinically in a direct manner expressed his unconscious feelings symbolically. He objected strenuously to the flowers in the analyst's office. He hated them, "because it's so feminine—flowers are," he said with great disgust.

kids." The night before, he had watched a segment of the TV show *M*A*S*H*. In an operating room scene, a nurse's face looked pretty with "the bottom half masked but when she unmasked it, it was structurally not as attractive." *Half mask* reminded him of a hymen. Here, the hymen was a mask or a veil that covered the vagina made dangerous by projected sadomasochistic impulses. The analyst was experienced as a "ripping bird of prey." The emphasis on aggression in defloration motivated his forgetting the name of the flower.

A 70-year-old man in analysis spoke of having a "long and interesting" dream. In it, a young lady offered him an apple that he didn't want and was afraid of. Nevertheless, he ate part, which he found to be warm, and threw the rest away. The patient thought "it was long" sounded like talking about penis size. "The thought I have is of putting my penis in your mouth, and that is not certain." He was reminded of Adam and Eve who became aware of their nakedness and were embarrassed by it. "Apples are a nice and tasty fruit. . . . After sharing the apple, they got sexual and God got mad at them. I want to stay away from this topic. It arouses an erotic feeling. The thought of taking a bite— I'm not sure. I sliced it with my knife and threw away half. It sounds castration-like."

The patient recalled how early in the analysis he had experienced the analyst "like a spider spinning a web," because it seemed to him that she had a veiled or disapproving look. Veiled reminded him of a hymen—"a membrane shaped like a cobweb, thick and translucent, not completely attached to the walls with gaps in it. Hymie may be the plural—that's a joke." (The patient was aware that the analyst was Jewish and had a number of anxiety-provoking thoughts that he labeled anti-Semitic.)

> Hymens come in different shapes, most are incomplete. I have never seen one. Maybe that's what half an apple means. I had named it the serpentine apple. The serpent encouraged them to partake, and a serpentine apple sounds like a red chili pepper. Dangerous—the thought of putting my penis in your mouth and maybe someone would take a bite. In California, therapists and

patients get involved. . . . This could be a trap. It could be a way of getting people involved.

Here, with the analyst as a seducer, the hymen is represented as a trap, a spider web as well as flower and fruit. The serpentine-shaped apple equated with a red chili pepper, hot and phallic shaped, is an interesting bisexual image. It amalgamates an alluring feminine apple with a dangerously spicy and phallic-shaped chili pepper. In this case, the imagery is dominated by oral sadistic fantasies. Feared retribution for the projected aggression onto the analyst is met in this case, as it was in the previous one, by a secondary level of aggression appearing as anti-Semitism. Again, the image of Eve appears to express the fear of the seductive analyst.

In the following chapter we will examine clinical data that are derived from the analyses of female patients.

11

❧

Defloration and the Hymen in Female Patients

THE HYMEN, GENITAL ANXIETIES AND VULNERABILITY

The loss of virginity and the breaking of the hymen often revive early anxieties about the integrity and attractiveness of the female genitals and a related sense of vulnerability in being a female. The following are examples of this dynamic.

In this case the major presenting complaint was vaginismus, which is a severe tightening of the muscles of the vagina. Anxiety about the genitals being damaged, in which the hymen plays a prominent role, lies beneath the symptom in this case. A young woman suffering from vaginismus was terrified of the idea of intercourse with her husband. The few times in her life when she had tried to engage in intercourse had been excruciatingly painful. She had almost no memories of her childhood, and no clues as to what could account for her symptoms. She had no major complaints about her mother or father. A few months into her psychoanalytic treatment she recalled her first visit to a gynecologist, during her twenties. The gynecological examination was difficult and painful for her. At that time she had never had intercourse. "I seem to recall that the female gynecologist said that my hymen was torn. I'm not sure that she said that. Maybe she did. It could not have been torn, though. I don't remember. No she did not say anything. . . . Maybe she said it could have been broken in sports; I don't know."

The use of negations and equivocations is astounding; they attest, at the very least, to this woman's extreme anxiety. Later she revealed that she had persistent and obsessive thoughts that intruded into her mind while attempting intercourse. These thoughts centered on her fear of older male relatives and co-workers. While she was having intercourse she had older father figures in her mind. Thus, one possible understanding of her symptom is that it defended against incestuous feelings that she tried unsuccessfully to keep out of her thoughts. The punishment for the incestuous wishes was the pain she inflicted upon herself. With her vaginismus she closed men out of her body. Similarly, seeing the analyst as a dangerous intruder, she attempted in the treatment to close her out her mind by trying to instigate intellectual discussions and arguments, skipping sessions, and coming late.

Fear of pain and vulnerability also characterizes the following case. A young woman dreamed of the entrance to the analyst's office "across which someone is building something delicate and old." *Old* made her think of her mother's antiques. The patient described her favorite as "the best piece." She had gone shopping for rings for her upcoming wedding. Her thoughts went to the shape of the construction in the dream, which reminded her of arches. She loved arches, which are "entries to rooms." Arches were like arcs. Arcs were associated with penises. She then thought of sobbing or crying, which she would "never—not ever" do in front of her mother. If she were to do so, her mother would be reminded of the patient's femininity. The patient would once again be vulnerable, open to hurt and rejection, since her mother preferred her brother. The delicate covering of an entrance also reminded her of losing her virginity and the breaking of her hymen, which had made her cry. She contrasted this sad event with the extravagant and joyful celebration of the ritual circumcision of her favored younger brother. Once again we see an unconscious link between the hymen and the foreskin.

Here, the delicate decoration across the entrance of the analyst's office was seen as representation of feminine permeability and vulnerability to pain (the breaking of the hymen), as well as its inviting loveliness. Females were seen as "open" and vulnerable. Tears (and other secretions) differentiate them from males who are "closed" and more prized. Hence, she would wish to be the preferred male. Arches and arcs merge to express a bisexual wish, the wish to be both female and male. She associated "arch" to the entrance to the female genitalia and "arc" to the penis.

Another young woman, who also had just become engaged, reported that soon after getting her engagement ring, she lost sexual interest in her fiancé. The ring had been presented to her in an elaborate set of boxes, placed on the finger of a long white glove. In this context, she dreamed that she was working with her father doing manual labor and looked down to see that her ring was broken, scratched, and "all mucked up." She went on to speak of her feelings of sadness and disappointment since her engagement. Now she lamented the earlier loss of her virginity and purity. Is her disappointment that she has not "saved" her virginity for her father? Does her sense of loss cover over a more dangerous, libidinalized attachment to her father? Cavities, circles, or holes would often be interpreted as vaginas (Freud 1916b, p. 156). It is plausible in this context to see it as a "broken, scratched" hymen, encircling the vagina. We have found that the broken circle frequently stands for the hymen, intact or broken. There is an allusion, in the "manual" work, that is, doing something with the hands, to worries about damage from manual masturbation as well. As we can observe in these two cases, and as we might expect, an upcoming marriage serves as a ready precipitant for the emergence of fantasies about defloration and virginity. We have found that this is the case whether the woman is actually a virgin or not.

In the following example, a middle-aged woman who knew of the analyst's interest in the topic of the hymen and defloration dreamed that the analyst was giving a lecture about the topic of female sexuality, Judaism, and honeymoons. In association to the dream, she volunteered her knowledge of Orthodox Judaism's views and practices on the subject of the hymen:

> The hymen is never spoken about when one is talking about sexual issues. There is this cloth that they use after menstruation, and they make sure that the woman is not bleeding any more. The *mikva* is to make sex more spiritual. I think they use a cloth after the breaking of the hymen, too. The Orthodox don't go on a honeymoon because I think they have to wait seven days after the hymen is broken to have sex. And they have huge parties after the marriage so they will keep the couple away from each other.

(We believe this is erroneous. The only time couples must wait to have intercourse is when there is a question as to whether the blood is menstrual.)

The patient continued with a string of negations: "As for myself, I never spoke of the hymen. I never thought of it. I never talked about it. A little with my girlfriends, after the first time. I remember there was a little girl who lived across the street. My cousin told me that she fell off a rocking horse and supposedly broke her hymen. It was strange. She was being sexual, and I didn't know it existed [the hymen]. A 3-year-old being sexual, as opposed to someone just cutting herself." The patient assumed that the little girl was masturbating by stimulating herself by rocking.

What is striking about this material is that in spite of her being forearmed with the knowledge of the analyst's interest in the hymen, the patient, just like everyone else, does not avoid the insistent use of negations and denials in talking about the subject. She *never* heard of it. In her mind the blood of defloration and menstruation are linked to forbidden and potentially damaging sexual activities. In association to a dream about blood, a 60-year-old woman said, "One time when I had relations with my lover and I bled, he became very upset." When the analyst asked about what, the patient replied, "I didn't have my period. I didn't know what was happening, but there was blood all over." She then went on to tell of her doctor friend who told her how during a delivery blood had covered him and the walls. "Delivery and a period are the only times a woman bleeds like that." The analyst asked, "Is there any other time?" The patient replied "Never." In spite of this denial, her thoughts turned to the first time that she had sexual relations.

> Nothing is simple for me. My hymen did not break right, and after I had relations I was very sorry I did it. It was painful, and it stayed painful for a year or more. There was blood. I went to the doctor who said only half of it had broken and the other half was still there. My lover drove me nuts. He hated it. He wanted me to get rid of it, the piece of the hymen. I didn't want to. It didn't bother me. It didn't cause the bleeding. The bleeding could have been caused by a tear or a polyp.

In spite of her lover's protestations, this woman wanted to hold on to a hanging piece of her hymen. Throughout her analysis this woman had worked on her feeling of resentment and envy about her preferred older brother. We can speculate that her desire to keep the hanging piece of hymen reflected her wish for a phallus and fear of further surgical pain while repairing her sense of deficit.

With this woman, as with many of our cases, bloody experiences, menstruation, childbirth, and defloration were linked affectively with loss and pain. The sense of bodily integrity is threatened and a feeling of inadequacy is prevalent. In a published case by Sheila Gray (1985) fantasies of genital damage seemed linked to the hymen. The female patient, a scientist, suffered from persistent "vaginal anorgasmia" and an inhibition to publishing her work under her own name. In the second year of analysis, she dreamed: "I was preparing to give a dinner party with [my husband]. I was setting the table, and I went to the cabinet where my party dishes are stored. I found they were all broken. It was frightening. I woke up and found my period had begun. I was bleeding profusely" (p. 620).

The patient's first association was that the dishes were her wedding china. Her parents had pressured her into the marriage after they discovered that she had become sexually active. They wanted to "put a lid on her id." The patient passively accepted their decision and the plans for the shower and wedding. She adopted her mother's and grandmother's china patterns as her own. "Dinner party" brought to mind *The Dinner Party*, the traveling art exhibit of Judy Chicago during the 1970s. She had been impressed with the avant-garde nature of the explicit vaginal symbols depicted artistically in a conventional women's medium, china painting.

Gray felt that the dishes in the dream, "china," clearly stood for "vagina," and communicated this to the patient. The patient recalled that as a little girl she had called vagina *china*. She communicated her belief that her body was defective. In the following sessions, the patient remembered her menarche and her persistent fantasy that menstruation proved that her genital had been, in Gray's words, "irreparably damaged through a process outside her control. . . . [T]he dream confirmed to the patient her continuing, unconsciously held belief that her female organ, which was represented by the highly condensed symbol of her wedding china, had been permanently damaged. It was therefore unavailable for effective use in the marriage relationship, represented in the dream by the dinner party she was preparing with her husband" (pp. 621–622). Gray concluded that a decline in the patient's capacity to view herself as an autonomous, sexually and intellectually competent, feminine person seemed temporally related to the events that culminated in her marriage.

We would offer another, additional reading to this interesting and convincing account. The patient's many references to weddings, to the profuse current bleeding and memories of menarche, and to china that was damaged or broken strongly evoke images of defloration. We have demonstrated that weddings, blood, and china or glass often represent aspects of a scene of defloration. We also have found that menstrual and hymeneal bleeding are intertwined unconsciously. The marriage arranged to keep the "lid on the id" also is very reminiscent of stories like "Pandora's Box." What is interesting is Gray's implication that it was the patient's fear of her own feminine sexuality (and not penis envy) that was the underlying motivation for her inhibitions. Thus, the patient's marriage and her defloration, whenever it occurred, also evoked feelings of genital damage that contributed to the symptoms of sexual inhibition. Another symptom, not using her own name, may be related to her not being able to name correctly her own genitalia, and to the reported common mislabeling or nonlabeling of female genitalia in general (Lerner 1977).

BLOOD, MENSTRUATION, AND CHILDBIRTH

A woman in her ninth month of pregnancy was dealing with fears of delivery. In this material were allusions to the breaking of membranes, which the analyst did not take up in terms of the hymen. This decision was made out of a wish not to impose her own interests onto the material. The feeling was that the more timely interventions were needed to address the upcoming childbirth and issues in the transference. Retrospectively, however, we think that this decision also reflected the general unconscious inhibition against mentioning the hymen that we find so frequently. The language and the images in this patient's associations are very evocative of fantasies about the breaking of the hymen and the loss of virginity.

She spoke of her fears of the water breaking. "Would it hurt?" she asked. "Can I stop here? But there's no going back." This idea of not going back is a central feeling about the loss of virginity, the idea of "nevermore." She continued, "Sometimes they do it to you [break the water] and it seems like a violation, breaking a membrane." The patient talked anxiously about how residents' hands are "up you all the time."

A few sessions later, she reported a dream and noted that she had been feeling guilty, as if she were going to be punished for all her past sexual behaviors. As she was to put it later, "I was a rotten kid and I would have to be punished." In the dream, she had gone to the bathroom and there was blood. She associated to her Lamaze class in which the dangers of childbirth and medical conditions in which "you'd start bleeding" were described. The blood, she felt, was "like punishing myself for having sex." In her dreams during this time there were repeated themes of precariousness and danger, of being a victim of the elements, or of being broken or broken into, of violent attack, and of valuables being stolen. For example, she was in a bedroom and the doors were unlocked downstairs. Her mother seemed indifferent. Then two men on horseback came right into the house, upstairs, riding their horses into the room. The patient associated the scene with a kind of sexual attack. Thus, in the transference, the analyst was viewed both as the forbidding or attacking mother and as the mother who could not protect the girl against sexual attack. The setting reminded her vaguely of the analyst's office. The patient longed for protection against her fears and the anticipated pain. Behind the fears was highly conflicted sexual excitement. Alternately, the mother was seen as an intrusive invader. "I need a barrier against my mother," she said. She thought of anesthesia "like a barrier." The idea of a protective barrier may also be a reference to the hymen, as we have found in many anthropological and literary sources. The principal dynamic was the fantasy of punishment for masturbation by genital damage, inflicted through childbirth in a sadomasochistic scenario. The subtext was the breaking of the hymeneal membrane, also seen as punishment. In both, there is a reality to the fears of painful rupture.

THE HYMEN, PROTECTION,
AND THRESHOLDS

Breaking of the hymen and defloration, as we have seen, are experienced as the crossing over a threshold and the penetration of a barrier against harm. In the above case the mother was perceived as not providing protection for the daughter against the dangers inherent in adult sexuality. In the following case, the father is rebuked for similar reasons. A middle-aged designer began her session by complaining of beginning her menstrual period and bleeding profusely. Thus she had had no sex with her husband the night before. She had been at a professional meeting in which her boss had approached her and wanted to use some of her designs for a presentation he was to make. He approached her in what she felt was an obviously seductive way so that she felt used and manipulated. Also the day before, her car had broken down in the pouring rain. Her husband, who usually bailed her out of such jams, was unreachable. She had to get the car towed. In the middle of the night there had been a phone call, either a phony call, or a wrong number, which startled her out of her sleep. She went back to sleep then awakened from a dream with her heart pounding, frightened, and she could not return to sleep. She reported the dream:

She was on the twentieth floor in an apartment building with her two children who were grade-school age. It was a flimsily built, but brand new building. She was in the back part of the apartment when there was a knock at the door. When she went to see who was there she was horrified to see that her children had let in some strangers, a menacing group of eight or ten men and one woman, all of whom she knew meant harm. She tried to get them out, to push them out the door. The woman and one man were the last to be pushed out. She said to the woman, "He is just using you, you know," even though she knew that saying that would provoke the man. Then the largest of the men, tall and dark, tried to get back in. She managed to push him out, closed the door and tried to lock it. He was banging on the door which, because it was flimsy, did not seem secure. The whole door was shaking. Then he put his hand through the mail slot and grabbed one of her hands. She was yelling at her son to get the scissors so that they would cut off the end of the man's finger, which was sticking through the slot. Then she thought to herself, "Oh no, that's too violent." As she was trying to hold the door, she was yelling to her children to call her husband, who was not there, but the phone line was busy and they could not get through. She felt that maybe she should get on the phone because they were so young and couldn't get the right number to call the police, but the children were not strong enough to hold the door against this tremendous shaking. Then she told them to go to the windows along the back wall to yell for help to the people below.

Her associations went to the events of the day before. The windows reminded her of a documentary she had seen recently about Anne Frank. Anne Frank's father had tried to save the family from the Nazis by hiding them in an apartment on the top floors above his business in Amsterdam. The window looked out the back to the church and to the life below, and Anne could see the people out the window. But in the end Anne was not saved, and the Nazis broke into their secret hiding place through the door, which was disguised by a bookcase that could swing around. That is, it was not really sealed. She had thought as she watched the program that the Frank father had not been able to save Anne, that somehow he should have done something differently. She had felt very emotional about this thought. She associated the twentieth floor to being 20 years old, the age at which she lost her virginity. The night of this dream she had been talking with a friend about how old they were when they lost their virginity. The idea of being used in the dream reminded her of being used by her boss who wanted to use her material for himself. Then she returned to the worry of her husband being away and not being able to help her with the car being broken-down and leaving her exposed to the elements. Also, she had been annoyed with him because she had been "bugging" him to put in an air filtering unit into their house, as she is prone to allergies. She felt that pollens, that is, foreign substances, were invading the house. A mail slot made her think of a "male" slot—the female genital, the slot for the male.

Thus, the experiences of the day, which left her feeling unprotected, the discussions with her girlfriend about the loss of virginity, and her profuse bleeding brought up unconscious feelings about defloration. Defloration means, for this woman, an invasion by a dangerous man. The angry desire to castrate by cutting off the man's fingers is disavowed by saying "it's too violent." Men are seen as trying to possess women sexually and use them for their own purposes. Here the hymen is pictured as a false door covered by camouflage, a flimsy seal, and a filter that protects badly against the invasion of foreign substances. Here is one instance of Freud's assertion that women wish to castrate the men who have deflowered them. Anger is also aimed at a father and a husband who do not protect the female from "foreign substances," from painful attacks/defloration, and death.

As we noted in the material on psychoanalytic process, expectations of being opened up, exposure, and hurt frequently accompany the opening stages of analysis and can evoke fantasies about defloration and the hymen. A middle-aged woman in the beginning phase of her analysis was talking about a wished-for surgery: a face-lift and a brow-lift. She had a fantasy that a bone would be found that didn't belong, that was extra, "like an extra membrane. This may have something to do with my brain." She then remembered a dream in which her father, who had been dead for a number of years, was saying, "My daughter is not dumb." (Note even here the negative "not dumb.") The patient spoke of how she feared and hated to get rid of things and couldn't throw anything away. "Having an extra part, needing to get rid of something is something I'm afraid to do. Once you take it out, it's gone forever. You can never get it back. If you need it you can get it back somehow, if it's in a box and in storage." She linked the surgical removal of something extra with the idea that she would lose some of her intelligence: "They would take it out and then something that should have been there would leave a hole. . . . What happens after you die?" she mused.

Her thoughts went to a membrane and she wondered what it looked like. "Not paper-thin, but like a lump that was inside of me all those years." She thought of a hymen and said, "I used to think about it when I was little. That once it's gone you can never get it back again. It was so irreversible. Once you had sex you could never go back to being the way you were before." She continued obsessionally negating and undoing the feelings about this event. "I remember I thought it would really be a big deal and at the time it wasn't. I wasn't so different. I was in high school. I can't remember much of it. I didn't like the sex at all . . . I wished I hadn't done it . . . I had built it up to being such a big deal and it happened in a split second . . . It wasn't bad. Well, it was bad. It hurt me physically, but it was not that bad emotionally."

While this can be conceptualized in familiar terms of the displacement upwards of genital anxiety to the brain and intellect, there are other ways to view this material. The wished-for surgery may be a metaphor for the desire for the mind to be changed for the better (structural change) by the analyst and the analysis. In addition, there are unconscious, warded-off wishes for erotic pleasures. The negations in the patient's retelling of the time she lost her virginity, and the minimization of the experience—"no big deal"—are minimizations of the wish for, and the experience of, erotic pleasure.

She reported another dream in which there was one spot on her head. "There was a scab on it and it was yucky." It made her think of an earlier dream in which her whole head was shaved. "It meant exposing everything in treatment and my fears about it." She said, "A scab is what covers over a wound. Usually there is blood. It protects the area from anything getting in. Bleeding reminds me of menstruation. The hymen is a covering that bleeds when it's ruptured. A scab may mean covering something up, like you were caught hiding something.

A scab is someone who crosses over the line and goes where they shouldn't."

This woman fears getting rid of, or losing, "an extra part." The loss represents castration of the inner phallus, experienced as an intellectual power that brought her father's approval. Here the hymen is also seen as a protection from exposure and penetration: a scab, as a container of the fantasized hidden phallus, an inner "lump," and as a line over which one should not cross—the forbidden threshold. The meaning of *nevermore* in this context is that nevermore can there be a return to the previous, unbroken, unopened state. The forbidden threshold opens the way into adult sexuality and all its pleasures. Finally, a step across the threshold from childhood to adulthood is a step toward death.

THE HYMEN AND GUILT
ABOUT MASTURBATION

The breaking of the hymen is often associated with guilt and worries about masturbation. The following session occurred after a young married housewife received a report of a questionable Pap smear. Gynecological or other medical procedures and test results that indicate something may be wrong can generate both old and new bodily and genital anxieties.

The patient characteristically worried about being not in control of her feelings, both aggressive and sexual. At this session the patient appeared unusually anxious. She announced that she had had several dreams:

> I was walking to a bakery I've been to before. I was walking from my house in PJs. Old. Real, real old. I bought some muffins at the bakery. Someone stopped me, my mother, and said that I had a stain on the back of my PJs from my period. But then I looked at the PJs and they had changed. They were white. They really are white, but in the dream they were like tie-dyed. I said "No, I didn't stain these. That's part of the design." But I looked, and I had stained my underwear. And then I thought, "How could she

see that?" Then I was going back to my undergraduate dorms and there were two women there who were going to be my roommates. . . . I showed them my rings and I said, "Look what happened when I was gone. I got married and went on my honeymoon. ". . . Then it all changed. All of a sudden there was this cat. It was the same room. The cat was a maniac. Wild. There was also a child, like a baby, scratching. It was like wailing on you. . . . Then it turned into a little man. A dwarf. This man and another person started to abuse me in all ways. Brainwashed and manipulated me. I went crazy. I became catatonic. I went on trial to be judged whether I was sane. . . . I chose what I was going to wear. I wrapped this aluminum kind of holey blanket around myself with small holes—like see-through—from front to back. . . . I didn't have anything on underneath it. I felt that I could never make a case for myself. In fact, I was a walking zombie. Then there was an awful man who looked at me. He reminded me of you. I wouldn't be believed that I was the victim and abused mentally and physically.

What happened was that I got a call from the doctor after seeing you yesterday. I got a positive Pap smear. I have to have further tests done. And maybe I'll have to have a biopsy. [She becomes very upset here and cannot focus.] When I told my husband, I became tearful. There's something about myself being damaged. Something is the matter with me. It really hurts. [She is crying.] I feel so scared. Afraid I won't be able to have children.

The patient was not able to focus and to associate to her dream, as she usually was. The analyst said that while there was always cause to be concerned with a report such as she had received, that clearly there were some other feelings, some irrational feelings about herself, that were making it more difficult for her. There was a sense of being damaged that came through in the dreams and interfered with her being able to focus on them.

The patient responded,

Yes. There's someone else. Something else. Someone ripping something out of me. Hurting me. Almost a distortion, like the doctor is doing the damage. And that the damage didn't come first, before the doctor, but that the doctor caused the damage. What I think of is my 5-year-old little niece who had been in a car accident and was badly hurt. She felt that the hospital is what hurt her, not the accident. I think I blame people who are attempting to help me, instead of what might have done the damage to begin with.

"What damage?" the analyst asked. The patient answered, "Sex caused the damage. Intercourse. I think that's it." The analyst pointed out the stain of blood in the dream and asked if she remembered her first intercourse. The patient said,

It did not hurt. No, there was no blood when I first had intercourse. He was very gentle. Had my hymen been broken before, I wonder? It was scary.

I have my period right now. I have had stains that have shown. Since I've been on the pill it's been better. Before it used to be at night that I would really bleed a lot and stain the sheets. I'd have to put towels underneath me. I stained those pajamas once. Actually they're like a long T-shirt. That's how it got stained. It was so long.

My mother damaged me, too, by putting one of those . . . what it makes me think of in the dream is vaginal covers. Muzzles come to my mind. A vaginal cover is a chastity belt. You could say that my mother damaged me by making me feel inhibited and guilty about sex, muzzling me. What happened to me in the dream is how I try to cope with things typically. I shut down. [She has become visibly calmer.]

I know that anatomically I mix things up. I don't know what my cervix does, but I get the clitoris mixed up with the cervix. Although I know perfectly well that they are different. And I know they serve two different functions.

The analyst said, "You feel that your cervix according to the Pap smear is damaged but you are being punished because of what you have done to your clitoris" [that is, by masturbating]. The analyst suggested that what the dreams were saying was that the patient felt very guilty that she had damaged herself by the "craziness" of her sexual feelings. That idea was represented in the dream by the wild cat, which represented the wild, sexual side of herself, and also by the dwarf. She personified that side and tried to put it outside of herself because she felt so frightened by it. Then throughout the dream she was trying to say that she was not guilty, that she was the victim. It was not she, but it was someone else doing something *to* her. She feared she had damaged herself through masturbating and through the strength of her sexual desires.

The patient: "Yes. [Pause] I feel overwhelmed."

This long and extensive dream is characterized by chaos and confusion, signs of resistance. The reference to a place she's been to before indicates that these are old anxieties from childhood, aroused by the current medical crisis. There is a switch back and forth between the bloody and stained to the white and unstained. This alternation and switching is characteristic of the psychological mechanisms of defense called *doing and undoing*, in which a two-stage act symbolically expresses a sexual or aggressive wish and its reversal or undoing (Moore and Fine 1968, p. 31). The multiple transitions may also communicate events that reoccurred repeatedly, such as masturbation and menstruation. The one event that does not happen more than once, however, is defloration. The reversal reflects her wish to make herself a virgin again, a wish for circumstances that could be done and undone, such as the medical test. (The patient had earlier stated a sense of regret about the losing of her virginity and for not saving it for the "right" man.) The dream included references to her wedding and the honeymoon and by allusion to defloration: "Look what happened while I was gone." There are symbolic references to genitals in the cat and the dwarf, which the patient's associations to her genitals and to the cervix and clitoris confirm. In the transformation from a cat ("pussy") to a dwarf-phallus she may be expressing the wish to be male so that she would not have to worry about scary things such as Pap smears. We frequently see an intensified wish by women to be a male as a defense against the pressure of genital medical dangers. She goes on to fears of a biopsy, fears of being damaged, fears that she cannot have children, and a fear of castration in the basic sense of a loss of the capacity to procreate. She is afraid that her female genital and reproductive system are inadequate. Her associations to a "holey blanket" are chastity belt and muzzle. The image of the muzzle is a rich one, a representation and condensation of many conflicts and ideas. It both defends against sexuality—holy—as a chastity belt and lets sexual action through—holey. Being holy it states the patient's wish for a relief against guilt about the underlying sexual impulses. It also is a physical representation of a membrane. She is afraid she is crazy, wild with impulses that she wishes to shut down or muzzle. Finally, the analyst/mother is perceived as a figure who, by inflicting a chastity belt, damages, muzzles, and punishes her.

In the following session the patient reported that she had talked to her mother about the medical report and found her attempts at reassurance not very helpful. "In some way I ended up calming my mother, as usual." Over the weekend she had thought again that maybe her masturbation had been responsible for the negative report. She felt some sexual feelings and had the urge to masturbate, but stopped herself. If she got excited it might make more trouble and maybe she could never have another orgasm in her life. "I can never masturbate again. Like in my fantasy I damaged myself or something was done to me."

The analyst said that it was difficult for the patient to talk to her, which suggested that the patient was afraid that the analyst, like the doctors, would damage her sexually. The patient agreed and went on to elaborate the idea that the woman is damaged in intercourse. "Especially from my education. Like what I learned about breaking the hymen." The analyst asked, "What was that?"

"That it would be hurtful. That the hymen would be damaged. Damaged women. I don't remember where . . . what . . . no, I don't know where I learned it. Maybe in undergrad class about women's issues? It was enlightening. I don't know. . . ."

The fear of genital damage is evident in many cases. A woman in analysis was excited that her friend was getting married. She reported a dream of wearing glasses cracked in half. "They are big like saucers. Someone says, 'you should have stopped before you got injured.'" The patient in a recent session had told the analyst the joke of the father who tells the child, "Don't masturbate. You'll go blind." The child says, "Can I just do it till I need glasses?" The patient associated to the dream: "I don't remember being afraid of doing something that would break something. Did I masturbate and fear I would break something? My mother would say get your hand out of your tail. Tail is what we called vagina and cracked is another term for the vagina." She associated cracked glass with a broken hymen. Her thoughts went to her Bat Mitzvah, a ritualized rite of passage, and then to how she accidentally broke a glass holding red wine at a friend's wedding. She went on to think about menstruation.

According to some rabbis, the cracking of a glass by the bride-groom at a Jewish wedding refers to the destruction of the temple in 70 A.D. Yet in this woman's mind it represents the breaking of the hymen. She links this event unconsciously with something being broken and with menstruation, which also may have a similar evocation to her. We have found connections between rites of passage, such as baptisms, communions, ritual circumcisions, Bar Mitzvahs, and weddings. All are crossings of thresholds and often involve bodily transformations and developments.

The breaking of the hymen, commonly called "breaking the cherry," is suggested by the following: in the midst of struggling with an awareness of sexual feelings toward the analyst, a young woman remembered fighting with her mother as an adolescent. Then after a pause she said: "I remember that when I was about 5, my dad brought home some chocolate-covered cherries, and I was sitting on his lap and I was eating one. Instead of just putting the whole thing into my mouth, I bit into it, and all the stuff squished out. He was angry with me, and pushed me off. I was embarrassed and upset." In the same session she went on to talk about her guilt about her childhood masturbation and her fear that she would damage herself. She had had the fantasy that she had "plugged up a hole," and that she had only two holes "down there." She had heard some girls saying there were supposed to be three. Embarrassment and shame are associated here with forbidden erotic, oedipal wishes and pleasureful masturbation. There is shame about anal impulses, as well, in the making a mess and a "plugged-up hole." Her childhood confusion about her feminine anatomy is also evident.

THE HYMEN AND THE ROLE OF THE MOTHER

Very often the affect associated with the loss of virginity is shame, as in the above, but other common feelings among women are disappointment and loss, along with pain. Typically, in women's minds, mothers are the object of these feelings of disappointment and blame.

An inhibited, frightened woman, who had memories of sexual abuse by an older brother, resisted the increasing evidence that her alcoholic father had also been involved in some abuse. She reported having repetitive dreams after the previous session in which she insisted that Woody Allen could not be guilty of any crime. With a great deal of shame, hesitation, and reluctance, she recounted one of the dreams. "I don't know why it's so hard. You and I were in this place and I went to the bathroom, a shared bathroom. I had left in the sink . . . why can't I say it . . . It's so horrible . . . a douche bag. I left the bathroom and realized you would go in and see it and I was so embarrassed. . . ." The dream made her think of an incident she had never told to anyone. At the age of 12, she had gotten what she now thought was a vaginal discharge. Her father took her to the hospital where for some reason she did not understand, she was catheterized. The nurse in a harsh tone asked, "Are you active?" "Sexually active?" the analyst asked. "No, I think physically. I wonder if my hymen was broken." The patient recalled that she was found to have had a yeast infection, for which there was medicine to be applied vaginally with a plunger. The mother applied the plunger in a ritualistic manner. As she continued, the patient began to obsess about whether an aunt was always present. She complained to the analyst how "this was all humiliating." Then the patient recalled how she had first used pads, not tampons, when she began to menstruate. When later in the session the analyst asked if the patient had any discomfort or bleeding with her first intercourse, the patient replied, "No. Never. Not at all. Never. It was nothing. I don't even remember when I had intercourse for the first time." She had made herself dead drunk every time she had sex in college. Obsessing, she recounted how the first time might have been with this boy, or perhaps it was somebody else. . . . In this instance the doubting, denial, and negation surrounding the memory of the breaking of the hymen is clearly associated with protection against guilt-laden oedipal memories of traumatic familial experiences and fantasies, all with strong sadomasochistic meanings. There are strong hints of childhood sexual abuse by her father. In this case, as in many, not to know who was the first lover both expresses and defends against incestuous masochistic wishes toward the father. The harsh nurse is the embodiment of the forbidding mother who denies the girl her desires. In the transference she re-created the scene with the analyst as the passive onlooker to her humiliation, and also cast her again as the forbidding and intrusive mother.

In the above, bleeding from menstruation and from the breaking of the hymen are inextricably linked, as they are in this next case. A woman had been talking about her difficulties and feelings of inadequacy in being a mother and giving her prepubertal daughter guidance. In the transference, she had been expressing wishes that the analyst help her to be a woman, give her sexual guidance, and so on. Her lack of memories of her own mother she labeled a "black hole" or a "hole in my development." She mused about who had taught her to use tampons. Not her mother, certainly. In fact, her mother was strongly opposed to their use. It was the era. Again we encounter the image of the mother who forbids the girl to be penetrated by the tampon/penis and holds her back from a readiness to enter sexual maturity. When the analyst questioned her about this, the patient expressed the idea that the tampon would interfere with the hymen. She added, "But I don't know about that stuff. What is the hymen? I don't know. I still don't know what it is." The analyst asked, "Did you bleed when you had sex for the first time?" "No! Not like a period. It wasn't vivid."

In the context of the analyst's upcoming vacation, a young Catholic woman recalled her wedding. She was a virgin. As she and her husband were leaving the wedding she remembered feeling as if she were going to the guillotine. Her mother looked very sad. Looking around at a vase of flowers on the analyst's desk, she suddenly remarked, "Those are pretty flowers. They look like a wedding bouquet. My wedding was beautiful and I was terrified. Chop. Chop. I felt guilty. It was a real separation going on. I was leaving her and didn't want to. I missed my mother during my honeymoon and wanted to go home." Although this woman knew about sex intellectually and had been instructed about sexual matters by her mother, she felt her own active and mature sexuality was unacceptable. "I never got permission to be a sexual being. I felt I was stepping over a line." The analyst asked, "In what way?" The patient replied, "By becoming a married woman. Each step I take is like a leaving, going from her. I guess I feel if I step over the line there is a struggle, because the connection to my mother is to me as a child, not as an adult. I feel there has been a loss."

This clinical material speaks eloquently of the girl's sense of loss and separation from the mother. As in the cross-cultural and literary data, this patient describes how defloration marks the stepping over the threshold into adult sexuality and leaving the mother and childhood behind.

Women commonly blame their mothers not only for not protecting them but also for keeping them ignorant sexually. A married woman described how surprisingly pleasurable sex was with her husband. She praised the analyst's sensitivity to, and respect for, her female concerns such as menstrual cramps, and

so on. She said that this being understood was a novel experience for her. She spoke of a series of firsts—being the first in
her class academically, the first time she menstruated, and her
first intercourse at fifteen, which was "very, very, very painful.
It was never any better; it never felt any good. He was as inexperienced as I. I knew nothing about the details of my body. I
didn't know I had a clitoris. Later, I learned by looking in a
mirror. I was so angry at my mother—enraged. Why didn't she
tell me about this? All she said was 'Wear Kotex, don't use tampons, and don't get pregnant.' The real stuff she didn't tell me
and I felt stupid." We see here that for many females their sense
of faulty intellect, feeling "stupid," is linked not only to a sense
of the female genital as "inadequate" but even more important
to inadequate knowledge of it and its capabilities. The mother's
inadequate preparation of the girl also implies to her a prohibition against sexual pleasure.

A 23-year-old inhibited woman commented on the beautiful
spring flowers she noticed as she was coming to her analytic
session. She said, "All kinds of flowers on the sidewalk. It's very
pretty. Last time I was talking about blood, and I thought after-
ward that in some way I heard or just knew that babies are born
in blood. I remember even having some mixed up feeling at age
11 that if someone saw blood on me they'd think I had a baby.
I don't know but I linked blood with my mother. I think I have
seen menstrual blood or something like that. When you're a kid
and you're hurt, your mother is the doctor." She went on to talk
of negatively tinged memories of her mother and her own body
and her mother's critical attitude toward the patient's body. She
ended the session with details about her reputation in the family as reckless, and with a description of the first time she had
intercourse.

The patient's associations link flowers with blood and defloration. This is an example, other than the countless literary and
anthropological ones, that shows the symbolism of flowers for
defloration. The mother, and the analyst in the transference, are
blamed for the patient's dislike of the female body. At the same

time there is an implied yearning for the analyst, with her proximity to beautiful flowers, to undo the feelings of negativity and to show the patient the way to a happier sense of her femininity and her female body. In women patients the predominant affective tones throughout are loss and sadness, often overshadowing pleasure. In contrast, men's experiences of defloration are colored by fear and rivalry over being the first lover. The oedipal constellations, which differ for men and women, are played out differently in their experiences of defloration. The rivalrous same-sexed parent achieves prominence in the minds of the patients in their concerns about defloration. For men the foremost concern is one of retribution through bodily damage: castration at the hands of the father or the luring and/or revengeful women. For women there is fear of genital damage and loss of security in their relationships to their mothers as a consequence of their sexuality. We do not see the concern about separation and abandonment in men's material as we do in women's. These fears and feelings about abandonment are not necessarily preoedipal, but often represent reactions to oedipal rivalries with the mother. The psychic realities play an important part in these different conflicts. A man must penetrate the body of a woman; it is the woman's body and hymen that are penetrated, at times painfully. We will discuss the implications of these findings for psychoanalytic theories of female psychosexual development and sexuality in the final chapter.

CHAPTER

12

ぷ

Conclusions

$\mathcal{D}$efloration is an important milestone for both sexes. Sexual drives, as well as social and psychological imperatives, urge its realization. Potentially troublesome for both males and females, this task calls upon various ego functions and adaptive capacities. Both libidinal and aggressive lines of development contribute to its complexities. Prior conflicts, fixations, and traumas also create vulnerabilities that can make the experience of defloration even more difficult. A young man has to feel assertive and confident enough to pursue, penetrate, and possibly hurt the object of his desire, in spite of his anxieties. The young woman, on the other hand, has to want to be intimately penetrated and to overcome momentary discomfort for future and unknown pleasure. As one of our male patients said, "A man has to do; a woman just has to be." We do not mean to imply that men must be active and women must be passive, but that their sexual experiences are different and each role carries with it its own imperatives.

TRANSITIONS

Grete Bibring and co-workers (1961) spoke of the three major transitions for females: puberty to adulthood, pregnancy to motherhood, and menopause to aging, as crises involving profound endocrine, somatic, as well as psychological changes. These crises represent important developmental steps and have in common a series of characteristic psychological phenomena. According to Bibring, "All three are significant turning points in the life of the individual" (p. 12). The interdependence between the psychological and the biophysiological crises gives them a quality of inevitability, "the point from which there is no return" (p. 13). We think that defloration, with its characteristic sense of irreversibility, should be added to these three turning points. While it is not accompanied by endocrine and biophysiological changes, it is marked by characteristic psychological changes relating to other developmental transition points. Defloration, perhaps more than other transition points, seems to elicit the dramatic and persistent denials, negations, and "nevers" that we have observed clinically.

For example, in the following excerpt (our translation) from an autobiographical French novel *Moi d'Abord*, Katherine Pancol (1979) writes of the loss of her virginity. "My first time. From now on, I will never be the same. I tiptoe into the world of adults. I leave the sweetness and warmth of childhood" (p. 25). Even in another language, we see the striking presence of "never," the concept of nevermore, and the threshold phenomenon.

Negations come up in our clinical material with adult patients as they talk about their experiences with defloration retrospectively or currently. These phenomena occurred, regardless of the characteristic defensive style of the patient. That is, this form of expression is related to the content of defloration. Defloration typically comes during the adolescent stage. Our psychoanalytic colleagues who specialize in adolescents have reported that the topic of defloration is a manifest preoccupation with their patients.[1] Since consolidating a sexual identity and incorporating sexuality into one's life are major tasks of adolescence, this preoccupation is not surprising. Negations and doubts also accompany adolescents' reports of defloration, however, as can be seen in reports of interviews with teenage girls about their first sexual experiences (Thompson 1990), adolescents' queries to newspaper advice columns, and current films (see Chapter 1).

In adult analyses and psychotherapies the *Sturm und Drang* of adolescence is often silenced or ignored, on the part of the patients and often by the psychoanalysts and therapists as well. Frequently in adult treatments not enough attention is given retrospectively to the period of adolescence. Conflicts about sexuality and specifically defloration may contribute to this avoidance. Adults forget, perhaps would like to forget, the disconcerting intensity of sexual and romantic feelings that they experienced as adolescents. Even after a few years, defloration experiences may be subject to retrospective defensive negating and denials. Freud's case of Dora (1905) documents an 18-year-old girl's conflicted reminiscences from an earlier period in her adolescence. Dora needed to forget frightening and sexually charged episodes with Herr K. who had tried to seduce her. The analysis revealed that Dora was fearfully obsessed about the loss of her virginity with Herr K.

Issues of self-esteem so salient during adolescence also are at play here. The sense of adequacy can become tied to sexual performance as well as to comparisons along this dimension with adolescent peer groups. We think that narcissistic vulnerabilities and hurts are important motivations to the negations surrounding the experience of defloration. For example, adolescent girls commonly express a feeling that finally they have ap-

1. Our thanks to Drs. Karen Chapin, Leon Hoffman, Purnima Mehta, Judith Ruzumna, and Alan Zients for their helpful comments and suggestions.

proached their ideal of more sophisticated or superior women after the loss of their virginity. We see this clinically and in literary works, such as the passage from *The Beggar Maid*, in which the heroine, pleased with herself, proclaimed that she had done what others did. Disappointed in the sexual experience, however, she tried to fake a passionate response. In the novel *Wartime Lies*, the adolescent boys bragged about their sexual experiences and exaggerated the size of their penises. They joked brashly about the blood that comes with defloration. This behavior served their need to cover their anxieties about their inexperience and their bodily capacities, and to reinforce their self-esteem. They needed to deny these anxieties. At the same time, the sense of masculinity is often bolstered by accomplishing sexual relationships.

As we have shown, social support and the internal valence for loss of virginity is less conflicted for boys than for girls. In the current American scene, girls, like boys, often insist that they have no anxiety about the loss of virginity and are eager to be unencumbered by its restraints. Our impression, however, is that this stance is often a counterphobic façade. Further psychoanalytic data from adolescents may throw more light on these questions and on the meaning of the retrospective negations we have observed in our adult patients.

NEVERS

Our first task in this book was to answer the question of why negations and nevers appear so frequently in relation to the hymen and to defloration. Second, in answering this question, we also discovered more about the experience of defloration and the meanings of the hymen as well. We turned for help and inspiration to classical mythology, anthropology, fairy tales, and literature to see what, if anything, was written there about our subject. These areas have traditionally been useful sources to psychoanalysts in understanding human nature and behavior.

The emphatic and exaggerated use of double negatives can be likened to a dream within a dream. A dream within a dream serves as an overstated denial of the reality of the sources beneath the dream's content, such as a memory of a traumatic childhood event. It is as if the dreamer is doubly emphasizing, "This is only a dream and never happened." The reality in this case is the loss of virginity and the breaking of the hymen and what these experiences mean to the individual. Negation and doubting are characteristic accompaniments to thoughts about defloration and represent defensive reactions to underlying conflicts and anxieties. In addition, many hopes, fantasies, and expectations precede the event in the minds of young men and women. They expect to be transformed magically, to be swept away by romance and pleasure, to become part of an idealized union or couple, never to feel excluded or left out again. When these expectations are not met, there are disappointments, which are often negated or denied defensively: "It was no big deal . . . it was good . . . no, it was not good."

BISEXUALITY

We have noted that the mental representation of the hymen is a useful vehicle for the expression of, and the defense against, conflicts and wishes around bisexuality, an important dynamic in many of our cases. Both men and women use the hymen and defloration to express fantasies about bisexuality. For example, we found that the hymen can take on both masculine and feminine attributes in the minds of patients and thus expresses hidden bisexual fantasies. One patient imagined the hymen to be like a serpentine apple, which for him was both phallic-shaped and feminine. In this way he unconsciously endowed the woman with a penis. A female patient imagined her hymen as a tiny hidden phallus, which she did not want to lose. At the same time it had significant feminine meanings for her, which were also cherished.

Another example of the bisexual meanings attributed to the hymen was in its equation with the foreskin, which we found in several patients, both men and women. There is data that ritual circumcisions, both male and female, express a culturally shared need to classify and consolidate gender definitively (Assaad 1980). According to ancient Egyptian beliefs about the bisexuality of the gods, the feminine soul of man was thought to be located in the foreskin and the masculine soul of women in the clitoris. Thus in initiation to adulthood the feminine portion of the male has to be shed as does the male portion of the female. The cultural and conscious fear is of bisexuality, fueled by the ubiquitous unconscious wish to be both sexes (Kubie 1974). In some of our cases we found an unconscious mental equation between circumcision of the foreskin and the rupture of the hymen. One woman directly linked a joyful ritual circumcision with the tearful remembrance of defloration. It is interesting that during the 1970s there was a movement among Jewish feminists searching for equality to find a ritual for girls to be the counterpart for the ritual circumcisions for boys. Their idea was to perform symbolic breakings of the hymen. Interestingly, however, this idea concretely links the foreskin with the hymen.

Another example of the linkage of hymen and foreskin is furnished by the man who associated the hymen with the piece of skin removed during circumcision. He felt, "circumcision makes a man like a woman." That is, the foreskin was a feminine piece of himself, which he shed. Simultaneously, since the foreskin was also equated with a hymen, he identified himself with a deflowered woman. We were surprised to find such a concrete unconscious connection between foreskin and hymen in the minds of our male and female patients. This finding is somewhat different from a previously expressed notion in the psychoanalytic literature that vagina and foreskin can be unconscious equivalents (Jaffe 1976, Nunberg 1947, Roheim 1945).

Such a fantasy allows either sex to identify unconsciously with the other. In our clinical material patients unconsciously assumed both male and female identifications in the defloration drama. In their minds they could be both the one who entered or penetrated or the one who was opened or penetrated. This form of bisexuality involves internal enactments with intrapsychic object representations, as contrasted with images that are bisexual by virtue of having physical or psychological characteristics attributed to both sexes combined into one figure.

DEFLORATION EXPERIENCES: DIFFERENCES BETWEEN MEN AND WOMEN

Our material confirms Yates's (1930) suggestion that the meanings of the hymen and defloration are different for men and for women, although we would elaborate these differences in the following way. In women, feelings of sadness, disappointment, and loss are associated with the end of virginity. The loss is twofold, loss of youth, innocence, or purity, and loss of the mother's protection and love. The loss of virginity and the breaking of the hymen revive feelings from earlier stages of development. These feelings encompass loss of a fantasized penis, loss of female genital integrity, and fears of genital damage and mutilation. Breaking of the hymen often evokes feelings of vulnerability and permeability: not the feared loss of openness, the "female castration complex" posited by Elizabeth Mayer (1985), but rather the fear of suffering a permanent opening, being exposed.

With many females, the blame placed on an unprotecting mother who does not prepare her daughter for adult sexuality is clearly evident. We did not find this idea generally in the material of our male patients. These feelings of anger and resentment toward their mothers in the female patients could be seen as representations of oedipal or preoedipal ties that under stressful situations, such as defloration, are re-evoked. The feeling of the loss of mother's protection also can be defensive. It covers an unconscious and guilty sense of achievement over taking the mother's place as the girl moves into active rivalry with mother and into the pleasures of adult sexuality. The revengeful hostility and binding to the man who deflowers the woman, which was reported in the early psychoanalytic literature, were not present in our female cases. Rather, strong negative feelings seemed to center around their mothers. Anger toward men, when present, came because they felt that the men had abandoned them after defloration, either emotionally or physically. Thus, expectations for intimacy and hopes for a permanent relationship were shattered. With the exception of instances of forced penetration or rape, it was not the defloration *per se* that aroused women's anger and the need for revenge.

The fact that the female genital or parts of the female genital have been misnamed and unnamed is also a cause for women's blame of the mother. Feeling that their sexuality had been undeveloped and their eroticism lost, women held their mothers responsible. In spite of intellectual knowledge, girls often do not know the function of the parts of the genitals. This blame reflects the perception and/or reality of the mother's need to keep the girl a child, "dumb" and nonsexual. Although both males and females claimed not to know of the hymen's existence, the narcissistic element of "feeling stupid" about it was characteristic only for the women.

Other affects associated with defloration in females are those of shame and humiliation. The various cultural traditions and traumatic situations that force exposure to others of the state of the girl's genital, as in the ritual deflowering ceremonies, produce or intensify these affects of humiliation and shame. Men's needs to humiliate and overpower women may underlie such public rituals and institutions. Lupton (1993) has discussed cultural taboos about blood as representing the feared and envied power of woman. Blood symbolizes her fertility and her life-giving force. Perhaps a meaning of a man's wish to "deflower" a woman is to seize the flower from her, in the sense of her flower being an envied and feared female sexual or life force. (In slang a "flower" means the female genital.)

For many women a sense of shame attaches to their genitals. Many writers have written about the meanings and origins of shame and other negative feelings about the female genital. For example, Arlene Richards (1992) and Marion Oliner (1988) have linked these feelings to confusions between genital and anal sensations, stemming from early childhood. Horney (1933) traced girls' fantasies of genital damage to oedipal conflicts and fears about penetration by the father's penis. Doris Bernstein (1990) has elaborated specific feminine genital anxieties of "penetration," "access," and "diffusivity." Earlier writers focused on a woman's sense of deficit stemming from her lack of a penis, being "castrated" (Abraham 1922). Phyllis and Robert Tyson (1990) argue that a woman's feelings of shame about her body are multiply determined. Defloration, with its usual accompanying appearance of blood, or with even the expectation of blood, accentuates feelings of mutilation, damage, dirtiness, or sinfulness that may be present.

One of our prominent findings in women regarding the breaking of the hymen and bleeding was the revival of guilt for masturbation and other perceived sexual misdeeds with consequent fantasies of having damaged the genitals. This phenomenon is linked intrapsychically with menstruation, which induces similar anxieties. Some of the differences in meaning and affect between men and women about the hymen stem from the fact that the hymen and bleeding are real parts of the female genitalia and experience.

With men, the affects associated with the hymen and virginity are somewhat different. The obsessional doubting observed in men was a defense against positive oedipal anxieties aroused at the idea of being "the first" with a woman (unless all of the reported women were lying about being virgins). We did not see in men the predominance of the sense of loss and sadness as with women. Rather, the feelings shift more to unconscious fears of castration and destruction by their father and/or mothers perceived as retaliating. Guilt-ridden unconscious sadomasochistic fantasies are often stirred up in men's minds by the act of penetration and defloration. Such fantasies can "up the emotional ante" for men and must be counteracted by negations and denials. In addition, the doubting reflects anxiety about the unresolved dilemma of two conflicting images of mother, Madonna/virgin versus whore/used and fallen woman. There are indications that the idea of the perpetual virgin is motivated by many of these conflicts in men. These male reactions to female virginity are obviously different from those surrounding the loss of their own male virginity, which we have not addressed in this book.

Men's images of defloration and female sexuality parallel the biblical story of Adam and Eve. This story is the introduction of sexuality and sin to mankind, similar to the Greek myth of Pandora. In the religious doctrines men have expounded over the centuries, in the literature they write, and in the conflicted fantasies they reveal to their analysts, women frequently appear as evil, luring temptresses. Ultimately, in men's minds, trouble, castration, and even death follow the scene of defloration. Satan tempts man through woman: man sins and so dies on that very day (Jeffrey 1992). We see that the unconscious sin in man is the oedipal one, which carries with it his aggressive impulses, springing from all earlier stages of development. The tree of knowledge is called the tree of death. To know sexually is to die.

Another dominant theme for men is possession, control, and ownership of women. De Beauvoir (1974), whom we quoted in the first chapter, described this idea of possession as it is translated into the idea of deflowering. Speaking of men's needs to possess their wives and lovers, she writes, "it is always impossible to realize positively the idea of possession; in truth, one never has any thing or any person; one tries then to establish ownership in negative fashion" (p. 174).

REPRESENTATIONS OF THE HYMEN

Unconscious fantasies that we have elaborated above give rise to the multitudinous images of the hymen that appear in clinical, literary, and cross-cultural material. The multiplicity of representations of the hymen of our clinical cases fell generally into three categories: those centering on oral imagery such as apples, chili peppers, or cherries; those that are organized in terms of visual representations, such as glass or veils; and those that convey the idea of a physical barrier/trap, such as spider webs or wire. These categories convey the multidetermined defensive meanings and underlying aggressive and libidinal impulses attributed to defloration and the hymen by our patients.

Certain common rituals in current daily life that seem symbolically to represent defloration are launching a ship by breaking a bottle prior to its "maiden" voyage, cutting a ribbon to inaugurate a new venture or building, ground-breaking ceremonies by an important man like the mayor, and the wrapping of gifts to cover secret treasures. Around weddings there are many rituals that allude to the defloration to come: the superstition that it is bad luck to cut the ribbons of gifts at a wedding shower, flower girls strewing petals before the bride as she walks down the aisle, breaking the glass at a Jewish wedding or crockery at betrothals, the rule that the wedding ring must be an unbroken circle in its design, carrying the bride over the threshold, the veil worn by the bride, the custom of wearing virginal white or, in some cultures, red, by the bride, and so on.

NAMING AND EDUCATION

Anxieties about the physical reality of defloration have implications for education. The same tendency toward a collusion of silence between patient and analyst about the subject frequently exists between educator and student. There is also a general circumvention between mother and daughter about sexual knowledge. Imparting information about the defloration and/or the hymen is a unique case in that defloration is associated with possible pain and may evoke sadomasochistic associations. Defloration also is associated concretely with a step into adult sexuality. This step can be viewed ambivalently by mothers and daughters, as we have shown. Thus, in general, the facts of female sexuality and anatomy are not clearly recognized or delineated. Frequently, sexual education is held back from girls as if it would harm them. The inhibition in verbalizing, teaching, and thus knowing about the hymen is also enhanced by the ready connection of sadomasochistic meanings around the event of defloration.

In the Judaeo-Christian tradition, knowledge and carnality are linked in the Adam and Eve story and with the use of the verb *to know* to mean possession in a sexual sense. Thus, part of the inhibition of verbalization and education about the female genitals is connected to the deep anxiety that to know means to act, in this case sexually, and that thought equals the deed. Kulish (1992) has argued that the nonnaming of, and the practice of excising, the clitoris are attempts to curb female sexual appetite and desire. Naming also gives power and mastery over that which is named. Similarly, the hymen's rupture means the pathway to adult female sexuality is open.

Herbert Tucker (1993), in an essay on the poet Browning, wrote about the unrepresentability of the concept of virginity and its loss. "To 'know' [that is, also 'no'] virginity is to undo it . . . the knowledge even of one's own virginity seems to entail a partial loss of innocence, as it transgresses the frontier of pure being that is virginity's metaphysical correlative" (p. 68). This fear of a loss of innocence even conceptually is yet another reason for the lack of acknowledgment and naming of the hymen.

At one point in the case of Dora, Freud (1905) says, "There is *never* [italics ours] any danger of corrupting an innocent girl. . . . For where there is no knowledge of sexual processes even in the unconscious, no hysterical symptom will arise; and where hysteria is found there can no longer be any question of 'innocence of mind' in the sense in which parents and educators use the phrase" (p. 49). After stating that he calls sexual organs and processes by their correct technical names, he uses French in a double entendre: "J'appelle un chat un chat." (That is, I call a cat a cat.) He also says at that point, "Pour faire une omelette, it faut casser des oeufs." (To make an omelet, it is necessary to break eggs.) With these phrases Freud undoes and negates what he declares he is attempting to do, that is, to talk in a straight-forward manner about sexuality. He links a typical reference to the female genitals, the vulgar term *pussy* or *chat*, with a possible allusion to the hymen and defloration, "eggs breaking." Unwittingly Freud implies girls can be hurt by sexual knowledge, even while intellectually he is trying to say the opposite, "There is never any danger of corrupting an innocent girl." Also there may be an attempt to negate the idea of the possible hurt or harm done to the woman in defloration.

TECHNICAL CONSIDERATIONS

A preponderance of both males and females presented material relating to the hymen in associations to dreams. We wonder, is the tendency for this conflict-laden anatomical fact to remain repressed the determinant for its emergence as latent dream content or simply an artifact of our population or analytic styles? Or is there a connection between the fact that a dream is often presented as a gift to the analyst, just as virginity may be perceived as a gift? As a young colleague suggested, is it that the dream has a hymeneal representation in itself, being veil-like, a manifest covering over underlying secrets and mysteries, "the royal road to the unconscious"?

There are several clinical questions that emerge from our research. Since this material was gathered by female analysts, we wonder if it was shaped in any way by our gender. We suspect that it was. For example, male patients frequently experienced the analyst as a seductive, dangerous temptress; female patients frequently saw the analyst as the silent, uncaring mother who was passive or forsook them in their danger or as the jealous rival who appropriates sexuality for herself. The gender of the analyst seemed to facilitate these images. Would a male patient imagine "deflowering" his male analyst in the maternal transference and/or would the male analyst readily recognize such imagery? One male analyst did report clinical material in

which his male patient felt opened up or deflowered by him
through the process of analysis. In a dream this same patient
expressed the corresponding fantasy of deflowering the analyst.
Defloration and the breaking of the hymen can become a
metaphor for the entire analytic process, as our clinical material illustrates. Like defloration, analysis is an opening up that
can change one forever. Both men and women identify with the
virgin in terms of opening up, exposing themselves in an inti-
mate situation, being penetrated, and acquiring knowledge (that
is, knowing or being "known"). On the opposite side, patients
often identify with the penetrator who, for example, wishes to
penetrate the veil of secrecy of the analyst. These feelings can
become potent sources of resistance within the transference.

We have found that processes of internalization or identification are intensified during certain periods of change and flux.
Such processes of internalization can be experienced in fantasy
as a defloration, in the sense of a taking in of something from
the outside. One such period of active internalization and identification is the termination phase of psychoanalysis, as has been
suggested by Hans Loewald (1988). We have found that termination brings concrete contents about defloration and the loss
of virginity. Another period of flux that encompasses active internalization and consolidation of identifications is adolescence.

While deflowering and being deflowered might appear as
central metaphors in some cases, their clinical importance is
more generalized. The hymen and defloration constitute part of
the reality of sexual relationships and the female's body. Thus
material about the hymen is revived and then reoccurs in many
mental scenarios. With its conscious signal "never," the hymen
is linked to unconscious fantasies elucidating childhood and
adolescent sexual conflicts. (As Freud said, the unconscious
knows no "nevers.") Because of the hymen's dynamic and ge-
netic importance, it is necessary that we be aware of and sensitive to its many appearances and meanings in clinical material.
Ignoring or missing these meanings sacrifices understanding and
empathy with our patients. An emphasis on castration/penis envy

can lead to a one-sided, facile view of female sexuality and a loss of a richer understanding that the concept of the hymen and its role contributes.

Our material emerged in most cases spontaneously or with little direct questioning. Like the physical reality of the hymen, the topic in our clinical material seems to lie just below the surface and requires little technical activity to allow its emergence. The paucity of analytic literature around this one-time phenomenon may echo a mutual collusion or resistance by both patient and analyst to downplay its importance in the intrapsychic world. We have suggested some motivations for this resistance. This raises additional questions: Is a more active questioning by the analyst sometimes required to confront the patient's denials and negations about these realities? If we hear material that seems to signify defloration, for example, weddings, broken china, or translucent membranes appearing in the same context, and we name it or ask about it directly, are we technically in error? Are we detouring around a necessary analysis of patients' resistances? Is this a penetrating intrusion in itself, breaking roughly through the veil of resistance? Or are we colluding with patients' consistent denials and negations by not naming the unmentioned? Are we joining Freud when he said, "J'appelle un chat un chat?"

In a discussion of our ideas about the hymen and defloration, one senior male analyst volunteered his reactions. As he listened to our clinical material he mused to himself, "I have never heard material like this. This has not been my clinical experience." He then realized that his musings exemplified and paralleled the responses of our patients, especially our male patients, who made comments like, "This was not an experience I had." He was astonished and amused to find this reaction in himself. Upon further reflection he felt that it was not possible that material on this subject had been absent in his many years of experience. In casual conversations with other colleagues and friends, both men and women, most initial reactions are of this sort, either a negation or a response that totally ignores the subject.

IMPLICATIONS FOR THEORIES OF FEMALE
SEXUALITY AND PSYCHOSEXUAL DEVELOPMENT

Contemporary revisions of psychoanalytic theories of female sexuality have emphasized a female line of development, a primary femininity, and the uniqueness of the female genitalia. Earlier classical psychoanalytic understandings of female development and female sexuality were modeled on those of the boy. In fact it has been said that the earlier theories were based on Freud's fantasies about females, for example, that girls were castrated beings. The former ideas did not take into account the unique developmental experiences and tasks of the little girl based on bodily perceptions, psychological factors like narcissism and identification, the early infant–mother relationship, and object relations in general. Moreover, the entire forward development of the girl into the oedipal, latency, and adolescence periods, and ultimately motherhood, was thought to hinge on her sense of deficit from not possessing a penis. Certainly developmentally a girl desires to have a penis, to possess that which she does not have, just as boys desire breasts, or the womb, that which he does not have (Lax 1994). With environmental, familial, societal, and/or institutional support for these notions, the girl's feelings of deficit or the desire for a phallus will have a greater saliency or permanency for her.

Early writers confused male fantasies with reality and made theory out of them. Unfortunately, some of the most strident voices defending Freud's theories, such as Bonaparte (1953) and Deutsch (1945), closed forces against the ideas of people like Horney (1933), Clara Thompson (1942), and Jones (1935), who stressed ideas of primary femininity and cultural influences. It was as if the early defenders of Freud were afraid that his brilliant insights into the unconscious mind would be diluted or lost by the invasion from outside forces or clashing ideas. We feel that in order to champion and save the efficacy and saliency of the discovery of the Oedipus complex in the human psyche, conflicting clinical insights or observational data about early child development tended to be disregarded, oversimplified, or ignored. Contemporary psychoanalytic contributions have attempted to correct the earlier phallocentric and erroneous perspectives. Newer ideas about feminine development have emphasized preoedipal factors. These ideas have enhanced earlier views, which did not have a place for the role of narcissism, or the early mother–child relationship, separation-individuation, and so on.

In our clinical data, separation from the mother and the maternal relationship are highly prominent in the minds of our female patients as they think about defloration. As we have elaborated in earlier chapters, the social and cultural realities are important determinants for this feeling of loss and separation. In many societies marriage brings separation, sometimes total separation, of the girl from her mother, family, and home. Called upon to move into a new role and identity, she leaves past and childhood behind.

As psychoanalysts, however, we are interested in and more qualified to delineate the intrapsychic factors. Theorists such as Nancy Chodorow (1978) have suggested that separation is especially difficult and salient for the little girl as compared to the little boy. She posits that in the course of development, the girl must separate from the primary object, the mother, while she has the task of identifying with her, the same-sexed object. Identifying with the opposite-sexed object, the father, on the other hand, helps boys with separation from the mother, but leaves them more vulnerable to an exaggerated need for autonomy. These suppositions, however, are open to question, as they seem to us to be both overly generalized and simplified.

We do not feel that the observation about the prominence of the role of separation from mother around defloration for women *necessarily* demonstrates a regressive or preoedipal interpretation of feminine psychology. Frequently separation material is erroneously or automatically construed as infantile or preoedipal.

Rather we would say that separation themes occur at all stages of development. The female oedipal configuration carries earlier conflicts with it, just as the male configuration does.

Our topic of heterosexual defloration necessarily focuses on oedipal issues for both men and women. We think that these separation issues seen with women are more clear and poignant, not necessarily because of a heavier loading of preoedipal issues of separation, but because of the special shape of the oedipal situation for the girl. What is unique to the feminine positive oedipal organization derives from the fact that rivalry occurs with the same-sexed parent, the mother, who is generally the primary caretaker. The girl has to maintain a relationship with her mother/caretaker, while at the same time competing with her. Similarly, Person (1982) stresses that the little girl is more intimidated than the little boy during the oedipal period because her rival is also her source of dependent gratification. In contrast, in the positive oedipal configuration, the boy is not confronted with competition with the major caretaker/mother on whom he must depend. We would stress that this gives to the girls' oedipal phase a coloring of separation that should not always be read as infantile or preoedipal. It reflects the complexity of the highly sensitive psychological tasks facing the little girl as she traverses the oedipal period.

The contents of the superego for women that differ from those of men, as noted by Bernstein (1990) and Carol Gilligan (1982), reflect the uniquely complex task of the female in maintaining both friendly and rivalrous relations with the primary caretaking parent. In general, the girl is more interested in moral issues governing relationships and feelings than the man, who is more concerned with abstractions and univerals. Harold Blum (1976) first suggested the importance of distinguishing between origins, functions, structure, and content of the superego. He emphasizes that the female ego ideal has a maternal core. Thus, the feminine ego ideal may extol the endurance of suffering, which should not be equated with masochism.

Conclusions 223

These considerations about the girl's oedipal issues bear upon the questions of education about defloration raised above. An important contribution to the mother's reticence about what is said or taught to the girl about sex is related to the unconscious perception of her daughter as rival. A definitive moment for the girl in terms of stepping into the role of an adult, and competing with her mother, is defloration and the breaking of the hymen.

Finally, the experience of defloration for both women and men can become entwined with sadomasochistic meanings, as our clinical data illustrate. At the same time, our data suggest that these meanings reflect individual patients' idiosyncratic conflicts and anxieties and are not intrinsic to the sexual experience of either gender. The first psychoanalytic writings about defloration were embedded in the theoretical context of female sexuality seen as inevitably or innately masochistic. We wholeheartedly concur with Horney (1935) who said of these ideas: "These biological functions have in themselves no masochistic connotation for women, and do not lead to masochistic reactions; but if masochistic needs of other origin are present, they may easily be involved in masochistic fantasies" (p. 232).

This book is a beginning attempt to explore an area that has received little attention. Contemporary ideas have not sufficiently taken into account the importance and the reality of the hymen as the representation of the entry into adult female genital sexuality. The representation of the hymen is frequently repressed and often suppressed and serves as an organizing image around which fantasies and conflicts are elaborated. Female sexuality as portrayed in early and classical psychoanalytic literature was distorted by attention to what was not there rather than what was there. Beginning with the general collusion about the notion of there being no knowledge of the vagina in the child, which became a crucial part of the psychoanalytic theory of female sexual development, followed by the overemphasized line of phallocentric interests, a clearer understanding of the female genital experience has been obstructed and delayed. A more complex and clear understanding comes from an appreciation of the contributions of both male *and* female genital experiences. This study represents an addition to a line of contemporary psychoanalytic thought that is attempting to reevaluate and articulate uniquely feminine genital experiences. (Bernstein 1990, Chasseguet-Smirgel 1970, Kestenberg 1968, Mayer 1985, Richards 1992, Tyson 1989). We hope further data on these subjects will help to lift "the veil of secrecy surrounding the dark continent."

References

Abraham, K. (1922). Manifestations of the female castration complex. *International Journal of Psycho-Analysis* 3:1–28.

Abraham, R. C. (1933). *The Tiv People*. Lagos: The Government Printer.

Aeschylus. (1938). *Agamemnon* and *The Choephoroe*. In *The Oresteia of Aeschylus*, ed. G. Thomson. Cambridge: Cambridge University Press.

Albee, E. (1995). *Three Tall Women*. New York: Dutton.

Ames, D. W. (1953). Plural marriage among the Wolof in the Gambia: with a consideration of problems of marital adjustment and patterned ways of resolving tensions. Unpublished Ph.D. dissertation. Evanston, IL: Northwestern University.

Andersen, H. C. (1926). *Andersen's Fairy Tales*. Philadelphia: John C. Winston.

Anzieu, D. (1986). *Freud's Self-Analysis*. New York: International Universities Press.

Arlow, J. (1979). Metaphor and the psychoanalytic situation. *Psychoanalytic Quarterly* 49:363–385.

Assaad, M. B. (1980). Female circumcision in Egypt: social implications, current research, and prospects for change. *Studies in Family Planning* 11:3–16.

Austin, L. (1934). Procreation among the Trobriand Islanders. *Oceania*, vol. V: 103–113. Sydney: Australian National Research.

Balmer, J., ed. (1993). *Sappho Poems and Fragments*. New York: Carol Publishing Group.

Becher, H. (1960). The Surara and Pakidai, two Yanoama tribes in northwest Brazil. *Hamburg, Museum fur Volkerkunde, Mitteilungen*, vol. 26, pp. 1–133. Hamburg: Kommissionsverlag Cram, De Gruyter and Co.

Begley, L. (1991). *Wartime Lies*. New York: Knopf.

Bennett, W., and Zingg, R. H. (1935). *The Tarahumara: An Indian Tribe of Northern Mexico*. Chicago: University of Chicago Press.

Bernheimer, C., and Kahane, C., eds. (1985). *In Dora's Case: Freud–Hysteria–Feminism*. New York: Columbia University Press.

Bernstein, D. (1990). Female genital anxieties, conflicts, and typical mastery modes. *International Journal of Psycho-Analysis* 71:151–165.

Bettelheim, B. (1954). *Symbolic Wounds: Puberty Rites and the Envious Male*. Glencoe, IL: Free Press.

———— (1975). *The Uses of Enchantment*. New York: Random House.

Bibring, G. L., Dwyer, T. F., Huntington, D. S., and Valenstein, A. F. (1961). A study of the psychological processes in pregnancy and of the earliest mother–child relationship. *Psychoanalytic Study of the Child* 16:9–24. New York: International Universities Press.

Blake, W. (1789). The Book of Thel. In *The Portable Blake*, ed. A. Kazin, pp. 279–286. New York: Penguin, 1976.

Blum, H. (1976). Masochism, the ego ideal and the psychology of women. *Journal of the American Psychoanalytic Association* (supplement) 24:157–192.

Bolinder, G. (1925). *The Indians of the Tropical Snow-capped Mountains: Investigations in Northernmost South America*. Stuttgart: Strecker und Schroder.

Bonaparte, M. (1953). *Female Sexuality*. New York: International Universities Press.

Bonierbale-Branchereau, M. (1985). Le premier rapport sexuel. (The first sexual encounter.) *Genitif* 6:39–56.

Bouris, K. (1993). *The First Time.* Berkeley, CA: Conari.

Bouroncle-Carreon, A. (1964). Contribution to the study of the Amara. *America Indigena* 24:129–169, 233–269.

Breuner, N. F. (1992). The cult of the Virgin Mary in southern Italy and Spain. *Ethos* 20:66–95.

Briffault, R. (1927). *The Mothers.* New York: Macmillan.

Bulfinch, T. (1979). *Bulfinch's Mythology.* New York: Crown.

Burgos, N. M., and Diaz-Perez, Y. I. (1986). An exploration of human sexuality in the Puerto Rican culture. *Journal of Social Work and Human Sexuality* 4:135–150.

Burling, R. (1963). *Rengsanggri: Family and Kinship in a Garo Village.* Philadelphia: University of Pennsylvania Press.

Caldwell, J. C., and Caldwell, P. (1992). The family and sexual networking in sub-Saharan Africa: historical regional differences and present-day implications. *Population Studies* 46:385–410.

Carson, A. (1990). Putting her in her place: woman, dirt, and desire. In *Before Sexuality: The Construction of Erotic Experience in the Ancient Greek World,* ed. D. M. Halperin, J. J. Winkler, and F. I. Zeitlin, pp. 135–169. Princeton: Princeton University Press.

Chasseguet-Smirgel, J. (1970). Feminine guilt and the Oedipus complex. In *Female Sexuality: New Psychoanalytic Views,* ed. J. Chasseguet-Smirgel, pp. 94–134. Ann Arbor: University of Michigan Press.

——— (1976). Freud and female sexuality: some consideration of the blind spots in the exploration of the "dark continent." *International Journal of Psycho-Analysis* 57:275–286.

Chodorow, N. (1978). *The Reproduction of Mothering: Psychoanalysis and the Sociology of Gender.* Berkeley, CA: University of California Press.

Christensen, J. B. (1952). *Double Descent Among the Fanti.* New Haven: Human Relations Area Files.

Cohen, R. (1960). *The Structure of Kanuri Society.* Dissertation, University of Wisconsin. Ann Arbor: University Microfilms Publications, no. 60-986.

———— (1967). *The Kanuri of Bornu*. New York: Holt, Rinehart and Winston.

Darling, C., Davidson, J. K., and Passarello, L. C. (1992). The mystique of first intercourse among college youth: the role of partners, contraceptive practices, and psychological reactions. *Journal of Youth and Adolescence* 21:97–117.

Darnton, J. (1993). In Sweden, proof of the power of words. *The New York Times*, December 8, Section C, p. 17.

De Beauvoir, S. (1974). *The Second Sex*. New York: Vintage.

Decker, H. S. (1982). *Freud, Dora, and Vienna 1900*. New York: Free Press.

Delaney, J., Lupton, M. J., and Toth, E. (1988). *The Curse: A Cultural History of Menstruation*. Urbana, IL: University of Illinois Press.

de Lorris, G., and de Meun, J. (1275). *The Romance of the Rose*, ed. C. Dahlberg. Hanover and London: University Press of New England, 1983.

Derrida, J. (1981). The double session. In *Dissemination*, ed. B. Johnson, pp. 173–286. Chicago: University of Chicago Press.

Deutsch, H. (1945). *The Psychology of Women: A Psychoanalytic Interpretation, vol. II*. New York: Grune & Stratton.

Devereux, G. (1950). The psychology of feminine genital bleedings. *International Journal of Psycho-Analysis* 31:237–257.

Dickemann, M. (1979). The ecology of mating systems in hypergynous dowry societies. *Social Science Information* 18:163–195.

Diner, H. (1965). *Mothers and Amazons*. New York: Julian.

Dinesen, I. (1983). The blank page. In *Last Tales*, pp. 99–105. New York: Random House.

Doolittle, H. (H.D.). (1983). *H.D. Collected Poems 1912–1944*. New York: New Directions Books.

Douglas, M. (1966). *Purity and Danger: An Analysis of the Concepts of Pollution and Taboo*. New York: Praeger.

Dreiser, T. (1900). *Sister Carrie*. New York: Signet Classics, 1980.

Duras, M. (1985). *The Lover*. New York: Pantheon.

Efron, A. (1977). Freud's self analysis and the nature of psychoanalytic criticism. *International Review of Psycho-Analysis* 4:253–280.

References   229

Ellmann, R. (1975). *Selected Letters of James Joyce, vol. II and III.* London: Faber & Faber.

Elms, A. (1980). Freud, Irma, Martha: sex and marriage in the dream of Irma's injection. *Psychoanalytic Review* 67:83–109.

Ericksen, K. P. (1989). Female genital mutilations in Africa. *Behavior Science Research* 23:182–204.

Erikson, E. (1954). The dream specimen of psychoanalysis. *Journal of the American Psychoanalytic Association* 2:5–56.

Erlich, G. C. (1992). *The Sexual Education of Edith Wharton.* Berkeley and Los Angeles: University of California Press.

Erlich, V. S. (1966). *Family in Transition: A Study of 300 Yugoslav Villages.* Princeton: Princeton University Press.

Euripides. (1960). *Ion.* In *Ten Plays,* trans. M. Hadas and J. McLean. New York: Bantam.

Faergeman, P. M. (1955). Fantasies of menstruation in men. *Psychoanalytic Quarterly* 24:1–19.

Federn, H., and Nunberg, H. (1912). *Minutes of the Vienna Psychoanalytic Society,* vol. IV. New York: International Universities Press, 1975.

Firth, R. (1936). *We, the Tikopia: A Sociological Study of Kinship in Primitive Polynesia.* London: George Allen & Unwin.

Foley, H. P. (1994). *The Homeric Hymn to Demeter.* Princeton, NJ: Princeton University Press.

Fonseca, I. (1995). *Bury Me Standing.* New York: Knopf.

Freud, S. (1893). Studies on hysteria. *Standard Edition* 2.

——— (1895). On the grounds for detaching a particular syndrome from neurasthenia under the description 'anxiety neurosis.' *Standard Edition* 3:86–117.

——— (1899). Screen memories. *Standard Edition* 3:301–322.

——— (1900). The interpretation of dreams. *Standard Edition* 4/5:339–627.

——— (1901). On dreams. *Standard Edition* 5:631–686.

——— (1905). Fragment of an analysis of a case of hysteria. *Standard Edition* 7:3–122.

——— (1912). On the universal tendency to debasement in the sphere of love. *Standard Edition* 11:179–190.

——— (1913). Totem and taboo. *Standard Edition* 13:1–161.

—— (1914). On the history of the psychoanalytic movement. *Standard Edition* 14:3–66.

—— (1916a). Some character-types met with in psychoanalytic work. *Standard Edition* 14:311–333.

—— (1916b). Introductory lectures on psychoanalysis. *Standard Edition* 15.

—— (1917). Introductory lectures on psychoanalysis. *Standard Edition* 16.

—— (1918a). The taboo of virginity. *Standard Edition* 11:191–208.

—— (1918b). From the history of an infantile neurosis. *Standard Edition* 17:3–122.

—— (1922). Some neurotic mechanisms in jealousy, paranoia and homosexuality. *Standard Edition* 18:221–259.

—— (1933). New introductory lectures on psychoanalysis. *Standard Edition* 22:3–182.

Fulero, S. M., and Delara, C. (1976). Rape victims and attributed responsibility: a defensive attribution approach. *Victimology* 1:551–563.

García Lorca, F. (1941). *The House of Bernarda Alba* and *Blood Wedding*. In *Three Tragedies*. New York: New Directions.

Gardiner, M. (1955). Feminine masochism and passivity. *Bulletin of the Philadelphia Association of Psychoanalysis* 5:74–79.

Gilligan, C. (1982). *In a Different Voice: Psychological Theory and Women's Development*. Cambridge, MA: Harvard University Press.

Gluckman, M. (1950). Kinship and marriage among the Lozi of Northern Rhodesia and the Zulu of Natal. In *African Systems of Kinship and Marriage*, ed. A. R. Radcliffe-Brown and D. Forde, pp. 166–206. London: Oxford University Press.

Goldman, I. (1963). *The Cubeo: Indians of the Northwest Amazon*. Urbana: University of Illinois Press.

Goodenough, W. H. (1949). Premarital freedom on Truk: theory and practice. *American Anthropologist* 51:615–620.

Gray, S. (1985). "China" as a symbol for vagina. *Psychoanalytic Quarterly* 54:620–623.

Grenville, K. (1994). *Albion's Story*. New York: Harcourt Brace.

Grimm, J. and W. (1973). *The Grimms' German Folk Tales*, trans.

F. P. Magoun and A. H. Krappe. Carbondale, IL: Southern Illinois University Press.

Grinstein, A. (1995). *The Remarkable Beatrix Potter*. Madison, CT: International Universities Press.

Gubar, S. (1981). "The Blank Page" and the issues of female creativity. *Critical Inquiry* 8:243–263.

Hacker, S. (1994). The freep; let's talk about sex. *The Detroit Free Press*, May 27, p. 1G.

Halpern, J. M. (1958). *A Serbian Village*. New York: Columbia University Press.

Hansen, H. H. (1961). *The Kurdish Woman's Life: Field Research in a Muslim Society, Iraq*. Copenhagen: Copenhagen Ethnographic Museum Record, 7.

Hanson, A. E. (1990). The medical writer's woman. In *Before Sexuality: The Construction of Erotic Experience in the Ancient Greek World*, ed. D. M. Halperin, J. J. Winkler, and F. I. Zeitlin, pp. 309–338. Princeton: Princeton University Press.

Hardy, T. (1891). *Tess of the D'Urbervilles*. London: Penguin, 1985.

Hartman, F. (1983). A reappraisal of the Emma episode in the specimen dream. *Journal of the American Psychoanalytic Association* 31:555–585.

Hassan, M., and Shuaibu-Na'ibi, M. (1952). *A Chronicle of Abuja*. Ibadan, Nigeria: Ibadan University Press.

Hastrup, K. (1995). *A Passage to Anthropology: Between Experience and Theory*. London: Routledge.

Hebbel, F. (1840). *Judith: A Tragedy in Five Acts*. Boston: R. G. Badger, 1914.

Honnet, E. P. (1990). Rites of passage for college students: the psychological meaning of the experience of first sexual intercourse. *Dissertation Abstracts* 51:452–453.

Horney, K. (1933). The denial of the vagina. *International Journal of Psycho-Analysis* 14:57–70.

——— (1935). The problem of feminine masochism. In *Feminine Psychology*, pp. 214–233. New York: Norton, 1967.

Hugh, R. (1989). *Wicked Words*. New York: Crown.

Hurault, J. (1961). *Les Noirs Refugies Boni de la Guyane Francaise*. Dakar, Sudan: IFAN.

Hutchinson, H. W. (1957). *Village and Plantation Life in Northeastern Brazil*. Seattle: University of Washington Press.

Jaffe, D. S. (1976). The masculine envy of woman's procreative function. *Journal of the American Psychoanalytic Association* (Supplement) 24:361–392.

James, G. P. R. (1841). *The Jacquerie*. New York: Harper, 1942.

Jeffrey, D. L. (1992). *A Dictionary of Biblical Tradition in English Literature*. Grand Rapids, MI: William B. Eerdmans.

Jones, E. (1935). Early female sexuality. *International Journal of Psycho-Analysis* 16:263–273.

——— (1953). *The Life and Work of Sigmund Freud*. New York: Basic Books.

Joyce, J. (1922). *Ulysses*. New York: Vintage Books, 1961.

Kanekar, S., and Kolsawalla, M. (1977). Responsibility in relation to respectability. *Journal of Social Psychology* 102:183–188.

Kanekar, S., and Vaz, L. (1988). Attribution of causal and moral responsibility to a victim of rape. *Applied Psychology* 37:35–49.

Kaplan, L. J. (1991). *Female Perversions*. New York: Doubleday.

Kemp, P. (1935). *Healing Ritual: Studies in the Technique and Tradition of the Southern Slavs*. London: Faber & Faber.

Kent, D. (1993). Virgin territory: why your sexual status is such a big deal; sex & body. *Seventeen* 52:66.

Kestenberg, J. (1968). Outside and inside, male and female. *Journal of the American Psychoanalytic Association* 16:457–510.

Kharuzin, A. N. (1898). *The Judicial Customs of the Yakuti. Etnograficheskos Obozrenie* 10:37–64.

Kofman, S. (1991). *Freud and Fiction*. Boston: Northeastern University Press.

Kubie, L. (1974). The drive to become both sexes. *Psychoanalytic Quarterly* 43:349–426.

Kulish, N. (1991). The mental representation of the clitoris. *Psychoanalytic Inquiry* 11:511–536.

Lambek, M. (1983). Virgin marriage and the autonomy of women in Mayotte. *Signs* 9:264–281.

Landes R. (1938). *The Ojibwa Woman*. New York: Columbia University Press.

Lang, A. (1994). *A World of Fairy Tales*. New York: Dial Books.

Lax, R. (1994). The vicissitudes of boy's envy of mother, and the consequences of his narcissistic injury. Paper presented at the meeting of the American Psychoanalytic Association, New York, NY, December.

Leick, G. (1994). *Sex and Eroticism in Mesopotamian Literature*. London and New York: Routledge.

Lerner, H. E. (1977). Parental mislabeling of female genitalia as a determinant of penis envy and learning inhibitions in women. In *Female Psychology: Contemporary Psychoanalytic Views*, ed. H. Blum, pp. 269–283. New York: International Universities Press.

Levine, D. N. (1965). *Wax and Gold: Tradition and Innovation in Ethiopian Culture*. Chicago: University of Chicago Press.

Lewin, B. (1948). The nature of reality, the meaning of nothing, with an addendum on concentration. *Psychoanalytic Quarterly* 17:524–530.

Lewin, E., and Lewin, A. E. (1994). *The Thesaurus of Slang*. New York: Facts on File.

Lewis, I. M. (1961). *A Pastoral Democracy: A Study of Pastoralism and Politics among the Northern Somali of the Horn of Africa*. London: Oxford University Press.

——— (1962). *Marriage and the Family in Northern Somaliland*. Kampala, Uganda: East African Studies, 15, East African Institute of Social Research.

Lewis, R. W. B. (1985). *Edith Wharton*. New York: Fromm International.

Lightfoot-Klein, H. (1989). *Prisoners of Ritual: An Odyssey into Female Genital Circumcision in Africa*. New York: Harrington Park.

Lincoln, B. (1991). *Emerging from the Chrysalis*. New York: Oxford University Press.

Litvak, F. E. P. (1984). *Le Droit Du Seigneur in European and American Literature*. Birmingham, AL: Summa Publications.

Loewald, H. (1988). Termination analyzable and unanalyzable. *Psychoanalytic Study of the Child* 43:155–166. New Haven: Yale University Press.

Longus. (1977). *Daphnis and Chloe*, trans. G. Moore. New York: George Braziller.

Lupton, M. J. (1993). *Menstruation and Psychoanalysis*. Urbana and Chicago: University of Illinois Press.

Mahoney, P. (1977). Toward a formalist approach to dreams. *International Review of Psycho-Analysis* 4:83–98.

Malcolm, J. (1981). *Psychoanalysis: The Impossible Profession*. New York: Knopf.

Malinowski, B. (1929). *The Sexual Life of Savages in Northwestern Melanesia*. New York: Liveright.

Mallarmé, S. (1945). Mimique. In *Oeuvres Completes*, p. 310. Paris: Pleiade. English translation: Derrida, J. (1981). The double session. In *Dissemination*, ed. B. Johnson, p. 175. Chicago: University of Chicago Press.

Marcus, D. M. (1963). The Cinderella motif: fairy tale and defense. *American Imago* 20:81–92.

Marcus, S. (1974). *The Other Victorians*. New York: Basic Books.

Masson, J. (1985). *The Complete Letters of Sigmund Freud to Wilhelm Fleiss, 1887–1904*. Cambridge, MA: Belknap.

Masters, W. M. (1953). *Rowanduz: A Kurdish Administrative and Mercantile Center*. Unpublished Ph.D. dissertation. Ann Arbor, MI: University of Michigan.

Mautner, B. (1991). Freud's dream: a psychoanalytic interpretation. *International Journal of Psycho-Analysis* 72:275–286.

Mayer, E. L. (1985). Everybody must be just like me: observations on female castration anxiety. *International Journal of Psycho-Analysis* 66:331–348.

Mernissi, F. (1982). Virginity and patriarchy. *Women's Studies International Forum* 5:183–191.

Mitra, C. L. (1987). Judicial discourse in father–daughter incest appeal cases. *International Journal of Sociology and Law* 15:121–148.

Mohacsy, I. (1988). The medieval unicorn: historical and iconographic applications of psychoanalysis. *Journal of the American Academy of Psychoanalysis* 16:83–106.

Moore, B. E., and Fine, B. D. (1968). *A Glossary of Psychoanalytic Terms and Concepts*. New York: American Psychoanalytic Association.

Moors, A. (1991). Women and the Orient: a note on difference. In *Constructing Knowledge*, ed. L. Nencel and P. Pels, pp. 114–122. London: Sage.

Munro, A. (1977). *The Beggar Maid*. New York: Vintage, 1991.

Nabokov, V. (1955). *Lolita*. New York: G. P. Putnam's Sons.

Nemecek, O. (1958). *Virginity: Pre-Nuptial Rites and Rituals*. New York: Philosophical Library.

Nencel, L., and Pels, P. (1991). *Constructing Knowledge*. London: Sage.

Nilsen, A. P. (1990). Virginity: a metaphor we live by. *Humor* 3:3–15.

Nunberg, H. (1947). Circumcision and problems of bisexuality. *International Journal of Psycho-Analysis* 28:145–179.

Obermeyer, G. J. (1969). *Structure and Authority in a Bedouin Tribe: The 'Aishaibat of the Western Desert of Egypt*. Dissertation. Indiana University. Ann Arbor: University Microfilms.

O'Brien, E. (1960). *The Country Girls Trilogy and Epilogue*. New York: Plume, 1987.

Oliner, M. (1988). The anal phase. In *Early Female Development: Current Psychoanalytic Views*, ed. D. Mendell, pp. 25–60. New York: S. P. Medical and Scientific Books.

Opie, I., and Opie, P. (1974). *The Classic Fairy Tales*. London: Oxford University Press.

Ortner, S. B. (1991). Narrativity in history, culture and lives. In *Transformations: Comparative Study of Social Transformations*, pp. 1–13. Ann Arbor, MI: CSST. Working Papers #66, The University of Michigan.

Ovid. (1955). *Metamorphoses*, trans. R. Humphries. Bloomington: Indiana University Press.

Pancol, K. (1979). *Moi d'Abord*. Paris: Seuil.

Partridge, E. (1958). *Origins: A Short Etymological Dictionary of Modern English*. London: Routledge & Kegan Paul.

Penman, S. K. (1991). *The Reckoning*. New York: Ballantine.

Person, E. S. (1982). Women working: fears of failure, deviance and success. *Journal of the American Academy of Psychoanalysis* 10: 67–84.

——— (1995). *By Force of Fantasy*. New York: Basic Books.

Peters, E. L. (1965). Aspects of the family among the Bedouin of Cyrenaica. In *Comparative Family Systems*, ed. M. F. Nimkoff, pp. 121–146. Boston: Houghton Mifflin.

Petty, T. (1953). The tragedy of Humpty Dumpty. *Psychoanalytic Study of the Child* 8:404–412. New York: International Universities Press.

Plath, S. (1971). *The Bell Jar*. New York: Bantam, 1972.

Poe, E. A. (1849). *The Raven and Other Favorite Poems*. New York: Dover, 1991.

Potter, B. (1902). *The Tale of Peter Rabbit*. London: Frederick Warne, 1987.

——— (1903). *The Tale of Squirrel Nutkin*. London: Frederick Warne, 1987.

——— (1904). *The Tale of Two Bad Mice*. London: Frederick Warne, 1987.

——— (1905). *The Tale of Mrs. Tiggy-Winkle*. London: Frederick Warne, 1986.

——— (1913). *The Tale of Pigling Bland*. London: Frederick Warne, 1987.

Rabine, L. (1990). The unhappy hymen. In *The Other Perspective in Gender and Culture*, ed. J. F. MacCannell, pp. 20–38. New York: Columbia University Press.

Ramsey, P. (1982). Do you know where your children are? *Journal of Psychology and Christianity* 1:7–15.

Rattray, R. S. (1927). *Religion and Art in Ashanti*. Oxford: Clarendon.

Reichel-Dolmatoff, G. (1951). *The Kogi: A Tribe of the Sierra Nevada de Santa Marta*, vol. 2. Bogota, Columbia: Editorial Iqueima.

Richards, A. K. (1992). The influence of sphincter control and genital sensation on body image and gender identity in women. *Psychoanalytic Quarterly* 61:331–351.

Rilly, J. O., and Udry, J. R. (1985). The influence of male and female best friends on adolescent sexual behavior. *Adolescence* 20:21–32.

Roheim, G. (1945). *The Eternal Ones of the Dream: A Psychoanalytic Interpretation of Australian Myth and Ritual*. New York: International Universities Press.

Rose, H. J. (1959). *Religion in Greece and Rome.* New York: Harper & Row.

Rossetti, C. (1862). The convent threshold. In *Poems*, pp. 111–116. New York: Knopf, 1993.

Sanday, P. (1981). *Female Power and Male Dominance: On the Origins of Sexual Inequality.* Cambridge: Cambridge University Press.

Sappho. (1958). Epithalamia. In *Sappho: A New Translation*, trans. M. Barnard. Berkeley: University of California Press.

Schur, M. (1966). Some additional day residues of the specimen dream of psychoanalysis. In *Psychoanalysis—A General Psychology*, ed. R. M. Loewenstein, L. M. Newman, M. Schur, and A. J. Solnit, pp. 45–85. New York: International Universities Press.

Sexton, A. (1964). "The Wedding Night." In *Live or Die*, pp. 60–61. Boston: Houghton Mifflin, 1966.

Shakespeare, W. (1989a). *Hamlet.* In *The Unabridged William Shakespeare*, ed. W. G. Clark and W. A. Wright. Philadelphia: Running Press.

——— (1989b). *Measure for Measure.* In *The Unabridged William Shakespeare*, ed. W. G. Clark and W. A. Wright. Philadelphia: Running Press.

——— (1989c). *Pericles.* In *The Unabridged William Shakespeare*, ed. W. G. Clark and W. A. Wright. Philadelphia: Running Press.

——— (1989d). *The Tempest.* In *The Unabridged William Shakespeare*, ed. W. G. Clark and W. A. Wright. Philadelphia: Running Press.

Shapurian, R., and Hojat, M. (1985). Sexual and premarital attitudes of Iranian college students. *Psychological Reports* 57:67–74.

Shaw, E. (1985). Female circumcision. *American Journal of Nursing* 85:684–687.

Sissa, G. (1990). Maidenhood without maidenhead: the female body in ancient Greece. In *Before Sexuality: The Construction of Erotic Experience in the Ancient Greek World*, ed. D. M. Halperin, J. J. Winkler, and F. I. Zeitlin, pp. 339–364. Princeton: Princeton University Press.

Sjoo, M., and Mor, B. (1987). *The Great Cosmic Mother.* New York: Harper & Row.

Slap, J. (1979). On nothing and nobody with an addendum on William Hogarth. *Psychoanalytic Quarterly* 48:620–630.

Slater, P. E. (1968). *The Glory of Hera.* Boston: Beacon.

Somchintana, T. R. (1979). The socio-cultural setting of love magic in Central Thailand. *Wisconsin Papers on Southeast Asia* 2:29–39.

Sophocles. (1988). *The Complete Plays of Sophocles,* ed. M. Hadas. New York: Bantam.

Spears, R. A. (1991). *Slang and Euphemism.* New York: Signet.

Sprengnether, M. (1985). Enforcing Oedipus: Freud and Dora. In *In Dora's Case: Freud–Hysteria–Feminism,* ed. C. Bernheimer and C. Kanane, pp. 254–275. New York: Columbia University Press.

Stone, M. (1976). *When God Was a Woman.* New York: Harcourt Brace Jovanovich.

Swan, J. (1974). Mater and Nannie: Freud's two mothers and the discovery of the Oedipus complex. *American Imago* 31:1–64.

Taylor, J. (1966). Foreword. In *The Journal of Beatrix Potter 1881–1897.* London: Frederick Warne, 1989.

———— (1989), ed. *Beatrix Potter's Letters.* London: Frederick Warne.

Terr, L. C. (1987). Childhood trauma and the creative product: a look at the early lives and later works of Poe, Wharton, Magritte, Hitchcock, and Bergman. *Psychoanalytic Study of the Child* 42:545–572. New Haven: Yale University Press.

Thompson, C. (1942). Cultural pressures on the psychology of women. *Psychiatry* 5:331–339.

Thompson, S. (1990). Putting a big thing into a little hole: teenage girls' accounts of sexual initiation. *The Journal of Sex Research* 27:341–361.

Tintner, A. R. (1980). Mothers, daughters, and incest in the late novels of Edith Wharton. In *The Lost Tradition: Mothers and Daughters in Literature,* ed. C. N. Davidson and C. M. Broner, pp. 147–156. New York: Ungar.

Titiev, M. (1971). *Old Oraibi: A Study of the Hopi Indians of Third Mesa.* New York: Kraus Reprint Co., reprint of 1944 edition, Harvard U., Peabody Museum of American Archaeology and Ethnology Papers, 22, no. 1.

Tordjman, G. (1981). *La Première Fois.* Paris: Editions Ramsey.

Tschopik, H. (1946). The Aymara. *Bureau of American Ethnology Bulletin* 2:501–573.

Tseelon, E. (1995). The Little Mermaid. *International Journal of Psycho-Analysis* 76:1017–1031.

Tucker, H. F. (1993). Representation and repristination: virginity in the ring and the book. In *Virginal Sexuality and Textuality in Victorian Literature*, ed. L. Davis, pp. 67–86. Albany: State University of New York Press.

Tyson, P. (1989). Infantile sexuality, gender identity, and obstacles to oedipal progression. *Journal of the American Psychoanalytic Association* 37:1051–1069.

Tyson, P., and Tyson, R. (1990). Gender development: girls. In *Psychoanalytic Theories of Development: An Integration*, pp. 258–276. New Haven, CT: Yale University Press.

Van de Velde, T. H. (1930). *Ideal Marriage: Its Physiology and Technique*. New York: Random House.

Wafer, L. (1934). *A New Voyage and Description of the Isthmus of America*. Oxford: The Hakluyt Society, ser. 2, no. LXXIII.

Walker, B. G. (1983). *The Woman's Encyclopedia of Myths and Secrets*. San Francisco: Harper & Row.

Warner, M. (1983). *Alone of All Her Sex*. New York: Random House.

———— (1995). *From the Beast to the Blonde: On Fairy Tales and Their Tellers*. New York: Farrar, Straus and Giroux.

Weis, D. L. (1985). The experience of pain during women's first sexual intercourse: cultural mythology about female sexual initiation. *Archives of Sexual Behavior* 14:421–438.

Weissman, P. (1964). Psychosexual development in a case of neurotic virginity and old maidenhood. *International Journal of Psycho-Analysis* 45:110–120.

Welldon, E. V. (1988). *Mother, Madonna, Whore*. New York: Guilford.

Wharton, E. (n.d.) "The Life Apart." Unpublished manuscript. Manuscript Department, Lilly Library, Indiana University, Bloomington, IN.

———— (1904). The house of the dead hand. In *The Collected Short Stories*, vol. I., ed. R. W. B. Lewis, pp. 507–529. New York: Charles Scribner's Sons, 1968.

———— (1905). *The House of Mirth*. New York: Charles Scribner's Sons.

———— (1910). The bolted door. In *The Collected Short Stories*, vol. II., ed. R. W. B. Lewis, pp. 3–35. New York: Charles Scribner's Sons, 1968.

———— (1911). *Ethan Frome*. New York: Charles Scribner's Sons.

———— (1912). *The Reef*. New York: Appleton.

———— (1917). *Summer*. New York: Appleton.

———— (1920). "Life and I," manuscript version of *A Backward Glance*. New Haven: Beinecke Rare Book and Manuscript Library, Yale University.

———— (1925). *The Mother's Recompense*. New York: Appleton.

———— (1929). *Hudson River Bracketed*. New York: Appleton.

———— (1933). *A Backward Glance*. New York: Charles Scribner's Sons, 1964.

Wharton, E., and Codman, O. (1902). The *Decoration of Houses*. New York: Norton, 1978.

White, B. A. (1991). *Edith Wharton: A Study of the Short Fiction*. New York: Twayne.

Wiggin, K. D., and Smith, N. A. (1909). *The Arabian Nights*. New York: Charles Scribner's Sons.

Wijenaike, P. (1963). My daughter's wedding day. In *The Third Woman and Other Stories*, pp. 115–128. Colombo, Sri Lanka: Salam Publishers, Ltd.

Wissler, C. (1918). *The Social Life of the Blackfoot Indians*. New York: The American Museum of Natural History, Anthropological Papers, 7, part 1.

Wolff, C. G. (1978). *A Feast of Words: The Triumph of Edith Wharton*. New York: Oxford University Press.

Wordsworth, W. (1799–1800a). Nutting. In *The Complete Poetical Works of William Wordsworth*, ed. A. J. George, p. 111. Cambridge: Cambridge University Press, 1904.

———— (1799–1800b). Strange fits of passion have I known. In *The Complete Poetical Works of William Wordsworth*, ed. A. J. George, p. 112. Cambridge: Cambridge University Press, 1904.

Yap, J. G. (1986). Philippine ethnoculture and human sexuality. *Journal of Social Work and Human Sexuality* 4:121–134.

References 241

Yates, S. L. (1930). An investigation of the psychological factors in virginity and ritual defloration. *International Journal of Psycho-Analysis* 11:167–184.

Young, K. Z. (1989). The imperishable virginity of Saint Maria Goretti. *Gender and Society* 3:474–482.

Zeitlin, F. I. (1990). The poetics of Eros: nature, art, and imitation in Longus' Daphnis and Chloe. In *Before Sexuality: The Construction of Erotic Experience in the Ancient Greek World*, ed. D. M. Halperin, J. J. Winkler, and F. I. Zeitlin, pp. 417–464. Princeton: Princeton University Press.

॰ॐ

Index

ABOUT THE AUTHORS

Deanna Holtzman, Ph.D., is a training and supervising analyst at the Michigan Psychoanalytic Institute. She obtained her doctorate from Wayne State University and completed a postdoctoral fellowship at Detroit Psychiatric Institute. Currently, she is in full-time private practice in Birmingham, Michigan. Dr. Holtzman is an adjunct clinical professor at the University of Detroit/Mercy, department of psychology, and adjunct assistant professor at Wayne State University, department of psychiatry. She is married and lives in Bloomfield Hills, Michigan.

Nancy Kulish, Ph.D., is a faculty member of the Michigan Psychoanalytic Institute. She obtained her doctorate from the University of Michigan. She is in full-time private practice in Birmingham, Michigan. Dr. Kulish is an assistant professor in the department of psychiatry at Wayne State University School of Medicine and an adjunct professor in the department of psychology at the University of Detroit/Mercy. She is married and lives in Bloomfield Hills, Michigan.